AMC
Maine Mountain Guide

9th Edition

The Hiking Trails of Maine
featuring Baxter State Park

Compiled and edited by
Peg Nation and Brenda Cummings

APPALACHIAN MOUNTAIN CLUB BOOKS
BOSTON, MASSACHUSETTS

Front cover photograph: Hikers on rocky ledges © Royalty-Free Corbis
Back cover photographs: TK
Cover design: Mac & Dent
Interior design: Eric Edstam
Cartography: Larry Garland

Distributed by the Globe Pequot Press, Guilford, CT.

Published by the Appalachian Mountain Club. No part of this publication may be repro-
duced or transmitted in any form or by any means, electronic or mechanical, including
photocopying and recording, or by any information storage or retrieval system, except as
may be expressly permitted by the 1976 Copyright Act or in writing from the publisher.
Requests for permission should be addressed in writing to Appalachian Mountain Club
Books, 5 Joy Street, Boston, MA 02108.

The paper used in this publication meets the minimum requirements of the American
National Standard for Information Sciences—Permanence of Paper for Printed Library
Materials, ANSI Z39.48-1984. ∞

Printed in the United States of America.
⊕ Printed on recycled paper using soy-based inks.

**Due to changes in conditions, use of the information
in this book is at the sole risk of the user.**

10 9 8 7 6 5 4 3 2   06 07 08 09

Contents

Locator Map

2. AROOSTOOK COUNTY

Presque Isle ●

(11)

1. BAXTER STATE PARK AND KATAHDIN (BSP)

3. GREATER MOOSEHEAD LAKE REGION

Millinocket ●

(201)
Greenville ●

4. 100-MILE WILDERNESS

(95)

(6)

11. RANGELEY/ STRATTON REGION

12. KENNEBEC VALLEY

10. WELD REGION

9. GRAFTON NOTCH/ MAHOOSUC RANGE

Newport ●

5. EAST OF THE PENOBSCOT

Eastport ●

(9)
Bangor ●

(2)

8. OXFORD HILLS/ EVANS NOTCH

Augusta
★

6. CAMDEN HILLS

(95) (295)

Portland ●

7. SOUTHWESTERN MAINE/ PLEASANT MOUNTAIN

Acknowledgments

The ninth edition of the *Maine Mountain Guide* is based on the excellent work done by the volunteers. We recognize their contributions, as well as the contributions from other chapter members who generously donated their time to review the trails in the eighth edition and provide updates for this edition. We thank all of you for your work.

We would like to extend our thanks particularly to the following individuals for their hard work, at times under difficult situations, in completing whole sections of the guide: George Brown, Craig Dickstein, Donna Johnson, Wayne Newton, Alix and Bob Pratt, and Dave Wood. Other individuals who contributed significantly to the guide include: Keith Chapman, Bob Child, Al Cressy, Ed Libby, Mary Lou Moulton, Scott Peterson, Peter Roderick, Eric Topper, Barbara Trafton, and Paul Wentworth.

Special thanks goes to Jean Hoekwater and her crew at Baxter State Park for taking the time to review and update the Baxter State Park and Kathadin section of the guide.

This edition of the guide would not exist without the tremendous assistance and support from Sarah Jane Shangraw and the rest of the AMC Books staff. We would also like to express our appreciation to Larry Garland for the excellent maps that he produced for this guide.

Peg Nation and Brenda Cummings, Co-Editors

Introduction

This, the ninth edition of the Appalachian Mountain Club's guide to the mountains and trails of Maine, describes nearly two hundred summits in all sections of Maine—from Mt. Agamenticus in the southwestern corner of the state to Deboullie Mtn. in northern Aroostook County, and from Mt. Aziscohos close to the New Hampshire line in northwestern Maine to Pocomoonshine Mtn. near the St. Croix River, which forms the New Brunswick border. Some examples are the compact and scenic Camden Hills, the low but frequently climbed hills in southwestern Maine, and the isolated and interesting mountains close to the Quebec and New Brunswick boundaries.

This guide is intended for use as a pathfinder; it therefore does not include extended historical references or descriptions of views. In general, it describes trail ascents. Any difficulties going down a trail that you would not have encountered going up are mentioned at the end of the description. Where a trail follows a range, this guide describes it for the direction usually traveled. Signs mark many paths, but hikers cannot rely on them, because they often fall down or disappear. Also, trails are constantly changing. Logging may destroy them; heavy storms, such as the ice storm of 1998, may obscure them; and new trails are occasionally added. Unless otherwise labeled, compass directions given in this text are based on true north instead of magnetic north. This is important information, because in Maine the compass needle points up to 20 degrees west of true north.

With reference to streams, the terms right bank and left bank mean right and left when you face downstream. Abbreviations used frequently in the text are listed on page xxiii.

This guide strives to remain current by adding or deleting trails or mountains depending on present conditions. For updates to the trail descriptions in ths guide, go to www.outdoors.org/publications/books/updates.

Trip Planning and Safety

Distances and Times

The distances and times that appear in the tables at the end of trail descriptions are cumulative from the starting point at the head of each table. Estimated distances are preceded by est.

Times are based on a speed of 2 mph, plus an additional half-hour for every 1000 ft. gained in elevation. Times are included only to provide a consistent measure for comparison among trails and routes. When no time is given, the route described may be considered a leisurely walk or stroll. With experience, you will learn how to correct these standard times for your own normal pace. Bear in mind, however, that if your average pace is faster than the standard time, it will not necessarily be so on trails with steep grades, in wet weather, if you are carrying a heavy pack, or if you are hiking with a group. And in winter, you should roughly double the time it would normally take for you to complete a hike.

Guidelines for Wilderness Hikers and Campers

AMC is a partner of Leave No Trace (see Appendix D). Below are some fundamentals of recreating in the outdoors. Following these simple rules will help preserve the backcountry for all to enjoy.

- Camp in Designated Areas. The backcountry can no longer withstand indiscriminate camping and hiking. Please cooperate.
- Bring Your Own Tent or Shelter. Shelter buildings are often full, so each group should carry all needed equipment for shelter, including whatever poles, stakes, ground insulation, and cord are required. Do not cut boughs or branches for bedding.
- Use a Portable Stove. In some camping areas, a "human browse line" is quite evident, because people have gathered firewood over the years: Limbs are gone from trees, the ground is devoid of deadwood, and vegetation has been trampled by people scouring the area. A carefully operated stove puts the least pressure on the forest.

- Help Preserve Nature's Ground Cover. If a shelter is full, or if you camp away from shelters, find a clear, level site on which to pitch your tent, away from trails and streams. Site clearing and ditching around tents are too damaging to soil and vegetation.

- Hammock Camping. Some campers use hammocks rather than tents. Hanging between trees eliminates even that crushing of ground cover caused by tents. (Hammocks, however, have certain limitations during bug season!) We can all practice low-impact camping by making conscious efforts to preserve the natural forest.

- Water for Drinking and Washing. Wash your dishes and yourself well away from streams, ponds, and springs. A handy practice is carrying a small screen or cloth to filter the dishwater, so that you do not leave food remnants strewn about the woods. Most hikers drink from streams without ill effect, and indeed, the pleasure of quaffing a cup of water fresh from a (presumably) pure mountain spring is one of the traditional attractions of the mountains. Unfortunately, in many mountain regions the cysts of the intestinal parasite *Giardia lamblia* are present in some of the water. A conservative practice is to boil water for 20 min. or to use an iodine-based disinfectant. Chlorine-based products, such as Halazone, are ineffective in water that contains organic impurities, and they deteriorate quickly in your pack. Remember to allow extra contact time (and use twice as many tablets) if the water is cold.

- Think About Human Waste. Keep it at least 200 ft. away from water sources. If there are no toilets nearby, dig a trench 6–8 in. deep for a latrine and cover it completely when you break camp. The bacteria in the organic layer of the soil will then decompose the waste naturally. (Do not dig the trench too deep, or you will be below the organic layer.)

- Carry In–Carry Out. Trash receptacles are not available in trail areas (except at some trailheads), and visitors are asked to bring trash bags and carry out everything—food, paper, glass, cans—they carry in. Cooperation with the "carry in–carry out" program so far has been outstanding, and the concept has grown to "carry out more than you carried in." We hope you will join in the effort.

- Use Special Care Above Timberline. Extreme weather and a short growing season make these areas especially fragile. Footsteps alone can destroy the toughest natural cover, so please try to stay on the trail or walk on rocks. And, of course, do not camp above timberline.

- Limit the Size of Your Group. The larger the group, the greater the impact on the environment and on others. Please limit the size of your group to a dozen or fewer.

Be Prepared

Hikers should always carry a map and compass, knife, waterproof matches, water, adequate food, a windbreaker, rain gear, a spare sweater or fleece, gloves or mittens, a hat, and extra socks. In addition, at least one member of the group should carry a lightweight survival kit that includes first aid supplies (Band-Aids, gauze pads, and adhesive tape; moleskin or a similar blister preventive; an antiseptic; and an analgesic), high-energy emergency food, a flashlight or headlamp with extra batteries, paper and a pencil, and a space blanket.

Before entering the woods, tell someone where you are going and when you plan to return, and get to know the area. Study a good map and know how to use your compass. Pick out reference points along the trail after you start your hike and check your compass from time to time. Dress for the terrain and weather. Do not depend on cotton clothing for warmth; once it is dampened by perspiration or precipitation, it will pull warmth from your body. Wool and some synthetics such as polypropylene provide better insulation even when wet. Dress in layers: Remember, you can always take off what you have on, but you cannot put on what you do not have with you.

Hypothermia

Hypothermia, the most serious danger to hikers, is the inability to stay warm because of injury, exhaustion, lack of sufficient food, or inadequate or wet clothing. Most cases occur in temperatures above freezing; the most dangerous conditions involve rain with wind. The symptoms are stumbling, poor coordination, garbled speech, amnesia, disorientation, and agitated behavior. Progressive lethargy, uncontrollable shivering, and coma will follow if no treatment is given. The result is death, unless the victim (who usually does not understand the situation) is treated, and it is not unusual for the victim to resist treatment and even combat the rescuers.

If you suspect a person is hypothermic, find the victim shelter from the wind and rain, and remove any wet clothing. Place the victim in a sleeping bag without clothes or with dry garments. Be sure to cover the head and neck, and provide insulation from the ground. If the victim is fully conscious, supply quick-energy food and warm (not hot), nonalcoholic drinks. Keep the victim inactive until signs of improvement appear. Allow adequate rest before moving on; do not hesitate to send for help if there is any doubt that the victim should proceed.

Uncontrollable shivering is evidence of advanced hypothermia. The shivering will eventually cease on its own, but its disappearance is an indication that the hypothermia is becoming even more severe. In severe cases, only professional treatment offers hope for survival. Reduce exposure to wind and rain, prevent further heat loss, and send for help. Do not try to re-warm in the field.

The prevention of hypothermia is infinitely easier than its treatment and should be a prime concern of hikers during any season. Sources of detailed information on causes, prevention, and current treatment are available through the AMC's Boston or Pinkham Notch headquarters and on the AMC's website, www.outdoors.org.

If You're Lost

If you get lost in the Maine woods, it is not necessarily a serious matter. First stop, sit down, and think. If you are familiar with the territory, you may be able to find your way back to the trail or to a high spot to survey the area. If you are unsure which direction to take, stay where you are! If you have informed someone of your trip plan, then you will probably be found quickly. Do not panic. If you have the proper equipment, you can improvise a shelter (near water if possible) and wait for help. Build a fire for warmth and to draw attention. (Be careful to keep the fire under control, of course.) The main thing to remember is to stay put and stay calm.

Search and Rescue

The Department of Inland Fisheries and Wildlife is empowered to conduct search-and-rescue operations in Maine. Call the nearest Warden District for more information, or the Maine State Police at 800-452-4664. The text of the relevant sections of Maine law is given below; for more information, write to the Department of Inland Fisheries and Wildlife, 41 State House Station, 284 State St., Augusta, ME 04333, or go to www.state.me.us/ifw.

Title 12, Sec. 7035, No. 4; Powers

Search and rescue. Whenever the commissioner receives notification that any person has gone into the woodlands or onto the inland waters of the State on a hunting, fishing or other trip and has become lost, stranded or drowned, the commissioner shall exercise the authority to take reasonable steps to ensure the safe and timely recovery of that person; except in cases involving downed or lost aircraft covered by Title 6, section 303.

A. The commissioner may summon any person in the State to assist in those search and rescue attempts. Each person summoned shall be paid at a rate set by the commissioner with the approval of the Governor and shall be provided with subsistence while engaged in these activities.

B. The expenses of the department in search and rescue efforts shall be paid from the General Fund. The Joint Standing Committee of the Legislature having jurisdiction over Inland Fisheries and Wildlife shall report out a bill during each regular session requesting General Fund monies for the full cost of the search and rescue.

C. The commissioner may enter into written agreements with other agencies or corporations, including commercial recreational areas, allowing partial search and rescue responsibility within specified areas.

D. The commissioner may terminate a search and rescue operation by members of his department when, in his opinion, all reasonable efforts have been exhausted.

Any person who has knowledge that another person is lost, stranded or drowned in the woodlands or inland waters of the State shall notify the Warden Service Division of the Department of Inland Fisheries and Wildlife.

Sec. 7036, No. 4; Prohibited Acts

Failure to notify. Except as otherwise provided through written agreement, a person is guilty of failure to report a lost, stranded or drowned person if he has knowledge that a person is lost, stranded or drowned in the woodlands or inland waters of the State and fails to give notice of the incident by quickest means to the Warden Service Division of the Department of Inland Fisheries and Wildlife.

Fires and Fire Closure

The following is a summary of regulations that govern building fires in various areas:

1. In Acadia National Park and in state parks, regulations permit fires at designated places only. In Acadia National Park, consult a park ranger before building any fire.

2. In the White Mountain National Forest, permits are no longer required, but hikers who build fires are still legally responsible for any damage they may cause.

3. In other areas:

    a. In organized territory (i.e., within the boundaries of a township with its own local civil government), fires may be kindled on private land only with written permission from the landowner. The landowner's permission must be presented to the town fire warden, who may then issue a permit.

    b. In unorganized territory (i.e., where the local government function is performed by state or county authorities), a permit for outdoor cooking and warming fires may be obtained free of charge from any MFS ranger.

    c. Fires may be built without a permit at the following places:

        (1) MFS-authorized campsites and lunch grounds
        (2) State Highway Commission roadside picnic areas
        (3) Appalachian Trail shelter sites
        (4) Baxter Park and Recreation campgrounds and campsites (but see park regulations and discuss with rangers)
        (5) Maine Bureau of Parks and Recreation campsites and picnic areas
        (6) Maine Bureau of Public Lands–authorized campsites

    d. Specific and detailed information on fire permits may be obtained from any MFS ranger or the Forest Service's Augusta office (telephone number: 207-287-2791).

During periods when the danger of fires is high, the governor, through proclamation, may prohibit all outdoor fires or may close the woods altogether. Check with the MFS before embarking on a trip for any restrictions that may be in effect. It will have the most up-to-date and accurate information regarding fires and required permits.

We cannot stress enough the importance of care when you use fire in the woods. Hikers as a group have compiled a fine record, but a forest fire traced to the carelessness of a hiker could result in the closing of much land and many trails.

Maine Forest Service Fire Towers

For years, the Maine Forest Service maintained fire towers on many mountains. The trails built to these summit towers made excellent hiking paths. During the last two decades, these towers have been abandoned as the MFS has switched to aircraft for forest fire patrol. Several of the towers have been removed or converted to other uses, such as microwave or cable television relay. Others have been tipped over and left in an unsightly mess.

Some of the fire wardens' cabins have been sold to private owners; others are in disrepair or have been vandalized or torn down. Do not expect to use them for camping or emergency shelter.

In many cases, continued use by hikers or adoption by volunteers has kept trails to fire towers open; in other, more remote regions, the trails are becoming overgrown. No group has offered to maintain them. Before you head for the more isolated areas with summit towers, check trail conditions with the local MFS office.

Camp Trip Leaders' Permits

Those who lead summer-camp trips in Maine should be aware of a law that regulates issuing permits for camp trip leaders. The text of the legislation is given below; for more information, write to the Department of Inland Fisheries and Wildlife, 41 State House Station, 284 State St., Augusta, ME 04333, ifw.webmaster@maine.gov.

Title 12, Sec. 7322; Permits for Camp Trip Leaders

Boys' and girls' camps licensed by the Department of Human Services, or located in another state and licensed in a similar manner, if the laws of the other state so require, conducting trip camping shall: provide at least one staff member over 18 years of age for each 6 campers and ensure that the staff member in charge of the trip holds a valid trip leader permit. Any person wishing a permit shall submit an application on forms provided by the commissioner and shall pay the application fee. To qualify initially for a permit, an applicant must show successful completion of an approved trip leader safety course or complete an application provided by the commissioner outlining in detail the applicant's experience and training as a trip leader; and meet any other requirements adopted by rule of the commissioner. Waiver of the course requirement by the commissioner on the basis of the applicant's experience and payment of the application fee shall qualify the applicant for a trip leader permit.

With the advice of the board, the commissioner shall review and adopt a trip leader safety course curriculum which shall include, but not be limited to: training in first aid; training in water safety, including life saving techniques as appropriate; and trip leader qualifications and required experience for the special waiver procedure in subsection 4. The commissioner shall publish the curriculum adopted or approved by the board and a current list of courses, with the approved curriculum, by name and address.

Wardens of the department and the rangers of the Forestry Service and rangers of the Bureau of Parks and Lands may terminate any trip which is considered unsafe or in violation of this section.

The initial qualifying fee for a trip leader permit is $18. The permit may be renewed upon payment of $13 if requirements of the department are met.

Winter Considerations

For those who are properly prepared, winter hiking and climbing in Maine offer challenge and satisfaction. The general comments in the *AMC White Mountain Guide*'s section on winter climbing apply equally well to winter climbing in Maine. An added factor in Maine winter climbing is that unplowed access roads frequently lengthen a trip. Many trips that take only a day in summer may take two or more in winter and require camping.

Snowshoes are a must. Climbers should also carry crampons if they are likely to travel on ice or "boilerplate" snow. Other required gear includes an ice ax or ski pole if you are climbing on open slopes. For brisk snowshoeing, a light shell over a wool shirt is usually sufficient, even in very cold weather. At rest or above timberline, you will usually need an insulated parka and wind pants, and perhaps a face mask and goggles. Be sure to carry spare pairs of wool socks and warm mittens along with an extra hat. Ordinary leather boots are inadequate. Waterproof insulated boots are recommended, and they should not be too tight.

Deep snow can make route finding difficult. In steep areas or when snow is not compacted, hiking time is much longer than in summer. Be prepared to make an early start and to return after dark using artificial light. Trips should be planned carefully.

The trail descriptions given in various sections of this guide usually apply in winter, with the qualifications that unplowed roads may add distance and trail markers may be hidden. Winter hikers should avoid high peaks and steep rocky slopes unless they have a lot of experience.

Any hikers climbing the higher and longer routes in winter should be fully aware of the danger of low temperatures and high winds. This danger is infinitely greater in winter than in summer. Consult a windchill chart for an indication of how cold your hike can be. Plan your trips with such weather in mind.

Note that Baxter State Park has very specific winter use registration requirements, including minimum size and experience level of group. See pages 4 through 8 of this guide. For more specific guidelines, go to the Park's website: www.baxterstateparkauthority.com.

Skiing

A number of Maine's downhill ski areas are mentioned briefly in the text. To locate them easily, refer to the index under Skiing.

In summer, ski trails offer routes that, because of their width and their usually zigzag course on the steeper slopes, are likely to have better views than do regular summer trails. On the other hand, ski trails are less shady, the footing may be poor and rough, and some of them cross swampy places.

Bushwhacking

This guide deals mainly with mountains in Maine that have trails, but it does include a few peaks where you must bushwhack for short distances. It leaves out countless other bushwhacking sites, ranging from rather low hills to mountains approaching 4000 ft. Some of these mountains are close to existing roads and trails, but many others are accessible only by water or long approach walks. Various topographic maps will show many of these named and unnamed trailless peaks.

Only people who are fully experienced in route finding, using a compass, and map reading should try to bushwhack the higher and more distant mountains. Bushwhackers can encounter a variety of problems and should take extra care to carry sufficient food, clothing, shelter, compasses, first aid equipment, and similar supplies. Bushwhacking is much more time consuming than ordinary hiking, and you should be prepared to spend the night out if necessary.

Since most trailless mountains are located on private property, you should obtain permission from an authorized person prior to starting out. You should also be extra careful to leave word with a responsible party of your routes and destinations.

Bushwhackers should not mark their routes. The usual markers, such as rags and tapes, deteriorate rapidly. Missing markers may mislead those who subsequently attempt to follow them. Markers also destroy the concept of a mountain without trails. If you plan to take the same route out that you take in and you want to mark it to save time on the return, please remove your markers as you leave.

Northern Maine Landowners' Policies

Maine's economy depends very much upon its woodlands. Traditionally, these lands have been owned by a large number of small-lot owners and by a small number of companies that own large areas. These private holdings include many of Maine's mountains; generally, owners allow recreational use of their land.

The opening of the Allagash Wilderness Waterway and improved highways and roads leading to northern and northwestern Maine have increased the flow of hikers, hunters, anglers, canoeists, and others to the forest country. At the same time, continuing technological advances in logging have led to greater use of trucks to haul lumber and pulpwood. The timberland owners constantly extend their system of private roads, many of which are open to the public. These roads offer access to many areas that used to be difficult to reach.

Each landowner or land-owning company has particular rules. Prior permission is often needed to use a company's roads. For instance, some companies do not allow trailers or RVs on their roads, and others limit vehicle length and width. Anyone coming from a distance to enter an area should check ahead of time with the companies concerned.

In 2003, the AMC purchased the 37,000-acre Katahdin Iron Works tract near Gulf Hagas in the 100-Mile Wilderness. The purchase is part of the AMC's Maine Woods Initiative, which seeks to address the ecological and economic needs of the Maine Woods region by supporting local forest products jobs and traditional recreation, creating new multiday backcountry experiences for visitors, and attracting new nature-based tourism to the region.

At time of publication, the AMC is developing a management plan to determine which portions of the Katahdin Iron Works tract will be managed for natural resource protection, recreation, certified sustainable forestry, and multiple use.

The tract is part of the KI-Jo Mary Multiple Use Forest, which is administered by North Maine Woods, Inc. (NMW).

The Maine Forest Service has transferred control and management of most of its forest campsites in this area to NMW, which operates gates on the major private roads into the area. Users must register at the gates and pay fees, which vary somewhat from year to year and are at times higher for out-of-state residents. There are also fees for use of campsites within the controlled area. The landowners have established some basic rules for their roads. Speed limits are posted. Trucks always have the right-of-way on these private roads. Do not leave unattended cars that block passage on any road; large logging trucks may need to pass, or access could suddenly be needed to fight a forest fire. Pull well off the road when stopping, even for a few minutes.

For a map showing the gates and for the latest regulations and information, access the North Maine Woods website, www.northmainewoods.org or call 207-435-6213. North Maine Woods, P.O. Box 425, Ashland, ME 04732. The Sportsman's Alliance of Maine, 205 Church Hill Rd., Augusta, ME 04330 (207-622-5503), www.samcef.org, offers information on public and private lands issues including access.

Cooperation

The AMC earnestly requests that those who use the trails, shelters, and campsites on public lands know the rules and follow them. The same consideration should be shown to private landowners; please be respectful while on private land. Note that some landowners require permission. The AMC appreciates landowners willingness to allow public access. Hikers should keep in mind that land ownership does change and trails that were previously open to the public may have been closed. The AMC will post any updates to the information in this guide at www.outdoors.org/amcbookupdates.

The New England Trail Conference advises that trails should not be blazed or cut on private property without the consent of the owners and definite provision for maintenance. Trails should not be cut or marked on public lands without the approval of the park or forest officials.

The main purpose of this book is to furnish accurate details, both in the text and on the maps; we will gratefully accept corrections from àny source. If you find inaccuracies, signs missing, obscure places on the trails, or a map that needs correcting, please send a report to Books Editor, Appalachian Mountain Club, 5 Joy St., Boston, MA 02108.

Maps and Resources

Extra copies of the maps at the back of this guide can be purchased separately from the Appalachian Mountain Club, 5 Joy St., Boston, MA 02108 or from the AMC's website, www.outdoors.org, or by calling 800-262-4455. Elevations of mountaintops and other points can be found on the maps. Remember, though, that a map cannot indicate the condition of a trail. This is a function of the text. Never assume the existence of a usable route merely because there is a dotted line on the map. Consult both the text and the map.

Among many maps and books covering the mountainous areas of Maine, the following may be particularly valuable.

- For coverage of Acadia National Park, see AMC's *Hiking, Biking, and Paddling Map to Acadia National Park.* AMC also publishes a comprehensive, multisport guide to the park, *Discover Acadia National Park* (Monkmans, Second Edition 2005).
- USGS topographic quadrangles have been published for all of Maine. The 7.5-min. series has replaced the old 15-min. series. In this book, the text indicates the quadrangle available for a given mountain. An index map showing all USGS maps is available at many sporting-goods stores and bookstores throughout the state. The index map and individual maps are also available from USGS Map Sales, Federal Center, Box 25286, Denver, CO 80225 (800-USA-MAPS).
- DeLorme Map Store, 2 DeLorme Dr., P.O. Box 298, Yarmouth, ME 04096 (207-846-7100 and 800-642-0970) publishes *The Maine Map and Guide*, an accurate and regularly updated map of Maine. *The Maine Atlas and Gazetteer*, from the same publisher, provides detailed sectional maps indicating roads, trails, and significant topographic features.
- The fourteenth (2004) edition of the *Appalachian Trail Guide to Maine* contains further information about the Appalachian Trail and maps (seven) for this trail's entire length in Maine. Copies are available at many retail outlets and from the Maine Appalachian Trail Club, P.O. Box 283, Augusta, ME 04330-0283.

- For further detail on Baxter State Park, see *Katahdin: A Guidebook to Baxter State Park & Katahdin*, by Stephen Clark, published by Clark Books, Shapleigh, ME 04076.
- Information about state parks, public lands, and fire permits can be obtained from the Maine Forest Service (207-287-2275); Bureau of Public Lands (207-287-3061); and Bureau of Parks and Recreation (207-287-3821).
- The AMC's journal, *Appalachia*, periodically publishes material on the mountains of Maine. *Appalachia*, America's longest-running journal of mountaineering and conservation, has been published twice yearly since 1876. To subscribe, call 800-262-4455, or go to www.outdoors.org.

Abbreviations

The following abbreviations are used in the trail descriptions:

min.	minute(s)
hr.	hour(s)
mph	miles per hour
in.	inch(es)
ft.	foot, feet
yd.	yard(s)
mi.	mile(s)
m.	meter(s)
km.	kilometer(s)
est.	estimate
jct.	junction
rt	round trip
lp	loop
Mt.	Mount
Mtn.	Mountain
AMC	Appalachian Mountain Club
AT	Appalachian Trail
BSP	Baxter State Park
CTA	Chatham Trail Association
FR	Forest Route
MATC	Maine Appalachian Trail Club
ME	Maine
MFS	Maine Forest Service
NH	New Hampshire
NPS	National Park Service
US	United States
USFS	United States Forest Service
USGS	United States Geological Survey
WMNF	White Mountain National Forest

Section 1

Baxter State Park and Katahdin

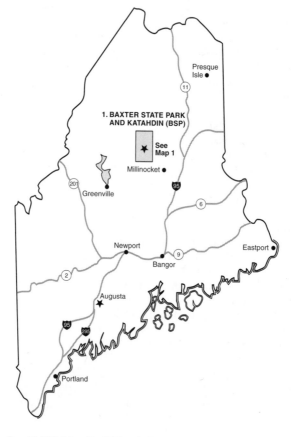

See AMC Maine Trail Map 1: Baxter State Park/Katahdin.

RECOMMENDED HIKES

Easy

Howe Brook Trail (rt: 6.0 mi., 3 hr.) A beautiful walk with little elevation change along a mountain brook, with chutes and potholes, ending at a small waterfall.

Lookout Ledge (rt: 2.6 mi., 1 hr. 45 min.) A short hike to a panoramic view of the inteior of the park.

Grassy Pond (Loop) Trail (lp: 3.1 mi., 1 hr. 30 min.) A beautiful wildlife walk, encompassing four ponds.

Foss & Knowlton Pond Trail (rt: 5.3 mi., 2 hr. 30 min.) Access to Foss & Knowlton Ponds for fly fishing.

Moderate

South Turner Trail (rt: 4.0 mi., 3 hr. 40 min.) This hike takes you past Sandy Stream Pond, which is frequented by moose, and ends on the summit of South Turner Mtn., where there are exceptional views of the park.

North Traveler Trail (rt: 5.0 mi., 4 hr. 40 min.) An interesting trail that traverses through alpine meadows, old woods, and ledges to an impressive view from the summit of North Traveler Mtn.

Strenuous

Abol Trail to Baxter Peak via Hunt Trail (rt: 7.6 mi., 7 hr.) This is believed to be the oldest route up Katahdin. The trail intersects with the Hunt Trail, first climbing up through the Old Abol Slide, then following the Hunt Trail (AT) up to Baxter Peak, where the northern terminus of the AT is.

Martston Trail–Mount Coe Loop (lp: 8.8 mi., 7 hr.) This loop hike provides access to North and South Brother, whose summits provide excellent views of the surrounding areas.

LIST OF MOUNTAINS

Katahdin, at 5267 ft. the highest mountain in Maine, is about 80 mi. north of Bangor, between the East and West branches of the Penobscot River. It is as wild and alluring as any mountain in the East. The name, in Indian dialect, means "greatest mountain." Katahdin lies within Baxter State Park (BSP), created by a gift of former governor Percival P. Baxter in 1931. By the time of his death in 1969, Governor Baxter had extended the grant to more than 200,000 acres. A condition of his gift—there are variant wordings and differing interpretations by Governor Baxter and others—is that the area "shall forever be left in its natural wild state, forever be kept as a sanctuary for wild beasts and birds and forever be used for public forest, public park and public recreational purposes."

Katahdin (5267 ft.)

Katahdin, an irregularly shaped mountain mass, rises abruptly from comparatively flat country to a gently sloping plateau above the treeline. It culminates on its southeastern margin in an irregular series of low summits, of which the southern two are the highest. These peaks are 0.3 mi. apart, and Baxter Peak (5267 ft.) to the northwest is the higher of the two. From the southeastern South Peak (5240 ft.) a long, curved, serrated ridge of vertically fractured granite, known as the Knife Edge, hooks away to the east and northeast. About 0.7 mi. from South Peak, this ridge ends in a rock pyramid called Chimney Peak. Immediately beyond Chimney Peak, and separated from it by a sharp cleft, is a broader rock peak, Pamola (4919 ft.), named for the Indian avenging spirit of the mountain. To the north, the broad rock mass of Hamlin Peak (4756 ft.) dominates the plateau or tableland, which ends in the series of low North (Howe) Peaks (4750–4612 ft.). Refer to the Katahdin map in this guide.

The first recorded ascent of Katahdin was in 1804 by a party of eleven, including Charles Turner Jr., who wrote an account of the ascent. There may have been unrecorded ascents during the next 15 years, but we know the mountain was climbed again in 1819 and 1820. After this date, ascents became more regular.

The tableland, nearly 4 mi. long, falls away abruptly from 1000 to 2000 ft. on all sides. After that, the slope becomes more gentle. Great arms stretch out to embrace glacial cirques, known locally as basins. The Great Basin, with its branch, the South Basin, is the best known. In the floor of the latter, at an altitude of 2910 ft., Chimney Pond lies flanked by impressive cliffs and bordered by dense spruce forest. It fills about eight acres and is a base for many varied mountain climbs. North of the Great Basin, but still on the eastern side of the mountain, is the North Basin (floor altitude 3100 ft.), whose high, smooth-ledged sides surround a barren, boulder-strewn floor. The nearby Little North Basin has few visitors. On the western side of the tableland, the little-known Northwest Basin lies at about 2800 ft., and farther south, there is a broad valley known as the Klondike. Klondike Pond rests in a small glacial arm of this valley, just below the plateau. At 3435 ft., it is 0.3 mi. long, deep, narrow, and remarkably beautiful.

From the peaks at its northern and southern ends, the tableland slopes gradually toward the center, known as the Saddle. From the eastern escarpment of the Saddle, the land falls off gently toward the dense scrub that carpets the northwestern edge. Many avalanches have scored the walls of the tableland, but only two of these scorings are now trails—the Saddle Slide at the western end of the Great Basin and the Abol Slide on the southwestern flank of the mountain.

Katahdin's isolated position makes for an exceptional view that takes in hundreds of lakes, including Moosehead; the many windings of the Penobscot; and, to the south, the hills of Mt. Desert Island and Camden. Mt. Washington seems to lie in a direct line behind Mt. Abraham and is not visible.

Katahdin is the northern terminus of the Appalachian Trail, which includes the Hunt Trail on Katahdin itself. The great mountain lies on the southeastern side of a scattered group of smaller mountains, many of which offer interesting climbs and good views, particularly of Katahdin. The text describes these mountains following the description of Katahdin and covers them in a clockwise direction—west, north, and then northeast.

West of Katahdin, the following mountains form an elbow-shaped range: the Owl, Barren Mtn., Mt. OJI, Mt. Coe, South Brother, North Brother, Fort Mtn., Sentinel Mtn., and the striking Doubletop Mtn. offer fine views from the western side of Nesowadnehunk Stream. Mullen Mtn. and Wassataquoik Mtn. are in the remote area between Fort Mtn. and Wassataquoik Lake. Sprawling Traveler Mtn. is the principal mountain in the northern section of the park. The South Branch ponds and campground sit at its western base. Turner Mtn. is to the northeast of Katahdin and offers magnificent views of it.

In all, there are at least 46 mountain peaks in the park. Eighteen of them exceed 3500 ft.

Camping facilities that accommodate about one thousand persons are available at 10 different public campgrounds, from which most trails are accessible (see the Katahdin/Baxter map). The campgrounds are: Roaring Brook, Abol, Katahdin Stream, Nesowadnehunk (Sourdnahunk), Kidney Pond, Daicey Pond, South Branch Pond, Trout Brook Farm, Russell Pond, and Chimney Pond. Russell Pond and Chimney Pond are accessible only by trail; the Park Tote Road serves the other eight. All the campgrounds have lean-tos (except Daicey Pond and Kidney Pond) and tentsites (except Chimney Pond, Daicey Pond, and Kidney Pond); some have bunkhouses. Daicey Pond and Kidney Pond have cabins only. All these sites offer only the most basic facilities. There are no hot showers, grocery stores, or gasoline stations, and the water is untreated throughout Baxter Park. Campers and visitors supply their own food and cooking utensils.

There are camping areas for groups of 12 or more at Avalanche Field, Foster Field, Nesowadnehunk Field, and Trout Brook Farm. Backcountry campsites for hiking parties of four or less are at Davis Pond, Pogy Pond, Wassataquoik Stream, Wassataquoik Lake Island, Little Wassataquoik Lake, Little East, Webster Stream, Long Pond, Middle Fowler Pond, Lower Fowler Pond, Upper South Branch Pond, Billfish Pond, Center Mtn., Hudson Pond, Matagamon Lake, and Webster Lake. Park headquarters in Millinocket, handles all reservations for park facilities. You can rent canoes at the South Branch Pond, Russell Pond, Kidney Pond, Daicey Pond, Trout Brook areas, Matagamon and Togue Pond Gates, Katahdin Stream and Vistor Center.

To preserve the wilderness environment, park authorities have begun limiting the number of visitors in the park. Reservations are strongly recommended and are the only way to guarantee space. Reservations must be confirmed and paid for in advance via mail or in person; phone reservations are confirmed with a credit card payment for last minute reservations 10 days or closer to the desired date. For reservations, write the Reservation Clerk, Baxter State Park, 64 Balsam Dr., Millinocket, ME 04462 (207-723-5140). When allotted spaces have been filled, no more overnight campers are allowed in the park. To avoid unnecessary driving and disappointment, campers without reservations should call the reservation clerk before starting a long trip to the park.

If camping facilities at Baxter State Park are filled, you can try a number of private sporting camps and campgrounds in the area around the park. The Maine Forest Service maintains several campsites in the general area.

The park is open to the public 12 months a year, although roads are not maintained for winter vehicle travel. There is a road fee for non-Maine vehicles. Nearly all of the 186 mi. of trails are blue-blazed. The only exception is the white-blazed Appalachian Trail. Remember that at various points on the tableland of Katahdin, and particularly near its summit, local variation in declination makes the compass somewhat unreliable.

For day use, hikers arriving at the Togue Pond Visitor Center will find announcements of trailhead closures posted outside the building as parking lots fill to capacity on busy days. When trailhead parking lots are filled, hikers will be directed to alternative trails and parking lots. Please be ready to choose a different hike if the trailhead for the trip you had planned is already full for the day. Early arrival is recommended.

Roads to the park run through Millinocket and Patten. These routes are shown on the official Maine Highway Map (or any other general highway map). Roads in the Baxter State Park area are indicated on the Katahdin/Baxter map with this guidebook. To reach the southern and eastern entrances to the park from points to the south, follow I-95 north to the Medway exit, and then go west on ME 157 to Millinocket and the park area; or continue on I-95 to Sherman Mills, and then follow ME 11 to Patten and ME 159 west past Shin Pond to the northern portion of the park.

Currently, the park has two entrances. As they enter or leave the park, all visitors must stop at the entrance gatehouse to register and to pick up or leave passes. You can also find out about the status of hiking trails on the mountains and get other information at the gate-house.

The southernmost gatehouse is just north of Togue Pond, about 18 mi. from Millinocket. Immediately past the gatehouse, the road forks. The right fork leads 8.1 mi. to the Roaring Brook Campground and trails to Chimney Pond and Russell Pond. The left fork leads to the Abol Campground (5.7 mi.), the Katahdin Stream Campground (7.7 mi.), and the Nesowadnehunk Field and Campground (16.8 mi.).

The second entrance is on Matagamon (First Grand) Lake on the approach road to the northeastern part of the park. It is 24 mi. from Patten and ME 11. Follow ME 159 west from Patten past Shin Pond. The Trout Brook Farm Campground is 2.6 mi. to the west on the Park Tote road. The South Branch Pond Campground is 9.6 mi. Drive west at first on the Park Tote road, and then south about 2.5 mi. on a well-marked turnoff.

You can reach most campgrounds and other facilities in the park from the Park Tote road. To meet the terms of former Governor Baxter's deeds of trust, park roads are unpaved and relatively unimproved. The Park Tote road extends 41.1 mi. from the Togue Pond Gatehouse to the Matagamon Gatehouse. It is a very narrow, winding, dirt or gravel road. Except in a few places, dense foliage along the road restricts the view. A trip to Baxter State Park is not really worthwhile unless you plan to hike or camp.

From the Togue Pond Gatehouse, the Park Tote Road first leads northwest and then generally north. It skirts the southern and western flanks of Katahdin. During the first five miles of the drive, the mountain is briefly visible a few times. After passing the Abol and Katahdin Stream campgrounds, the road reaches Foster Field, where you can see Doubletop, OJI, and other mountains in the range west of Katahdin. After that, the views are very restricted all the way to the Matagamon Gatehouse. Most of the Park Tote Road follows the routes of old logging roads. For clarity and consistency, the older, more colorful road names have been dropped in favor of the term "Tote Road."

People planning to camp, hike, and use the facilities in the park should know the rules and regulations, which are revised annually. They can be obtained by writing to Baxter State Park, 64 Balsam Dr., Millinocket ME 04462. The latest versions of the most important rules are summarized below. The Park's official website, www.baxterstateparkauthority.com, will provide the most current Park information available.

Camping is allowed only at authorized campgrounds or campsites. A responsible adult at least 18 years old must accompany groups that include five or more persons under 16 years of age; there must be one adult for each five minors. Larger camping groups may be restricted to authorized group-camping areas. The rules prohibit bringing pets into the park and also limit the entry and use of larger recreational vehicles. They also prohibit airplanes, motorboats, motorcycles, trail bikes, and other all-terrain vehicles. Currently, snowmobiles may be operated only on the Park Tote road. They may not be used on South Branch Pond, Daicey Pond, Kidney Pond, or Roaring Brook Rds., except by authorized park personnel.

Warning: Severe injuries and deaths have occurred in the Park. Visitors are responsible for their own safety as well as that of thier group in the Park's wilderness conditions. The upper summits are very high and are rugged and bare above the timberline, and the park is fairly far north. As a result, the weather and trail conditions can change very quickly, even in the middle of summer. The weather on Katahdin is similar to that on Mt. Washington, but longer access routes can make conditions even more dangerous in many cases.

Hikers planning to go to higher elevations should take plenty of food, water, and warm clothing. The trails on many of the routes are among the steepest and most difficult in New England. Hikers should be in good physical condition if they plan to climb the higher and more distant summits; those who are not in good shape should limit their activities accordingly. Do not leave the trails (unless bushwhacking is suggested in this guide), particularly on Katahdin or during severe weather or limited visibility.

Due to the high volume of trail use, please stay on the trail above treeline and in areas marked "Wildlife Area Only." Wildlife, if crowded, can become stressed; please respect their homes and habits by keeping a safe distance away. The alpine environment above the treeline in Baxter State Park is home to many rare and unusual plants and animals, including a few on Maine's Endangered Species List. Please help care for their fragile environment by staying on the marked trails.

Hikers entering the park via the Appalachian Trail must register at the trail kiosk as they enter the Park.

Hunt Trail (map 1: D1–D2)

The white-blazed Hunt Trail, the route of the Appalachian Trail up Katahdin, climbs the mountain from the southwest. It was first cut in 1900 by Irving O. Hunt, who operated a sporting camp on Sourdnahunk Stream. The trail leaves from the Katahdin Stream Campground. From the treeline to the tableland, this trail is steep and rough. Heed the warnings in the previous paragraphs.

The trail follows the northern side of Katahdin Stream. At 1.1 mi. from the campground, it passes the trail to the Owl on the left, then crosses Katahdin Stream; shortly after that, a trail leaves left to Katahdin Stream Falls. The trail steepens through the spruce and, at 2.7 mi., reaches two large rocks that form a cave, a nice place to enjoy lunch if you are hiking on a rainy day. There is a spring, undependable in dry periods, 50 yd. down the trail from this feature.

The trail passes through a growth of small spruce and, in 0.2 mi., emerges on the bare, steep crest of the southwestern shoulder of Katahdin, called the Camel's Hump. There, cairns mark the trail, which goes on to wind among gigantic boulders. The trail then traverses a broad shelf and climbs steeply 0.5 mi. over broken rock to the open tableland (at 3.7 mi.), where two slabs of rock mark the "Gateway." The trail continues east, following a worn path and paint blazes, until it reaches Thoreau Spring (at 4.2 mi.), an unreliable water source. At the spring, the Baxter Peak Cutoff trail goes off to the left and reaches the Saddle in 0.9 mi. This trail provides a loop route for travel from the summit to the Saddle via the Saddle Trail and back to Thoreau Spring and down the Hunt Trail to Katahdin Stream Campground. To the right, the Abol Trail descends

2.8 mi. to the Abol Campground. From the spring, the Hunt Trail climbs moderately northeast for 1.0 mi. to Baxter Peak, with its commanding panoramas and surprising view of the South Basin.

Distances from Katahdin Stream Campground

> *to* Owl Trail junction: 1.1 mi., 45 min.
>
> *to* cave: 2.7 mi., 2 hr. 55 min.
>
> *to* Gateway: 3.7 mi., 4 hr. 25 min.
>
> *to* Thoreau Spring and junctions with Abol Trail and Baxter Peak Cutoff: 4.2 mi., 4 hr. 35 min.
>
> *to* Saddle (via Baxter Peak Cutoff): 5.1 mi., 5 hr. 30 min.
>
> *to* Baxter Peak: 5.2 mi., 5 hr. 20 min.
>
> *to* Chimney Pond Campground (via Baxter Peak Cutoff and Saddle Trail): 6.8 mi., 6 hr. 30 min. *Note: Descending to Chimney Pond for an overnight necessitates descending to the Roaring Brook Campground, 16 miles from the Katahdin Stream Campground trailhead. A second vehicle must be spotted at Roaring Brook Campground; there is no shuttle service available. Returning to the summit of Katahdin from Chimney Pond and then returning via the Hunt Trail after overnighting at Chimney Pond is not recommended.*
>
> *to* Chimney Pond Campground (via Baxter Peak, the Knife Edge, and Dudley Trail): 7.6 mi., 7 hr. 45 min. This is a very difficult route, and should only be attempted by experienced hikers. *Note: Backpacking with overnight gear from one side of Katahdin to the other is not recommended by Park staff. Camping overnight on the mountain is not allowed and visitors are responsible for their own group safety as well as rescue costs if hiking against Park recommendations.*

Abol Trail (map 1: D2)

The Abol Trail is believed to be the oldest route up the mountain, and evidence exists that the first recorded ascent took place near this trail. It follows a great slide up the southwestern side of Katahdin.

Caution: This trail is dangerous because of its steepness and the great amount of loose rock and gravel in the slide. Climb and descend with great care.

The trail leaves the Park Tote road at the Abol Campground. It crosses through the campground and, at 0.2 mi., enters an old tote road and reaches the southern bank of a tributary of Abol Stream. It continues along the southern bank of the stream for 0.6 mi. The trail then bears right (northeast) away from the brook and leads sharply right. It reaches a gravel wash of old Abol Slide (1.3 mi.) and climbs the slide, reaching a more recent slide at 1.9 mi. Beyond this point, the slide is steeper and becomes entirely bare. Huge boulders and increasing steepness mark the latter part of this climb. On the tableland, paint blazes lead 0.1 mi. to Thoreau Spring and the Hunt Trail. Go right on the Hunt Trail and continue northeast up gentle slopes to the summit of Katahdin. Water at Thoreau Spring has become unreliable in recent years. It is possible to make a long but rewarding circuit using the Hunt and Abol trails. You can either leave cars at both the Abol and Katahdin Stream campgrounds or walk the 2.0 mi. between them on the Park Tote road. Going up by the Abol Trail is best.

Distances from Abol Campground

> *to* foot of old Abol Slide: 1.3 mi., 1 hr. 20 min.
>
> *to* tableland: 2.6 mi., 3 hr. 15 min.
>
> *to* Thoreau Spring and Hunt Trail junction: 2.8 mi., 3 hr. 20 min.
>
> *to* Baxter Peak (via Hunt Trail): 3.8 mi., 4 hr. 5 min. (descending, 3 hr.)
>
> *to* Katahdin Stream Campground (via Hunt Trail): 9 mi., est. 9 hr.

Roaring Brook Campground (map 1: D3)

This campground, at about 1480 ft., is on the southern bank of Roaring Brook at the northern terminus of Roaring Brook Rd. It is about 8.1 mi. from the Togue Pond Gatehouse. Trails to Chimney Pond and Russell Pond start here. Closer by are Sandy Stream Pond (where hikers often see wildlife) and South Turner Mtn.

Distances from Roaring Brook Campground

> *to* Chimney Pond (via Chimney Pond Trail): 3.3 mi., 2 hr. 30 min. (descending, 2 hr.)
>
> *to* Baxter Peak (via Chimney Pond and Dudley trails and the Knife Edge): 5.7 mi., 6 hr. 5 min. (descending, 4 hr. 40 min.)
>
> *to* Baxter Peak (via Chimney Pond and Saddle trails): 5.5 mi., 4 hr. 35 min. (descending, 3 hr. 15 min.)
>
> *to* Baxter Peak (via Taylor Trail and the Knife Edge): 4.3 mi., 5 hr. 15 min. (descending, 3 hr. 10 min.)

- *to* Hamlin Peak (via Chimney Pond, North Basin Cutoff, and Hamlin Ridge trails): 4.5 mi., 4 hr. 15 min.
- *to* North Basin (via Chimney Pond, North Basin Cutoff, and North Basin trails): 3.3 mi., 2 hr. 35 min. (descending, 1 hr. 50 min.)
- *to* Russell Pond (via Russell Pond Trail): 7.0 mi., 3 hr. 45 min.
- *to* South Turner Mtn. summit (via Russell Pond and South Turner Mtn. trails): 2.0 mi., 1 hr. 50 min.

Helon Taylor Trail (map 1: D3)

Much of this trail follows the route of the old Leavitt Trail. It provides a direct route from the Roaring Brook Campground to Pamola and follows the exposed Keep Ridge. This route provides the best sustained views of any trail starting from a road in the park, but it also exposes the hiker to the weather. Be careful. Avoid this trail in bad weather, particularly if you plan to go all the way to Baxter Peak via the Knife Edge. The Taylor Trail does not have dangerous footing, but it does require almost continuous climbing over rocks and boulders, so it can be fairly tiring.

The trail begins on the Chimney Pond Trail 0.1 mi. west of the Roaring Brook Campground. It climbs 0.5 mi. through mixed growth to a ridge crest. It then levels off for a short period, passing through scrub and a boulder field. After that, it climbs steeply through small birch, enters an old flat burn, and drops to the small Bear Brook, one of the branches of Avalanche Brook. Bear Brook offers the only water on the trail.

After Bear Brook, the trail ascends steeply through scrub, a fine stand of conifers, and a boulder field with wide views in all directions. It climbs over and between boulders to Keep Ridge and then along the open ridge—with a spectacular view of the Knife Edge opening up ahead—to the summit of Pamola.

Distances from Roaring Brook Campground

- *to* start (via Chimney Pond Trail): 0.1 mi., 5 min.
- *to* Pamola summit: 3.2 mi., 3 hr. 20 min. (descending, 2 hr. 15 min.)
- *to* Baxter Peak (via the Knife Edge): 4.3 mi., 5 hr. 15 min. (descending, 3 hr. 10 min.)
- *to* Chimney Pond Campground (via the Knife Edge and Cathedral Trail): 6.0 mi., 4 hr. 55 min.

Chimney Pond Trail (map 1: D3)

The Chimney Pond Trail begins at the ranger's cabin at the Roaring Brook Campground. Following the old Basin Ponds tote road, it climbs west along the southern bank of Roaring Brook. After 0.6 mi., it bears gradually away from the brook and climbs more steeply. A brook, the outlet of Pamola Pond, crosses at 1.0 mi. At 1.9 mi., the trail bears left; 50 yd. to the left is the site of the old Basin Ponds Camp, GNP Camp 3 (1921–1936). The trail then bears right and enters an overgrown clearing at 2 mi. At that point, Lower Basin Pond comes into view.

The trail follows the southern end of Lower Basin Pond and continues along its southwestern shore. At 2.2 mi., the trail goes left uphill into the woods. At 2.3 mi., the North Basin Cutoff goes off to the right. Stay left to continue on the Chimney Pond Trail. At 2.7 mi., it follows the side of a depression known as Dry Pond, which holds water in spring and after heavy rains. At 3.0 mi., the North Basin Trail to Hamlin Ridge and the North Basin leaves on the right, and at 3.2 mi., there is a bunkhouse, part of the Chimney Pond campground, on the left. The trail then goes downhill slightly to end at the shore of Chimney Pond.

Distances from Roaring Brook Campground

> *to* brook crossing: 1.0 mi., 35 min.
>
> *to* North Basin Cutoff junction: 2.3 mi., 1 hr. 30 min.
>
> *to* Dry Pond: 2.7 mi., 2 hr. 5 min.
>
> *to* North Basin Trail junction: 3.0 mi., 2 hr. 20 min.
>
> *to* Chimney Pond Campground: 3.3 mi., 2 hr. 30 min.

Chimney Pond Campground (map 1: D3)

Magnificently located on Chimney Pond (2910 ft.), this campground is an excellent base for climbing to the highest summits and the tableland area. Because of this campground's heavy use and fragile ecology, the park authority enforces several restrictions. No open fires are allowed; campers must use portable stoves. In addition, campers may not set up tents; overnight visitors must sleep in the bunkhouse or lean-tos. Early reservations are a must at this popular site.

Distances from Chimney Pond Campground

> *to* Roaring Brook Campground (via Chimney Pond Trail): 3.3 mi., 2 hr.

to North Basin (via Chimney Pond and North Basin trails): 1.2 mi., 45 min.

to Hamlin Peak (via Chimney Pond, North Basin, and Hamlin Ridge trails): 2.0 mi., 2 hr. 30 min. (descending, 1 hr. 45 min.)

to Davis Pond Lean-to (via Saddle and Northwest Basin trails): 4.4 mi., 3 hr. 30 min. (returning, 3 hr. 45 min.)

to Baxter Peak (via Dudley Trail and the Knife Edge): 2.4 mi., 3 hr. 45 min. (returning, 3 hr.)

to Baxter Peak (via Cathedral Trail): 1.7 mi., 2 hr. 30 min. (descending, 1 hr. 45 min.)

to Baxter Peak (via Saddle Trail): 2.2 mi., 2 hr. 15 min. (descending, 1 hr. 35 min.)

to Baxter Peak (via Chimney Pond, North Basin, Hamlin Ridge, and Saddle trails): 4.2 mi., 3 hr. 55 min. (descending, 3 hr. 5 min.)

to Katahdin Stream Campground (via Saddle Trail, Baxter Peak Cutoff, and Hunt Trail): 6.8 mi., 5 hr.

Dudley Trail (map 1: D3)

The Dudley Trail leads from Chimney Pond to Pamola. It runs from the ranger's cabin east across the outlet of the pond, bears right, climbs over huge boulders, and reenters the woods, where the route is well blazed. On the rocks, cairns mark the trail clearly.

At 0.3 mi. from the pond, a side trail to the left marked Pamola Caves leads past ledges, often streaming with water, and climbs to some caves that are about 0.4 mi. from the Dudley Trail. In the caves, you must worm your way through small winding passages to reach three remarkably straight, spacious corridors.

The Dudley Trail continues nearly due east from the junction, reaches a major cleft in the cliffs, and then climbs rapidly south. The soft granite has eroded into curious forms, and the trail becomes more difficult. Emerging above the timberline, the trail is marked by cairns, blue paint blazes on the rocks, and a well-worn path that traverses patches of heath and low spruce. The trail bears slightly right (southwest) nearly to the edge of the South Basin. Then it heads south again and on up the long northern slope of Pamola. The route's boulders rival those on the Hunt Trail, but the constantly changing view of the Great Basin below enhances the climb. After 30 min. among boulders, the going gets smoother and Index Rock (1.0 mi.) rises ahead. The trail passes just to the right of this landmark and continues less steeply 0.3 mi. to the peak of Pamola (4919 ft.). To reach Baxter Peak and points beyond, continue along the Knife Edge (see below). At Pamola, the Taylor Trail from the Roaring Brook Campground comes in over Keep Ridge from the east.

Descending, the left-hand (western) line of cairns should be followed from the summit of Pamola. Stay near the edge of the South Basin and pass just to the left of Index Rock. At 1.0 mi. from Pamola, the side trail to Pamola Caves goes to the right and the Dudley Trail descends to the left.

Distances from Chimney Pond Campground

> *to* side trail to Pamola Caves: 0.3 mi., 15 min.
>
> *to* Pamola Caves (via side trail): 0.7 mi., 1 hr.
>
> *to* Pamola summit: 1.3 mi., 2 hr. (descending, 1 hr. 30 min.)
>
> *to* Baxter Peak (via the Knife Edge): 2.4 mi., 3 hr. 45 min. (descending back to Chimney Pond, 3 hr.)

The Knife Edge (map 1: D3)

This narrow, serrated ridge tops the southern wall of the South Basin. Cliffs plummet down on the north, and the walls on the south are only slightly less steep. In places, the ridge narrows to only 2 or 3 ft. This is probably the most spectacular mountain trail in the East. The narrowness of the ridge, combined with the dizzying height and sheer cliffs, gives a sense of extreme exposure. This trail is not recommended for those afraid of heights.

From the summit of Pamola, follow the cairns that lead southwest. The trail drops abruptly into the sharp cleft at the top of the Chimney, then climbs the equally steep rock tower of Chimney Peak (4900 ft). From there, the route is fairly obvious. It traverses the Sawteeth, finally climbing the South Peak (5240 ft.) and continuing along the rocks of the summit ridge to Baxter Peak. *Caution: The Knife Edge is dangerous in a strong wind. Do not leave the trail. In recent years, several climbers have had accidents while trying to take unmarked "shortcuts" to the bottom.*

Distance from Pamola summit

> *to* Baxter Peak: 1.1 mi., 1 hr. 45 min.

Cathedral Trail (map 1: D3)

The three immense Cathedral Rocks extend from the summit ridge and partly separate the South Basin from the Great Basin.

A sign a few feet west of the ranger's cabin at Chimney Pond marks the start of this route to Baxter Peak by way of Cathedral Rocks. The trail climbs through a small, tangled spruce forest and passes into an old evergreen forest. At 0.3 mi., it goes by Cleftrock Pool, on the right. At 0.4 mi., by a large cairn, the trail turns right toward the Cathedrals, crosses a bridge of rock covered with low growth, climbs steeply through boulders to a high point, and from there, continues through low trees.

In 1967, a slide wiped out part of the next section of the trail, but with care you can still follow the route easily. Blazes mark the way around to the right, then up the steep side of the first Cathedral (0.8 mi.). The climb of the second Cathedral (0.9 mi.) is interesting and offers spectacular views of the Chimney and the Knife Edge. The route continues up the ridge to the top of the third Cathedral at 1.1 mi. At 1.2 mi., the trail forks. The right (northwest) fork is the Cathedral Cutoff and leads 0.2 mi. to the Saddle Trail. The Cathedral Trail bears left (southwest) 0.2 mi. over large boulders to the Saddle Trail (1.4 mi.), which it joins 0.8 mi. above the Saddle.

For one of the best circuits of the upper part of Katahdin, go up the Cathedral Trail to Baxter Peak; then either return to Chimney Pond via the Saddle Trail, or take the Knife Edge to Pamola and return to Chimney Pond via the Dudley Trail, or go on to the Roaring Brook Campground via the Taylor Trail.

Distances from Chimney Pond Campground

- *to* second Cathedral: 0.9 mi., 1 hr. 30 min.
- *to* Saddle Trail junction: 1.4 mi., 2 hr. 20 min.
- *to* Baxter Peak (via Saddle Trail): 1.6 mi., 2 hr. 30 min.
- *to* Chimney Pond Campground (via Saddle Trail): 3.9 mi., 4 hr. 5 min.
- *to* Chimney Pond Campground (via the Knife Edge and Dudley Trail): 4.1 mi., 5 hr. 15 min.
- *to* Roaring Brook Campground (via the Knife Edge and Taylor Trail): 6.0 mi., 5 hr. 40 min.

Saddle Trail (map 1: D3)

Climbers have taken this general route out of the basin since Saddle Slide occurred in 1899. Before that, they used an older slide just north of the present one.

The Saddle Trail is the least difficult route up Katahdin from Chimney Pond. From the ranger's cabin, the worn trail climbs a rocky path through dense softwoods. Beyond this stand, the trail swings to the right (north) and becomes smoother and flatter as it continues through an evergreen forest. It crosses a brook at 0.8 mi., then climbs steeply over large boulders. At 0.9 mi., the trail bears left up Saddle Slide and passes through stunted birches. At 1.0 mi., it emerges from scrub, and there is a scramble for 0.2 mi. up the loose, open slope of the slide. (Be careful of loose rocks.) At 1.2 mi., the trail suddenly reaches the top of the slide and the level, open tableland at the Saddle between the summits of Baxter Peak and Hamlin Peak. Go left (south) to reach Baxter Peak. The Northwest Basin Trail, to the right, leads to Caribou Spring, the Hamlin Ridge Trail, the North (Howe) Peaks Trail, the Northwest Basin, and all points on the northern end of the mountain.

The Saddle Trail to Baxter Peak continues south over gentle slopes. Cairns mark the well-worn path.

At 1.7 mi., the trail passes a large boulder. The northern end of the Cathedral Cutoff, which leads to the Cathedral Trail, is on the left (east); on the right (west) is the eastern end of the Baxter Peak Cutoff, which leads southwest along the base of the summit 0.9 mi. to Thoreau Spring and the Abol and Hunt trails. At 2.0 mi., the Cathedral Trail from Chimney Pond enters on the left. The Saddle Trail continues on to Baxter Peak at 2.2 mi.

Distances from Chimney Pond Campground

- *to* Saddle Slide: 0.9 mi., 40 min.
- *to* Saddle and Northwest Basin Trail junction: 1.2 mi., 1 hr. 25 min.
- *to* Cathedral Trail junction: 2.0 mi., 1 hr. 55 min.
- *to* Baxter Peak: 2.2 mi., 2 hr. 15 min.
- *to* Chimney Pond Campground (via Cathedral Trail): 3.9 mi., 4 hr.
- *to* Chimney Pond Campground (via the Knife Edge and Dudley Trail): 4.6 mi., 5 hr. 15 min.
- *to* Roaring Brook Campground (via the Knife Edge and Taylor Trail): 6.5 mi. (10.5 km.), 5 hr. 25 min.

Baxter Peak Cutoff (map 1: D3)

The trail leaves the Saddle Trail 1.7 mi. from Chimney Pond. It runs southwest over the open tableland along the base of Baxter Peak and ends at Thoreau Spring, which is on the Hunt Trail, 4.2 mi. from the Katahdin Stream Campground.

This trail makes it possible to hike a loop trail from one side of Katahdin to the other. In addition, the Baxter Peak Cutoff could provide an alternative path to a safer descent trail if caught on the mountain in bad weather.

Distances from Chimney Pond Campground

- *to* start of cutoff (via Saddle Trail): 1.7 mi., 1 hr. 45 min.
- *to* Thoreau Spring (Hunt Trail and Abol Trail junction): 2.6 mi., 2 hr. 15 min.

North Basin Trail (map 1: D3)

From Chimney Pond, follow the Chimney Pond Trail toward Basin Ponds. At 0.3 mi., the North Basin Trail starts on the left (north; look for sign). The trail runs through spruce forest to a junction with the Hamlin Ridge Trail on the left (west) at 0.7 mi. Then it passes across the foot of Hamlin Ridge to a junction, at 0.9 mi., with the North Basin Cutoff Trail. Signs and a large cairn mark this junction. The North Basin Trail continues to the lip of the North Basin and then reaches Blueberry Knoll, a few feet higher than the floor of the basin, where there is a sweeping view of both the North Basin and the South Basin, as well as the landscape to the east. From Blueberry Knoll, it is possible to bushwhack to the boulder-strewn floor of the North Basin, with its two little ponds. The northern wall is a tremendous sheer cliff.

Distances from Chimney Pond Campground

- *to* start (via Chimney Pond Trail): 0.3 mi., 10 min.
- *to* North Basin Cutoff junction: 0.9 mi., 30 min.
- *to* Blueberry Knoll: 1.2 mi., 45 min.
- *to* North Basin Pond (via bushwhack): 1.4 mi., 55 min.
- *to* Roaring Brook Campground (via North Basin Cutoff and Chimney Pond Trail): 3.9 mi., 2 hr. 45 min.

North Basin Cutoff (map 1: D3)

This trail from Basin Ponds to Hamlin Ridge and the North Basin forks right (sign) 2.3 mi. from the Roaring Brook Campground on the Chimney Pond Trail. It traverses an area of second-growth spruce, runs past several active beaver ponds, then climbs steeply through old growth to a junction with the North Basin Trail (0.7 mi.). To reach Hamlin Ridge, turn left (southwest); to reach Blueberry Knoll and North Basin, turn right (northeast).

Distances from Roaring Brook Campground

- *to*   start (via Chimney Pond Trail): 2.3 mi., 1 hr. 30 min.
- *to*   North Basin Trail junction: 3.0 mi., 2 hr. 25 min.
- *to*   Blueberry Knoll (via North Basin Trail): 3.0 mi., 2 hr. 35 min.
- *to*   Hamlin Ridge Trail (via North Basin Trail): 3.2 mi., 2 hr. 25 min.
- *to*   Chimney Pond Campground (via North Basin and Chimney Pond trails): 3.9 mi., 2 hr. 55 min.

Hamlin Ridge Trail (map 1: D2–D3)

The trail climbs, largely in the open, up Hamlin Ridge, which separates the North and South basins. The views are magnificent. From the Chimney Pond Campground, follow the Chimney Pond Trail 0.3 mi. to the North Basin Trail, then follow the North Basin Trail for 0.4 mi., to the start of the Hamlin Ridge Trail, which reaches the treeline after a climb of about 20 min. Then, after a short stretch of boulder-strewn slope, the trail rises to the backbone of the ridge. It follows the open ridge to Hamlin Peak (4756 ft.), and from there it goes on 0.2 mi. west across the open tableland and through a boulder field to Caribou Spring, which may have water in a spring on the right side of the trail near a large cairn. All water sources on Katahdin are unreliable; be sure to carry sufficient water. To the right from Hamlin Peak, the North (Howe) Peaks Trail runs along the headwall of North Basin and reaches Howe Peaks in just under a mile.

Distances from Chimney Pond Campground

- *to*   start (via Chimney Pond and North Basin trails): 0.7 mi., 20 min.
- *to*   Hamlin Peak: 2.0 mi., 2 hr. 30 min.
- *to*   Caribou Spring: 2.2 mi., 2 hr. 40 min.

Hamlin Peak Cutoff (map 1: D3)

Following a good path along the contour, this trail runs from the North Peaks, at a point in the col between North Peaks and Hamlin Peak, to the Northwest Basin Trail at Caribou Spring. By traveling north–south along the tableland, it avoids the climb over Hamlin Peak.

Distance from North Peaks

   to Northwest Basin Trail junction, Caribou Spring: 0.3 mi. (0.5 km.), 8 min.

Northwest Basin Trail (map 1: C3–D3)

This route climbs from the Russell Pond area to the Saddle through the wild and secluded Northwest Basin, with its virgin trees, glacial sheepback rocks, five ponds, waterfalls, and interesting central ridge. The lower end of the trail follows the route of the old Wassataquoik Tote Rd.

The trail begins at the Russell Pond Campground. It leads southwest from Russell Pond following the Russell Pond Trail for 0.1 mi. It then diverges right and crosses a dam at the foot of Turner Deadwater at about 0.3 mi. From there it goes on through the woods until it joins the route of the old Wassataquoik Tote Rd., at about 0.5 mi.

With Wassataquoik Stream on the left, the trail stays on the tote road and climbs gradually, crossing Annis Brook about 2.5 mi. from Russell Pond. The trail crosses a small brook that drains the eastern slope of Fort Mtn. It continues through thick woods and crosses Wassataquoik Stream at 3.6 mi. (*Caution:* Be very careful in high water.)

The trail climbs steadily, soon approaching Northwest Basin Brook. It runs along the brook bed for 300 ft. at about 4.4 mi. (Proceed carefully here; the rocks are very slippery.) Above the junction of the outlets from the first two ponds, Lake Cowles and Davis Pond, the trail leads steeply up to the northern shore of Lake Cowles. It then turns left and at 4.7 mi. crosses the outlet of Lake Cowles. Where it climbs to a heath-covered glacial sheepback rock, the path is becoming overgrown with blueberry bushes but is not hard to follow. From the sheepback, there are enjoyable views of the entire basin. The trail continues down to the Davis Pond Lean-to, at 5.1 mi. The shelter, rebuilt in 1987, is located on the northern side of Davis Pond.

From the Davis Pond Lean-to, the Northwest Basin Trail passes the so-called disappearing pond. (The fourth pond is 0.3 mi. below and on the outlet of Davis Pond; the fifth is hidden deep in the woods between the outlets of

Lake Cowles and Davis Pond.) The trail first goes southwest and then south as it climbs through a steep and rough area up the basin wall.

The trail emerges from the scrub and, at 6.2 mi., reaches a large cairn that marks a small peak (4410 ft.) near the western end of the Northwest Plateau. The Northwest Plateau reaches toward the west and is a flat extension of the northern tableland. It lies west of North Peaks and separates the Northwest Basin from Klondike Pond Ravine. Its lower slopes push their way far out into the Klondike. The Northwest Basin Trail climbs very gradually across the Northwest Plateau, passing through a belt of scrub at 6.8 mi. Then it continues more to the south across open tableland to Caribou Spring, at 7.3 mi. At the spring, the Hamlin Peak Cutoff leads sharply left to the North Peaks Trail, and the Hamlin Ridge Trail climbs left (east) to Hamlin Peak.

The Northwest Basin Trail descends south and at 8.3 mi., it reaches the Saddle. To get to Chimney Pond, descend east on the Saddle Trail.

Keep in mind that poor trail or weather conditions, heavy packs, and different levels of physical conditioning in hiking parties will increase the times given here.

Distances from Russell Pond Campground

>   *to* North Peaks Trail junction: 1.2 mi., 35 min.

>   *to* Annis Brook crossing: 2.5 mi., 1 hr. 30 min.

>   *to* Wassataquoik Stream crossing: 3.6 mi., 2 hr. 15 min.

>   *to* Davis Pond Lean-to: 5.1 mi., 3 hr. 15 min.

>   *to* peak of Northwest Plateau: 6.2 mi., 4 hr. 50 min.

>   *to* Hamlin Ridge Trail and Hamlin Peak Cutoff junction, Caribou Spring: 7.3 mi., 5 hr. 35 min.

>   *to* Saddle and Saddle Trail junction: 8.3 mi. (13.3 km.), 6 hr.

Russell Pond Trail (map 1: C3–D3)

This trail runs from the Roaring Brook Campground northward between Katahdin and Turner Mountain to the Russell Pond Campground. It is the principal approach to the Russell Pond area.

After leaving the Roaring Brook Campground, the trail crosses Roaring Brook. At 0.2 mi., it turns left (northwest; look for sign). To the right, the South Turner Mountain Trail leads to Sandy Stream Pond and South Turner Mtn. In the next half-mile, the Russell Pond Trail crosses several brooks while gradually climbing the low height-of-land between Sandy Stream Pond and Whidden Pond. The trail descends and passes to the east (right) of the latter, where there is an extensive view of the basins and peaks on the east side of Katahdin. At 1.1 mi., the Sandy Stream Pond Trail comes in on the right. At 1.4 mi., an opening yields good views; after this point, the trail moves into denser forest. Between 2.3 mi. and 3.1 mi., it crosses several brooks, and at 3.3 mi., it reaches a junction on the right with the Wassataquoik Stream Trail, which leads 2.5 mi. to the two Wassataquoik Stream lean-tos and rejoins the Russell Pond Trail at 3.9 mi. At 3.4 mi., the Russell Pond Trail crosses the Wassataquoik South Branch and soon crosses another brook. There are no bridges here; the crossing is knee-deep in dry weather, dangerous after rain.

The trail, now on the western side of the valley, passes under an overhanging rock at 3.8 mi. Moving away from Wassataquoik Stream, it passes several brooks and springs and climbs gently for nearly two miles to a spruce grove. Then the trail gradually descends, with the impressive, high, forested slopes of Russell Mtn. on the left. At 6.3 mi., it crosses the main branch of Wassataquoik Stream. At 6.5 mi., it crosses the old Wassataquoik Tote Rd. with the abandoned clearing for New City Camps on the right. A trail on the right leads 1.4 mi. to the two lean-tos on Wassataquoik Stream. Immediately beyond the tote road, the Russell Pond Trail crosses Turner Brook (North Branch of the Wassataquoik).

At 6.9 mi., the Northwest Basin Trail to the Saddle leaves on the left (west). Soon after, the trail reaches Russell Pond.

Distances from Roaring Brook Campground

> *to* Sandy Stream Pond Trail junction: 1.1 mi., 30 min.

> *to* Wassataquoik Stream Trail junction: 3.3 mi., 1 hr. 40 min.

> *to* Wassataquoik Tote Rd. junction: 6.5 mi., 3 hr. 10 min.

> *to* Northwest Basin Trail junction: 6.9 mi., 3 hr. 40 min.

> *to* Russell Pond Campground: 7.0 mi. (11.3 km.), 3 hr. 45 min.

Wassataquoik Stream Trail (map 1: C3)

Some once called this old route the Tracy Horse Trail or Wassataquoik South Branch Trail. It runs from the Russell Pond Trail along the South Branch of Wassataquoik Stream to the main branch of Wassataquoik Stream. It leaves the right (east) side of the Russell Pond Trail about 3.3 mi. north of the Roaring

Brook Campground, just before that trail crosses the South Branch. It leads to the junction with the main stream and continues along the southern bank of the main stream for about 100 yd.

The park authority maintains two lean-tos at the site of the old Hersey Dam (some remains of the dam are still visible). Reservations for them can be made as for any campsite.

To reach the Russell Pond Campground from the lean-tos, cross to the northern side of Wassataquoik Stream upstream from the lean-tos (no bridge) and look for a blue-blazed trail along the old Wassataquoik Tote Rd. In the downstream direction, this trail leads 1.6 mi. to a junction with the Grand Falls Trail at Inscription Rock. In the upstream direction, it leads 1.4 mi. to a junction with the Russell Pond Trail just south of the Turner Brook crossing. Turn right on the Russell Pond Trail to reach the campground, which is about 0.4 mi. away.

Distances from Roaring Brook Campground

> *to* start of trail to lean-tos (via Russell Pond Trail): 3.3 mi., 1 hr. 40 min.
>
> *to* lean-tos: 5.8 mi., 3 hr.
>
> *to* Russell Pond Campground (via Russell Pond Trail): 7.6 mi., 3 hr. 45 min.

Russell Mountain (2810 ft.)

This mountain is the northernmost extension of Katahdin. Its broad, trailless summit area is devoid of recognizable characteristics and so flat and full of boulders that you have to search for the summit cairn. But the summit offers excellent views in all directions. To reach it, bushwhack west from the Russell Pond Trail about 4.5 mi. north of the Roaring Brook Campground. Since there is no trail to the mountain and conditions change from year to year, check with the ranger at the Russell Pond Campground for the latest information. See also the section on Bushwhacking in the Maine Mountains in this book's introduction.

Russell Pond Campground (map 1: C3)

On the southwestern shore of Russell Pond (1333 ft.) in the heart of the wilderness north of Katahdin, this campground is a convenient and interesting hiking base. The wildlife in this remote area is especially intriguing. Facilities include tentsites, lean-tos, and a bunkhouse. The Wassataquoik Lake Cabin and the lean-tos on Wassataquoik Stream, Pogy Pond, and Little Wassataquoik Pond are administered from this campground.

Distances from Russell Pond Campground

> *to* Roaring Brook Campground (via Russell Pond Trail): 7.0 mi., 3 hr. 45 min.

> *to* Davis Pond Lean-to (via Northwest Basin Trail): 5.1 mi., 3 hr. 15 min. (descending, 2 hr. 45 min.)

> *to* Wassataquoik Lake (via Wassataquoik Lake Trail): 2.4 mi., 1 hr. 15 min.

> *to* Little Wassataquoik Lake (via Wassataquoik Lake Trail): 5.2 mi., 3 hr. 10 min.

> *to* Nesowadnehunk Campground: 14.3 mi. (relocated 1996)

> *to* Lookout (via Pogy Notch and Grand Falls trails): 1.3 mi., 50 min.

> *to* Grand Falls (via Grand Falls Trail): 2.8 mi., 1 hr. 30 min.

> *to* South Branch Pond Campground (via Pogy Notch Trail): 9.7 mi., 4 hr. 40 min.

> *to* Wassataquoik Stream lean-tos (via Wassataquoik Stream Trail): 1.8 mi., 1 hr.

Wassataquoik Lake Trail (map 1: C1–C3)

This trail connects the Russell Pond Campground with the Wassataquoik Lake area and continues on to the west to the tote road and the foot of Nesowadnehunk Lake. Most of the first part of this route was a logging road prior to 1878, and there is evidence it was cut out before 1845. The area was logged several times afterward. The west end of the trail follows a fairly new logging road built after the park was created. The former owners retained cutting rights for a period after they sold the property to Governor Baxter.

The trail leads north off the Pogy Notch Trail opposite Lean-to 4 at the northwestern corner of Russell Pond. At 0.5 mi. from Russell Pond, take the left fork (the right fork leads to Deep Pond). At 1.5 mi., the trail crosses a dam between two of the Six Ponds. It then crosses a brook at 2.0 mi., and at 2.2 mi., a side trail leads right (north) 300 ft. to a canoe landing for the island campsite on Wassataquoik Lake. The trail, relocated in 1994, parallels the southern shore of the lake. About halfway along, a trail leads left (south) uphill to Green Falls, one of the most beautiful spots in the park.

Near the head of Wassataquoik Lake, at 4.3 mi., the trail joins an old road. After crossing the outlet stream from Little Wassataquoik Lake several times, it reaches the lake itself. It then follows along the northern shore to the lake's western end (about 5.2 mi.). The trail heads west from the lake toward a col between Wassataquoik Mtn. and Lord Mtn. Shortly after leaving the lake, at 4.9 mi., the trail passes the Little Wassataquoik Lake Lean-to. The trail climbs to the col and then descends into the Trout Brook drainage area. From the col, the trail follows an old logging road for about a mile and a half before it leaves the road and turns left at about 6.3 mi. At 7.0 mi. the trail, relocated in 1996, swings left (south). Wet in places, it crosses a brook several times and, at about 8.2 mi., it crosses the South Branch of Trout Brook. The trail then skirts a series of small hills. At 9.7 mi., it reaches Center Pond, which has fine views of the Brothers. Ford and follow Little Nesowadnehunk Stream to the Nesowadnehunk Campground at 14.3 mi.

Distances from Russell Pond Campground

   to start (via Pogy Notch Trail): 0.2 mi., 5 min.

   to Deep Pond side-trail junction: 0.5 mi., 20 min.

   to dam at Six Ponds: 1.5 mi., 50 min.

   to side trail to Wassataquoik Lake: 2.2 mi., 1 hr. 10 min.

   to Green Falls (via side trail): 3.1 mi., 1 hr. 45 min.

   to Little Wassataquoik Lake: 4.6 mi., 3 hr. 10 min.

   to left turn off old logging road: 6.3 mi., 3 hr. 50 min.

   to Center Mtn. Lean-to: 7.9 mi., 4 hr. 20 min.

   to South Branch of Trout Brook: 8.2 mi., 4 hr. 30 min.

   to Center Pond: 9.7 mi., 5 hr. 20 min.

   to Nesowadnehunk Campground: 14.3 mi., 6 hr. 15 min.

Grand Falls Trail (map 1: C3)

This trail leads from the Russell Pond Campground to several interesting locations in Wassataquoik Valley. Its first part coincides with the Pogy Notch Trail.

From the campground, follow the Pogy Notch Trail around the western shore of the pond. The Wassataquoik Lake Trail leaves to the left soon after the start of the route. At 0.2 mi., the Pogy Notch Trail continues north (left) at a junction. The Grand Falls Trail takes the right fork, passes the ranger station, and continues to the next junction (0.4 mi.), where the trail to Lookout Ledges leaves to the left (north). The Grand Falls Trail continues ahead on the right through woods and over relatively level ground toward Wassataquoik Stream. As it nears the Wassataquoik, a side trail to the right leads 17 yd. to the bank of the stream and Inscription Rock, a huge boulder with a notice about logging in the area that was inscribed in 1883. A 1.6-mi. segment of the old Wassataquoik Tote Rd., from Inscription Rock to the Wassataquoik Stream Lean-tos, was reopened in 1983, allowing you to loop back to Russell Pond via the Wassataquoik Stream Trail and the Russell Pond Trail. From this junction, the main trail soon reaches the bank of Wassataquoik Stream near the Grand Falls of the Wassataquoik. These falls drop steeply through high granite walls and are impressive, particularly in high water. The ruins of a logging dam lie just upstream.

Distances from Russell Pond Campground

> *to* Lookout Trail junction: 0.4 mi., 10 min.

> *to* Inscription Rock (via side trail): est. 2.5 mi., 1 hr. 20 min.

> *to* Grand Falls: est. 2.8 mi. (4.5 km.), 1 hr. 30 min.

Lookout Trail (map 1: C3)

This high outlook (1730 ft.) offers views from Traveler Mtn. around to Katahdin and is easy to reach from the Russell Pond Campground. Follow the Pogy Notch and Grand Falls trails for 0.4 mi. and turn left at the junction. The trail climbs moderately and steadily for nearly a mile to the ledges.

Distances from Russell Pond Campground

> *to* start (via Pogy Notch and Grand Falls trails): 0.4 mi., 10 min.

> *to* Lookout Ledges: 1.3 mi. (2.1 km.), 50 min.

The Owl (3736 ft.)

This mountain is the first summit in the long, high range that runs west from Katahdin. Its southern face is especially steep.

The Owl Trail (map 1: D2)

The blue-blazed Owl Trail leaves the Hunt Trail 1.1 mi. from the Katahdin Stream Campground. The trail goes left from the Hunt Trail just before a crossing of Katahdin Stream and then follows the northern bank of a tributary. It turns sharply right (southeast) and crosses the tributary at 1.6 mi. (last source of water). The trail climbs gradually through dense spruce and fir and follows the western spur toward the summit. At 2.9 mi., the trail rises steeply through a ravine and then across the upper part of the Owl's prominent cliffs. At 3.2 mi., the trail reaches the first outlook. After a more gradual climb, it reaches the summit at 3.3 mi. Views in all directions are outstanding, especially those into the Klondike and across to the tremendous windrows in Witherle Ravine and on Fort Mtn.

Distances from Katahdin Stream Campground

> *to* start (via Hunt Trail): 1.1 mi., 45 min.

> *to* first outlook: 3.2 mi., 2 hr. 35 min.

> *to* the Owl summit: 3.3 mi. (5.3 km.), 2 hr. 40 min.

Barren Mountain (3696 ft.; 3681 ft.)

A high, wooded ridge, trailless Barren Mtn. has two well-defined summits and several lower humps. A blowdown that occurred in 1974 eliminated possible approaches from the south and southwest.

One route for a possible bushwhack of Barren Mtn. goes up the southeastern slide of OJI, then southeast into the col and up the Barren summit ridge. Scrub growth near the summits of OJI and Barren makes this route slow. It is also possible to climb from the Owl-Barren ravine, but blowdowns make this approach very difficult. See the section on Bushwhacking in the Maine Mountains in this book's introduction.

Mount OJI (3434 ft.)

Mt. OJI got its name from three slides on its southwestern slope that at one point suggested the three letters. After a major storm in 1932, however, the slides began to enlarge, and the letter shapes have become distorted. A fourth large slide came down in 1954; it is south of the so-called south slide. The north slide trail has been closed due to a number of serious injuries occurring on the wet slab sections. The south slide route is recommended.

Mt. OJI South Slide Trail (map 1: D2)

The trail leaves the tote road at Foster Field directly opposite the road to Kidney Pond and immediately crosses a brook. To follow the south-slide route, go right at the fork 0.4 mi. from Foster Field. The route follows an old road and, at 1.8 mi., continues on a narrow trail. As the gravel wash from the slide becomes noticeable on the forest floor, the trail bears right and soon reaches the open wash (2.0 mi.). Climb to the head of the slide and through brush and scrub to the summit ridge. Then go northwest to the summit (2.9 mi.), where a trail leads left to Old Jay Eye Rock, a fine observation point..

Another route is to approach the mountain by climbing the Mt. Coe slide. The OJI Link Trail, cleared in 1983, runs 0.5 mi. from the Mt. Coe slide across the col to a junction with the OJI South Slide Trail 0.2 mi. from the summit.

Distances from Park Tote Road at Foster Field

> *to* fork in trail: 0.4 mi., 10 min.
>
> *to* foot of south slide (via right fork): 2.0 mi., 1 hr. 10 min.
>
> *to* OJI summit (via south slide): 2.9 mi., 3 hr. 15 min.

Mount Coe (3795 ft.)

This peak, just north of Mt. OJI, has excellent views into the Klondike and is well worth the challenge of the climb.

Mount Coe Trail (map 1: C2–D2)

Follow the Marston Trail to the sign 1.2 mi. from the Park Tote Road. Turn right and follow the trail 0.2 mi. to the bottom of the Mt. Coe slide (it follows a stream). The climb is steady but moderate at first, then steep. At 2.6 mi., the trail bears left and begins to climb the left center of a wide slide area at 2.8 mi. (The OJI Link Trail leads right 0.5 mi. to the OJI South Slide Trail. It is 0.7 mi. to the summit of OJI via this trail.) At 3 mi., the trail enters scrub growth. At 3.3 mi. you will reach the summit.

An extension of the Mount Coe Trail, cleared in 1983 and further extended in 1987, rejoins the Marston Trail at a point 0.8 mi. from the summit of North Brother.

The trail descends the eastern ridge of Mt. Coe and proceeds toward South Brother. At 4.2 mi., you will pass two clearings with fine views of Mt. Coe. At 4.4 mi., the South Brother Side Trail leads right 0.3 mi. to the summit of South

Brother. At 5.1 mi., you will reach the junction with the Marston Trail. Ahead, it is 0.8 mi. to the summit of North Brother. To the left, it is 2.9 mi. to the tote road.

Distances from Park Tote Road at Slide Dam

- *to* start of Mt. Coe Trail (via Marston Trail): 1.2 mi., 50 min.
- *to* foot of Mt. Coe slide: 1.4 mi., 1 hr.
- *to* start of scrub: 3.0 mi., 3 hr. 45 min.
- *to* Coe summit: 3.3 mi., 4 hr. (descending, 2 hr.)
- *to* South Brother Side Trail junction: 4.4 mi., 4 hr. 45 min.
- *to* Marston Trail junction: 5.1 mi., 5 hr. 15 min.

The Brothers (North, 4151 ft.; South, 3970 ft.)

North and South Brother are open peaks that offer splendid views in several directions. *Caution: Early in the season—late May and the first half of June—climbers should expect to find deep snow at high elevations—a distance of 1.5 mi.*

Marston Trail (map 1: C1–C2)

The Marston Trail, the best approach for exploring the Brothers area, was relocated in 1987.

The trail leaves the Park Tote Road at the Slide Dam, 5.9 mi. north of the Katahdin Stream Campground and 3.6 mi. south of the Nesowadnehunk Campground. The trail starts from the road, nearly opposite the picnic shelter, and follows the northern bank of Slide Brook to an open, sandy area. At 0.2 mi., the trail bears left into a wooded area and over a slight rise into the drainage area of a second brook. Climbing steadily, the trail follows this brook closely for the next mile. At 0.8 mi., it crosses, and there are several more crossings in the next 0.4 mi. before the trail reaches the junction with the Mount Coe Trail at 1.3 mi.

The Marston Trail leads to the left and climbs gradually through extensive blowdowns. A small pond with fine views is reached at 2.0 mi. At 2.1 mi., you will reach the pond's outlet (last water). The trail then climbs steeply, passing several viewpoints. It levels off at 2.7 mi. and reaches the upper junction with the Mount Coe Trail at 2.9 mi. To the left, it is 0.8 mi. to North Brother. To the right, the Mount Coe Trail leads (1.0 mi. to South Brother via the South Brother Side Trail) 5.1 mi. to the Park Tote Road. After crossing this fairly level valley, it passes a spring at 3.1 mi. and then climbs steeply. At 3.6 mi., the trail leaves the scrub and continues among open boulders, reaching the summit of North Brother at 3.7 mi. Note particularly the view of the western slopes of Katahdin and, in the opposite direction, of the Nesowadnehunk Lake region and the interesting valley of Little Nesowadnehunk Stream.

Distances from Park Tote Road at Slide Dam

  to Mount Coe Trail, first junction: 1.3 mi., 50 min.

  to pond: 2.1 mi., 1 hr. 10 min.

  to Mount Coe Trail, second junction: 3.7 mi., 3 hr.

  to North Brother summit: 4.5 mi., 3 hr., 40 min. (descending, 2 hr., 50 min.)

Fort Mountain (3867 ft.)

This mountain, with its half-mile summit ridge, is northeast of North Brother. A high saddle connects the two. The best and easiest route to Fort Mtn. is a trail leading left into the bush from the summit of North Brother. This trail is rough, unmarked, and obliterated in sections by blown-down trees; it keeps to the southern side of the North Brother–Fort ridge most of the way. It emerges on the northwestern end of the Fort ridge. The distance is less than one mile.

Since the last printing, this trail is no longer in use. Hikers must now bushwack this trail at their own risk. The Park emphasizes that hikers must not cut brush or leave flagging at the end of their hike. Camping in Baxter State Park is in authorized sites only.

Distances from Park Tote Road at Slide Dam

  to North Brother summit (via Marston Trail): 3.7 mi., 3 hr.

  to Fort Mtn. northwestern summit: est. 4.7 mi., 4 hr. (descending, 2 hr. 45 min.)

Daicey Pond Campground (map 1: D2)

When the Baxter State Park (BSP) Authority terminated the private leases still existing in the park in the late 1960s, it decided to continue operations on a modified scale at the former Twin Pines Camps at Daicey Pond. There are 10 cabins for rent. Users must provide their own cooking equipment. Canoes can be rented. To reach Daicey Pond, follow the tote road for 2.7 mi. beyond the Katahdin Stream Campground and turn left (south). It is 1.5 mi. to the camps, which have beautiful views of the western side of Katahdin and the mountains to the west. From a canoe on the pond, you can get an excellent view of Doubletop.

The Appalachian Trail (AT) passes within a short distance of the campground and skirts the shore opposite the camp for 0.3 mi. Hikers entering the park from the south along the AT must register at the Abol kiosk and upon arrival at Katahdin Stream Campground. Katahdin Stream is 1.9 mi. northeast on the AT. South of Daicey Pond, the AT passes an old dam on Nesowadnehunk Stream and Little and Big Niagara falls. All are worth seeing and are within 1.3 mi. of the campground. The AT then leads out of the park near Abol Bridge on the West Branch of the Penobscot (see the MATC's *Appalachian Trail Guide to Maine* for details).

Daicey Pond is a good starting point for the climb to Sentinel Mtn (1842 ft). Trails also lead to the Kidney Pond area, and a lovely trail of about 1.4 mi. leads from the canoe landing on Daicey Pond, across from the cabins, to Lost Pond.

Grassy Pond (Loop) Trail (map 1: D2)

This 1.6 mile loop trail is a favorite of wildlife watchers, encompassing four ponds in a short hike. The trail is accessible by both the Park Tote Road and Daicey Pond. From the Tote Road, begin at the Appalachian Trail crossing. Heading south on the AT, cross the Tracy and Elbow pond outlets. The Grassy Pond Trail junction will leave the AT 0.5 mi. from the Tote Road. The trail begins in mixed conifer forests and ascends a hill that offers views of Mt. OJI and Doubletop Mtn. to the north and west. Descending the hill leads to the inlet of Grassy Pond, where there is a rental canoe available. There is also a canoe available at the outlet of Grassy Pond. Grassy Pond Trail meets the Nature Trail at the eastern side of Daicey Pond, and can be completed by beginning and ending at Daicey Pond Campground.

Distances from Park Tote Road AT crossing

  to Grassy Pond Trail junction with Appalachian Trail: est. 0.5 mi., 15 min.

Distances from Daicey Pond

      Complete loop, 3.1 mi., 1 hr. 30 min.

Foss & Knowlton Pond Trail (map 1: D2)

This trail heads south from Lost Pond to the AT and the West Branch of the Penobscot River. The trail utilizes fire roads from the Baxter fire of 1977. This trail goes through burnt over area that have been reclaimed by forest pioneer species such as white birch and aspen. The trail allows access to the Foss & Knowlton and Lost Ponds for fly fishing.

Distances from Daicey Pond at the Appalachian Trail

> *to* junction with Foss & Knowlton Pond Trail (via Lost Pond Trail): 1.4 mi., 40 min.

> *to* Foss & Knowlton Pond: est. 2.5 mi., 1 hr. 10 min.

> *to* junction with Appalachian Trail: est. 5.3 mi., 2 hr. 30 min.

Kidney Pond Campground (map 1: D1)

Formerly a private enterprise, the Kidney Pond Campground reopened under park management in 1990 for fishing, hiking, canoe rental on some of the surrounding ponds, and cabin rental. The campground is reached off the Park Tote road, with day-use parking available.

The Draper Pond Trail runs from the Doubletop Mountain Trail 0.5 mi. to a canoe landing on the pond's southern shore. Rocky Pond Trail (0.6 mi.) to the northwest reaches the pond where park canoes can be rented. A 0.6-mi. trail leads to Little Rocky Pond. From the western shore, the Polly Pond Trail runs 0.9 mi. to just outside the park border. From a canoe landing on the western shore of Kidney Pond, the Celia and Jackson Pond Trail reaches Celia Pond at 0.9 mi. At 1.1 mi., the Little Beaver Pond Trail starts south; it runs 0.7 mi. Jackson Pond, with park canoes, is reached at 1.3 mi.

Kidney Pond is girded east and south by its Outlet Trail (1.8 mi.), which heads east, then south, along Nesowadnehunk Stream and branches, left to the Daicey Pond Campground and right (west) to connect with the Sentinel Mountain Trail.

South of Kidney Pond, the Lily Pad Pond Trail goes to a canoe landing on a stream, which reaches the pond in 0.25 mi. From Lily Pad Pond's southern landing, the 1-mi. Windy Pitch Pond Trail heads south to the pond, passing Little and Big Niagara falls.

Distances from Kidney Pond Campground

> *to* Rocky Pond (via Rocky Pond Trail): est. 0.6 mi.

to Little Rocky Pond (via Rocky Pond Trail): est. 1.2 mi.

to Polly Pond (via Rocky Pond and Polly Pond Trails): est. 2.1 mi.

to Daicey Pond Campground (via Outlet Trail): est. 1.9 mi.

to Lily Pad Pond canoe landing (via Lily Pad Pond Trail on south side of Kidney Pond): est. 1.3 mi.

to Celia Pond (via Celia and Jackson Ponds Trail): 1.5 mi.

Sentinel Mountain (1842 ft.)

This low mountain rises over the northern bank of the West Branch of the Penobscot River and offers the finest view of the western side of Katahdin. From Kidney Pond Rd., skirt the western side of Kidney Pond, or paddle across it to the canoe landing (Sentinel Landing) on the southern side of the cove on the right (west).

Sentinel Mountain Trail (map 1: D1–D2)

From Daicey Pond, cross Nesowadnehunk Stream. Then branch left (west) from the trail to Kidney Pond at a point 300 yd. from that pond. The trail goes around the southwestern side of the pond to Sentinel Landing, which is about 0.7 mi. from Daicey Pond. (*Caution: Be careful to avoid several branch trails that are almost as clear as the main trail; some of them lead from a landing the main trail passes before it gets to Sentinel Landing.*)

From Sentinel Landing, the blue-blazed trail to Sentinel Mtn. leads southwest. At 0.3 mi. (sign), the trail bears right onto a section that was relocated to avoid beaver flow. At 0.7 mi., you will have to cross Beaver Brook on stepping-stones. The trail climbs the northeastern side of the mountain along a brook, which crosses the trail at 1.1 mi. and furnishes water nearly to the open summit ledges. The trail reaches the ledges at 2.2 mi. Follow the ledges to the right (north) to reach the actual summit (2.3 mi.).

From the actual summit at the western end of the summit ridge, the trail continues back along the southern side of the ridge, with an outlook over the West Branch, to form a loop. It rejoins the main trail about halfway between the first ledges and the true summit.

Distances from Sentinel Landing

to Beaver Brook crossing: 0.7 mi., 20 min.

> *to* second brook crossing: 1.1 mi., 40 min.
>
> *to* Sentinel summit: 2.3 mi., 1 hr. 30 min.

Doubletop Mountain (North Peak, 3489 ft.)

Doubletop's steep, slide-scarred eastern slopes make it easy to identify from many points in the Katahdin region. The views from its two peaks are impressive and are particularly helpful to anyone planning to climb South Brother, Mt. Coe, Mt. OJI, or Barren Mtn., or to hike into the Klondike.

Doubletop Mountain Trail, Southern Approach (map 1: C1–D1)

The Doubletop Mountain Trail, relocated in 1994, starts at Kidney Pond. At 0.3 mi., it reaches a junction with the Draper Pond Trail; the pond is 0.2 mi. beyond. Cross Slaughter Brook at 0.9 mi.; you will reach Deer Pond at 1.1 mi. At 1.3 mi., bear left on the old Slaughter Pond Tote Rd., which leads to the old Camp 3 clearing.

At the far end of the Camp 3 clearing, the trail to Doubletop forks right (north), leaving the clearing near its northwest corner. Watch carefully: This turn is hard to see. Straight ahead (west), an old road continues to Slaughter Pond. Turn right (north) before you reenter the woods or leave the clearing.

The trail follows an old road northwest up a valley, crossing a stream four times. The stream and trail run together for a while, which makes the route extremely wet and muddy. The trail passes close under the cliffs on Squaw's Bosom, the peak west of Doubletop, and then turns northeast at about 2.3 mi. Just after crossing the headwaters of the stream, it reaches uncut spruce woods and passes a spring at 3.1 mi. Turning north again, the trail climbs the saddle west of Doubletop. Then it slabs up a steep, timbered slope on the western side of the mountain to the South Peak (4 mi.), which is above the timberline. The trail continues from the South Peak 0.2 mi. to the North Peak. From the North Peak, the trail descends and leads north to the Nesowadnehunk Campground.

Distances from Kidney Pond

> *to* old Camp 3 clearing: 2.0 mi., 45 min.
>
> *to* South Peak: 4.6 mi., 3 hr. 20 min.
>
> *to* North Peak: 4.8 mi., 3 hr. 30 min.
>
> *to* Nesowadnehunk Campground: 7.9 mi., 6 hr. 30 min.

Doubletop Mountain Trail, Northern Approach (map 1: C1–D1)

The approach begins after passing the ranger station on your right. Cross over Nesowadnehunk Stream and turn left (south), walking along with the stream on your left (east). For the first mile, it follows a fairly level course, and then it turns southwest and ascends gradually in the valley of the brook draining the area between Veto Mtn. on the northwest and Doubletop on the southeast. After about 1.5 mi., the trail swings generally south once more to follow the northern ridge of Doubletop as it climbs more steeply and steadily to the North Peak.

Distances from Nesowadnehunk Campground

    to North Peak: 3.1 mi., 2 hr. 45 min.

    to South Peak: 3.3 mi., 3 hr.

    to Kidney Pond Campground road: 7.9 mi., 6 hr. 30 min.

Nesowadnehunk Campground (map 1: C1)

This campground on Nesowadnehunk Stream, although beautiful, is not a major hiking center. It is the base for the approach to Doubletop from the north. Anglers find this campground a convenient base.

Mullen Mountain (3463 ft.)

This rock-capped peak is north of the Brothers and south of Wassataquoik Mtn. The climb starts in the vicinity of Mullen Pond. Virgin spruce covers the northern slope, and the hiking is smooth. See the section on Bushwhacking in the Maine Mountains in this book's introduction.

The old Mullen Brook Tote Rd., up Mullen Brook to Mullen Pond, provides an approach from the Russell Pond area. (This route is not official—check for permission and trail conditions with the Russell Pond Campground ranger.) The old Mullen Brook Tote Rd. leaves the Northwest Basin Trail on the north, opposite where the Northwest Basin Trail joins the old Wassataquoik Tote Rd., about a half-mile from Russell Pond. The old Mullen Brook Tote Rd. is overgrown and hard to see from the Northwest Basin Trail. Beavers have dammed ponds along the route; where the trail skirts them, it is difficult to follow. Soon after leaving the Northwest Basin Trail, the route follows the edge of a swamp and then turns sharply left, skirts another swamp, crosses a brook, and returns to the old Mullen Brook Tote Rd. This road climbs gradually and then more steeply to Mullen Pond, about 3.5 mi. from the Northwest Basin Trail. To bushwhack to the summit from the eastern shore of the pond, turn left (south) and pass through open spruce woods to a collar of thick dwarf birches just below the open, rocky summit.

Distances from Russell Pond Campground

> *to* old Mullen Brook Tote Rd. junction (via Northwest Basin Trail): 0.5 mi., 25 min.
>
> *to* Mullen Pond: est. 4.0 mi., 2 hr. 15 min.
>
> *to* Mullen Mtn. summit: est. 5.0 mi., 4 hr. 30 min.

Wassataquoik Mountain (2984 ft.)

Hikers do climb this broad, wooded mountain from the southern shore of Wassataquoik Lake; see the section on Bushwhacking in the Maine Mountains in this book's introduction. (For the approach to the start of the route, see the description of the Wassataquoik Lake Trail.) The trail up Wassataquoik is not officially maintained. It starts west of the outlet brook of Green Falls, crosses the brook, and climbs steeply east of the falls. After several more crossings, it leaves the brook and climbs on up the mountain. Near the top, it is obscured by raspberry bushes and debris from a fire in 1959. From the southern and more precipitous edge of the summit, there is a good view of Mullen Mtn. and the country beyond.

Distances from Russell Pond Campground

> *to* start of trail to Green Falls (via Wassataquoik Lake Trail): est. 3.2 mi., 1 hr. 35 min.
>
> *to* Green Falls: est. 3.3 mi., 1 hr. 45 min.
>
> *to* Wassataquoik summit: est. 5.0 mi., 4 hr.

Strickland Mountain (2410 ft.)

It is best to climb this low, wooded summit from Camp Phoenix, on the eastern side of Nesowadnehunk Lake. This camp is an enclave of privately owned land surrounded by BSP and the lake. From the eastern side of the barnyard in the rear of the camps, cross the tote road and follow logging roads over the gentle slope to the point where it starts to get steeper. Beyond, there are no trails, but you can hike through mostly open, pleasant woods to the summit, from which there are good views toward Center Mtn. and the Brothers. Take a compass bearing on Camp Phoenix before descending. See the section on Bushwhacking in the Maine Mountains in this book's introduction.

Burnt Mountain (1793 ft.)

Burnt Mountain Trail (map 1: B2)

Trees are gradually blocking what were once excellent views from the summit of Burnt Mountain. The Burnt Mountain Trail begins at the Burnt Mtn. picnic area, 13.8 mi. west of the Matagamon Gatehouse or 8.8 mi. north of the Nesowadnehunk Gatehouse on the Park Tote Road.

Distance from Burnt Mtn. picnic area

> *to* Burnt Mtn. summit: 1.3 mi. (2.1 km.), 50 min.

South Branch Pond Campground (map 1: B3)

This campground is at the eastern end of Lower (northern) South Branch Pond (981 ft.). The South Branch ponds have perhaps the most spectacular surroundings of any in Maine, except the ones near Katahdin. They lie in a deep valley between Traveler Mtn. to the east and South Branch Mtn. (Black Cat Mtn.) to the west. The campground, the usual base for hiking in the Traveler area, has choice views of Traveler's peaks and ridges, of the pond, and of South Branch Mtn. Facilities include open-front shelters, tenting space, a bunkhouse, and rental canoes.

Distances from South Branch Pond Campground

> *to* Middle Fowler Pond: 4.0 mi., 2 hr. 30 min.
>
> *to* North Traveler summit (via North Traveler Trail): 2.5 mi., 2 hr. 20 min.
>
> *to* Peak of the Ridges (via Pogy Pond and Center Ridge trails): est. 3.5 mi., 2 hr. 50 min.
>
> *to* southern end of Upper South Branch Pond (via Pogy Notch Trail): 1.9 mi., 1 hr.
>
> *to* Russell Pond Campground (via Pogy Notch Trail): 9.7 mi., 4 hr. 40 min.

Pogy Notch Trail (map 1: B3–C3)

This trail leads from the South Branch Pond Campground around the eastern shores of the ponds, then south through Pogy Notch. It passes west of Pogy Pond and continues southwest to the Russell Pond Campground. The trail offers fairly easy access to the center of the park and the trails on Katahdin. Nice views enhance the hike.

From the South Branch Pond Campground, enter woods on the trail toward the eastern shore of the pond. The North Traveler Trail diverges left at 0.2 mi. At 1.0 mi., the trail reaches the delta of Howe Brook and the Howe Brook Trail, which leaves to the west. Soon it enters some woods, where it follows a brook route at first and then bears right (south) away from the brook. At 1.3 mi., the trail climbs over the end of the cliff between Lower and Upper South Branch ponds. The Center Ridge Trail goes left at 1.4 mi. The Pogy Notch Trail descends and passes an old campsite at the southeastern corner of the upper pond. The South Branch Mountain Trail comes in on the right at the old campsite (1.9 mi.). The Pogy Notch Trail continues south, passing through an alder swamp and beaver works at 2.8 mi. It crosses several brooks and rises and falls moderately in the next 0.5 mi. At 3.3 mi., the trail forks. Straight ahead is the old route to Traveler Pond; the Pogy Notch Trail turns right, climbs gradually, and passes through Pogy Notch.

Bear left at 3.9 mi. into a sparsely grown old burn. The trail then crosses a beaver canal and descends into the Pogy Pond watershed. It crosses a brook several times while passing out of the notch area and descending toward Pogy Pond. It then crosses several other brooks and reaches the head of Pogy Pond at 6.0 mi. (There are clear views of Traveler, Turner, and Katahdin mountains from the shore of the pond.)

The trail bears right, uphill, and at 6.1 mi., a side trail to the left leads 0.2 mi. to the Pogy Pond Lean-to. The main trail descends nearly to the pond (6.2 mi.), then bears right, away from the pond. (Be careful not to take a wrong turn onto a short spur trail to the west. Also, watch carefully for blazes, which are scarce in this area.) The main trail rises gradually, then descends through an old burn, traverses a series of shallow rises, and bears right. At 6.7 mi., it drops into the gully of the western tributary of Pogy Brook, crosses, and climbs up the opposite slope. Then it runs through a swampy hollow, climbs a rocky rise, and descends gradually to cross another brook (7.3 mi.). Immediately after this second brook, the trail bears right and climbs gradually through sparse mixed growth. It crosses a beaver meadow, reaches a rough boulder field at 7.8 mi., and descends through it. The trail descends toward Russell Pond, and at 9.4 mi., the trail to Grand Falls and Lookout Ledges leaves to the left. Just before the Russell Pond Campground, the Wassataquoik Lake Trail leaves to the right.

Distances from South Branch Pond Campground

   to North Traveler Trail junction: 0.2 mi., 5 min.

   to Howe Brook Trail junction: 1.0 mi., 30 min.

   to Center Ridge Trail junction: 1.5 mi., 45 min.

   to South Branch Mountain Trail junction: 1.9 mi., 1 hr.

   to Pogy Pond: 6.0 mi., 3 hr.

   to Grand Falls Trail junction: 9.3 mi., 4 hr. 30 min.

   to Russell Pond Campground: 9.7 mi., 4 hr. 40 min.

South Branch (Black Cat) Mountain (northern summit 2630 ft.; southern summit, 2611 ft.)

South Branch Mtn., or Black Cat Mtn. on USGS maps, is across the ponds from Traveler Mtn. It offers extraordinary views of Traveler as well as the region immediately to the west, and the climb can help you pick out routes up Traveler Mtn.

South Branch Mountain Trail (map 1: B3)

The South Branch Mountain Trail runs from the South Branch Pond Campground over both summits and down to the Pogy Notch Trail, which it joins at the southern end of the upper pond.

The trail (blue-blazed) starts at the northwestern corner of Lower South Branch Pond, across the outlet brook from the canoe rack (sign). The trail parallels a small brook, staying from 100 to 200 yd. away from it, for 0.3 mi. It then follows a ridge for 0.8 mi. to nearly flat lookouts with vistas of the ponds and the Traveler Range. After contouring for 0.3 mi., the trail turns abruptly right and climbs more steeply to the northern peak.

The southern peak is 0.5 mi. farther—an easy hike along the high saddle connecting the two summits. The trail from the southern peak was relocated in 1983. It descends over gentle meadows and rock fields to open ledges on the southern side of the mountain. At about three miles, it swings eastward and descends through mixed forests. There is a short, steep climb of about 0.1 mi., then the trail rejoins the old trail at about four miles. At 4.3 mi., it passes a side trail to the upper South Branch Lean-To, and at 4.5 mi., it crosses a brook with beaver works before joining the Pogy Notch Trail at the southern end of the upper pond. Turn left (north) for the South Branch Pond Campground and right (south) for Pogy Notch and Russell Pond Campground.

Distances from South Branch Pond Campground

> *to* lookouts: 1.1 mi., 45 min.

> *to* South Branch Mountain, northern peak: 2.0 mi., 2 hr.

> *to* South Branch Mountain, southern peak: 2.5 mi., 2 hr. 15 min.

> *to* Pogy Notch Trail junction: 4.5 mi., 4 hr.

> *to* South Branch Pond Campground (via Pogy Notch Trail): est. 6.4 mi., 5 hr.

Traveler Mountain (3541 ft.)/North Traveler Mountain (3152 ft.)

Traveler Mtn. is a great, starfish-shaped mountain with four high ridges sprawling out south, west, northwest, and north, and four shorter spurs between them.

Fires have ravaged the mountain, the last one in 1902, so that while its lower parts support hardwoods of some size, its upper slopes are mostly bare, and good for climbing. The bareness of these higher slopes makes for a uniform landscape that can be highly confusing in fog or darkness. Although the mountain's altitude is quite a bit lower than Katahdin's, the routes up Traveler from the South Branch Pond Campground are longer, partially without trails, and equally exposed; so treat the mountain with respect, start early, and allow a full day for the climb. Estimate time, distance, and the roughness of the terrain generously.

There are four main routes up Traveler from the South Branch Pond Campground. Three of them follow trails for part of the climb. The following sections describe the routes in order, from north to south.

North Traveler Trail (map 1: B3)

From the South Branch Pond Campground, follow the Pogy Notch Trail 0.2 mi. to the North Traveler Trail, which diverges left. The North Traveler Trail climbs through open woods to the crest of North Ridge, which it follows over bare ledges in places. The view improves until the trail enters birch woods. After that, the trail passes through lovely alpine meadows and fine old woods that alternate with steep ledges. At about 1.7 mi., in one of the wooded sections, a side trail leaves left to a good spring. After emerging from the last section of woods, the trail continues in the open up the ridge to the North Traveler summit at 3152 ft. The views are impressive.

Distances from South Branch Pond Campground

> *to* start (via Pogy Notch Trail): 0.2 mi., 5 min.
>
> *to* side trail to spring: 1.7 mi., 1 hr. 30 min.
>
> *to* North Traveler summit: 2.5 mi., 2 hr. 20 min.

Howe Brook Trail (map 1: B3)

The Howe Brook Trail begins at the southeastern corner of Lower South Branch Pond, where the rocky, fanlike delta of Howe Brook merges with the pond. This inlet is 1.0 mi. south along the Pogy Notch Trail from the campground. The trail follows the route of the brook to the first chutes and potholes. (Howe Brook is noted for its many pools, rock- and water-formed potholes, slides, and chutes, which continue for quite a distance up the valley.) The trail crosses the brook a number of times before it ends at a beautiful waterfall.

Distances from South Branch Pond Campground

> *to* start (via Pogy Notch Trail): 1.0 mi., 30 min.
>
> *to* waterfall: est. 3.0 mi., 1 hr. 45 min.

Center Ridge Trail (map 1: B3)

This route starts at the foot of Center Ridge at the northeastern corner of the upper pond, 1.4 mi. south on the Pogy Notch Trail from the South Branch Pond Campground. The Center Ridge Trail runs to the Peak of the Ridges. Diverging left (east) from the Pogy Notch Trail, it climbs steadily through woods and then across open ledges. There are excellent views of Howe Brook Valley and North Traveler. After climbing over many rocky knobs, the trail reaches the Peak of the Ridges (3254 ft.), where it ends. At the Peak of the Ridges, the route up Pinnacle Ridge comes in on the right.

Distances from South Branch Pond Campground

    to start (via Pogy Notch Trail): 1.5 mi., 45 min.

    to Peak of the Ridges: est. 3.6 mi., 2 hr. 50 min.

Loop Route (over Traveler and North Traveler) (map 1: B3)

The Traveler Mountain Loop includes three separate mountain summits in a 9.2 mile circuit that has a vertical rise of over 3,700 feet. The spectacular panoramic views from the summits of The Peak of the Ridges, Traveler Mtn. and North Traveler Mtn. must be experienced to be appreciated. The average round trip hiking time of fit hikers is 9–10 hours.

The 3.6 mile hike from the Lower South Branch Pond campground up the Center Ridge Trail to the Peak of the Ridges begins as a flat wooded hike parallel to the shoreline of the South Branch Ponds. The hike from Upper South Branch Pond to "The Peak of the Ridges" (Center Peak) has a vertical rise of 2,269 feet in over 2 miles. This is the most difficult portion of the Traveler Mountain Loop Trail. This vertical rise is only 84 feet less than the vertical rise from Chimney Pond to Baxter Peak on Mt. Katahdin. It is highly recommended that all hikers ascend Traveler Mtn. via the Center Ridge Trail and descend via the North Traveler Mountain Trail.

The hike from the Peak of the Ridges to Traveler Mtn. begins with a 2000 ft. hike across and down the "Little Knife Edge," a vertical spine of columnar rhyolite rock. At the base of this rock formation the hiker will cross a small alpine meadow and begin to climb through stunted coniferous forest and several small scree walls of stone.

Traveler Mountain is the highest volcanic mountain in New England (3,541 ft.) and possibly the highest on the entire East Coast. The upper portions of the Center Ridge Trail and "The Traveler" contain large rhyolite talus (loose rock) that is covered with the thin "map lichen" that becomes slippery when wet.

The hike from Traveler Mtn. to North Traveler Mtn. begins with a descent over open rock before dropping into another coniferous forest. A short ascent will bring the hiker to The Traveler Ridge (2,990 ft.), an open ledge of nearly a half-mile in length. A descent from Traveler Ridge passes through a scenic dwarf birch forest that gradually ascends up to the open ledges of North Traveler Mtn. The North Traveler Trail will take the hiker back to Lower South Branch Pond.

The Traveler Mountain Trail from the Peak of the Ridges to North Traveler Mtn. is 3.5 miles long. Nearly half of this distance is bare rock.

Traveler Mtn. was formed by a volcanic blowout similar to the Mt. Saint Helens explosion. Traveler Rhyolite is a fine grained and dense granite that is smoother in texture than Katahdin granite. Traveler rhyolite is essentially identical with the rhyolite of the Kineo flint in the Moosehead Lake region.

Suggestions for a safe hike on Traveler Mountain:

- Get an early start (7 A.M.)—sign the trail hiking sheet at the campground office.
- Travel with a friend—use the buddy system.
- Pick a dry day. Wet rhyolite is slippery.
- Carry at least 2 qts. of water and extra food per person.
- Use sturdy hiking boots and pack raingear or wind jacket and pants.
- Have a working flashlight with extra batteries.
- Turn around at 3 P.M. if you haven't reached the Traveler summit.
- Avoid all thunderstorms.
- Always ascend the Center Ridge Trail and descend the North Traveler Trail.

Distances from South Branch Pond Campground

   to Center Ridge Trail (via Pogy Notch Trail): 1.5 mi., 45 min.

   to Peak of the Ridges: 3.5 mi., 2 hr. 50 min.

   to Traveler summit: est. 4.8 mi., 4 hr.

   to North Traveler summit: est. 7.6 mi., 10 hr.

   to South Branch Pond Campground (via North Traveler Trail): est. 10.1 mi., 12 hr.

Pinnacle Ridge Route (map 1: B3)

This is the most spectacular of the four routes up Traveler, but there is no trail beyond the Pogy Notch Trail. From the southern end of the south pond, follow the Pogy Notch Trail about 0.8 mi. to a knoll where the slide on Pinnacle is plainly visible. Turn left (east) through pleasant woods and across older slides, and you will reach the Pinnacle slide. Climb up on the left to avoid the cliffs above. From the top of Pinnacle, a steady climb through open brush brings you to the Peak of the Ridges (3254 ft.). The distance from the Pogy Notch Trail to the Peak of the Ridges is about two miles.

Do not descend Pinnacle Ridge. If you are caught by bad weather as you climb up on the upper slope, there is an emergency way off via the so-called Escape Route down the broad gully between Pinnacle and Center ridges. It gets climbers off the exposed ridge quickly and allows them to follow the little stream and skirt the low cliffs near the bottom to the Pogy Notch Trail near the southern end of the upper pond. See the section on Bushwhacking in the Maine Mountains in this book's introduction.

Distances from South Branch Pond Campground

   to turn off Pogy Notch Trail: est. 2.7 mi., 1 hr. 25 min.

   to Peak of the Ridges: est. 4.7 mi., 3 hr.

   to Pogy Notch Trail (via Center Ridge Trail): est. 5.8 mi., 3 hr. 35 min.

   to South Branch Pond Campground (via Pogy Notch Trail): est. 7.2 mi. (11.6 km.), 4 hr. 20 min.

Trout Brook Farm Campground (map 1: A3)

Trout Brook Farm is on the site of a farm that once served logging operations. The campground is on the northern side of the perimeter road, about 27 mi. west of Patten and 2.6 mi. west of the Matagamon Gatehouse. It is 4.7 mi. east of the Crossing Lunchground, where the Park Tote Road crosses Trout Brook and where the road to the South Branch Pond Campground leads south. Trout Brook Farm has only tentsites. It is a starting point for many trips in the park, including canoe trips and hikes to Traveler Mtn. and other outlying mountains and hikes along the new trail system in the northern and northeastern sections of the park. Trails north of the Trout Brook Farm Campground are, for the most part, not on the map that accompanies this book. In addition to a handout, *Outlying Campsites*, available from BSP, hikers are referred to *A Guide to Baxter Park and Katahdin*, by Stephen Clark, and to DeLorme's *Map and Guide of Baxter State Park and Katahdin*.

Wadleigh Brook Trail (map 1: A2–A3)

This trail, opened in 1997, replaces the Webster Lake Trail. Combined with the Freezeout Trail, this makes a delightful two- or three-day circuit, which is the longest linear backpacking trip in the park. The many tentsites along the route permit flexibility in planning the trip. Although it does not involve mountain travel, it offers streams, ponds, and access to good fishing areas.

The trail leaves the Park Tote Road about a mile west of the Trout Brook Crossing Bridge. It follows Wadleigh Brook for a short way then turns northwest. At 1.5 mi., a side trail leads 1 mi. east to an old-growth forest area. At 4.3 mi., the Wadleigh Brook Trail follows the upper side of Wadleigh Bog, then crosses a brook leading from Blunder Pond. At 8.4 mi., the trail follows the eastern and northern sides of Hudson Pond, where there is a lean-to, then heads northwest toward Pine Knoll and meets the Freezeout Trail at 10.4 mi., near Hudson Brook. From this junction, the Freezeout Trail goes southwest to the eastern end of Webster Lake, passing the Webster Outlet campsite. In the other direction, the Freezeout Trail heads east-northeast along Webster Stream. (See Freezeout Trail for distances.)

Freezeout Trail (map 1: A1–A3)

The Freezeout Trail traverses a section of the park known as the Scientific Forest Management Area. This 28,000-acre parcel was specifically designated by Governor Baxter as an area to be managed by the "most modern methods of forest controls," and further as a "showplace for those interested in forestry" and forest management operations.

Caution: Ask at Park Headquarters or any facility in the northern end of the park for locations of the latest timber-harvesting operations. If you run into any equipment working in the woods, do not get too close. Questions and comments are invited; write the Park Forester at Park Headquarters.

The Freezeout Trail parallels the entire length of Webster Stream, which under the right conditions can be a challenging white-water experience (see the *AMC River Guide: Maine*).

The trail generally descends toward Matagamon Lake, paralleling Webster Stream. It sometimes bears away from the stream, but it always returns. At 1.8 mi. east of the junction at Hudson Brook, it passes the Webster Stream Lean-to, and at 5.8 mi., it passes the Little East Branch Lean-to, opposite the confluence of the East Branch of the Penobscot and Webster Stream. (To use lean-tos and tentsites, make arrangements with park officials in Millinocket or at one of the campgrounds.) From there, the trail makes a sharp right turn onto the remains of the old Burma Rd., an improved tote road last used in 1950. Follow it for the remaining 6.0 mi. to Trout Brook Farm, returning another 5.7 mi. by the tote road to the trailhead.

Distances from Park Tote Road trailhead at Wadleigh Brook

> *to* Freezeout Trail junction: 10.4 mi., 5 hr. 15 min.

> *to* Webster Lake outlet tentsite (via Freezeout Trail): 12.9 mi., 6 hr. 30 min.

> *to* Webster Stream Lean-to: 12.2 mi., 6 hr. 15 min.

> *to* Little East Branch Lean-to: 16.2 mi., 8 hr. 15 min.

> *to* Trout Brook Farm Campground: 22.2 mi., 11 hr. 15 min.

> Complete loop (not visiting Webster Lake): 34.0 mi., 17 hr.

Frost Pond Trail (map 1: A3–B2)

The Frost Pond Trail leaves the Freezeout Trail 4.3 miles from Trout Brook Farm. It ascends southwest gradually for 1.5 mi. until you reach the Frost Pond Lean-to. The Frost Pond trail continues from the lean-to south–southwest for 3.9 miles and connects with the Wadleigh Brook Trail.

This connecting trail offers a variety of scenic views and topography, including wetlands and a challenging ascent to the top of Wadleigh Mtn., with good views of the Travelers, South Branch Mtn., and other vistas to the south.

Distances from Trout Brook Farm Campground

> *to* trailhead (via Freezeout Trail): 4.3 mi.

> *to* Frost Pond lean-to: 5.8 mi.

> *to* Wadleigh Brook Trail: 9.7 mi.

Fowler Ponds Area

In conjunction with the development of the Trout Brook Farm Campground, some new official routes have been opened to several lakes in the area south of the tote road, west of Horse Mtn., and northeast of the South Branch Pond area. Between Barrell Ridge and Billfish Mtn. are the three Fowler ponds; in the next valley to the northeast are Billfish and Round ponds (which drain to the east) and High and Long ponds (which drain into Fowler Brook). Farther north, at the head of Littlefield Brook, is Littlefield Pond. For years, anglers kept routes to these ponds open from the tote road to the east and north. Official campsites are on the northern shore and outlet of Lower Fowler Pond and at the outlet and southern end of Middle Fowler Pond. See the ranger at the Trout Brook Farm or South Branch Pond campground for camping and trail information. The Clark guide and the BSP handout mentioned above under Trout Brook Farm would be most useful.

The Fowler Brook Trail leads south from the tote road about two miles west of the Trout Brook Farm Campground. It generally follows Fowler Brook and leads to the northern end of Lower Fowler Pond to join the Middle Fowler Pond link mentioned below.

Five Ponds Trail (map 1: A3–B3)

This trail has two branches leaving the southern side of the tote road at the Trout Brook Farm Campground. The southwest branch forks at about 1.8 mi. The left fork leads between High and Long ponds. It continues past Round Pond and Billfish Pond, then along Littlefield Pond; it then loops back to the Trout Brook Farm Campground as the southeast branch of the Five Ponds Trail. There are tentsites at Billfish and Long ponds.

After crossing a second brook, the right fork climbs a crest and reaches a second junction. The trail to the left goes to the Middle Fowler Pond outlet and its tentsites; to the right, the link reaches the northeastern shore of Lower Fowler Pond at about 2.5 mi., where it joins the Fowler Brook Trail back to the tote road.

Distances from Park Tote Road

Complete Five Ponds Loop Trail: est. 5.6 mi., 3 hr.

Trout Brook Mountain Trail (map 1: A3)

This trail also starts at the Trout Brook Farm Campground and climbs through mixed growth and hardwoods to open ledges with excellent views. After reaching the 1767-ft. summit at 1.3 mi., the trail drops between Trout Brook Mtn. and Horse Mtn., then joins the southeastern branch of the Five Ponds Trail to loop back 0.7 mi. to the tote road at the campground.

Distances from Park Tote Road

to Trout Brook Mtn. summit: 1.3 mi., 1 hr. 20 min.

Complete loop: 3.0 mi., 3 hr.

Middle Fowler Pond Trail (map 1: B3)

In 1987, a new route was opened from South Branch Pond to Middle Fowler Pond. It is considered to be an extension of the Middle Fowler Pond Trail, connecting the South Branch Pond and Trout Brook Farm campgrounds. The trail leaves the northern end of the South Branch Pond Campground and follows the Ledges Trail for the first 0.3 mi. The trail climbs gradually, following a small brook until open ledges are reached at 1.7 mi. From there, the trail proceeds through the gap between Big Peaked Mtn. and Little Peaked Mtn. It then traverses the northern slope of Traveler Mtn., providing occasional views. At 3.0 mi., the Barrell Ridge Side Trail leads 0.3 mi. to the open summit of Barrell Ridge. This summit has very fine views, especially of Traveler Mtn. From this point, the trail descends, and it reaches Middle Fowler Pond at 4.0 mi. (sign). To the left, it is 3.3 mi. to the tote road via the Middle Fowler Pond and Fowler Brook trails. To the right, it is 0.2 mi. to the southern campsite on Middle Fowler Pond.

Distances from South Branch Pond Campground

> *to* Middle Fowler Pond: 4.0 mi., 2 hr. 30 min.
>
> *to* Park Tote Road (via Middle Fowler Pond and Fowler Brook Trails): 3.3 mi., 1 hr. 45 min.

Horse Mountain (1589 ft.)

Horse Mountain Trail (map 1: A3–A4)

In the northeastern corner of BSP, this mountain rises above the western shore of First Grand (Matagamon) Lake. The trail leaves the southern side of the Park Tote Road 2.5 mi. west of the bridge over the East Branch of the Penobscot and just west of the Matagamon Gatehouse. It rises at an easy rate and, near the top, turns sharply left (east) to a viewpoint. The main trail continues on from this junction. After crossing the actual summit of Horse Mountain, former site of a fire tower, the trail continues on to Billfish Pond before ending at the Five Ponds Trail.

Distances from Park Tote Road

> *to* Horse Mtn. jct. with East Spur & summit trails: 1.2 mi., 1 hr. 5 min.
>
> *to* viewpoint via East Spur: 1.6 mi., 1 hr. 25 min.
>
> *to* Billfish Pond outlet: 2.2 mi., 2 hr.
>
> *to* Five Ponds Trail: 3.0 mi., 2 hr. 30 min.

Turner Mountain (northern summit, 3325 ft.; southern summit, 3122 ft.)

This mountain northeast of Katahdin is low compared to the great mountain. Turner offers magnificent views of Katahdin, however, and particularly of the basins. You can approach South Turner from the Roaring Brook Campground. The hike involves a moderate climb up the southwestern slide. North Turner is trailless. The two summits are more than two miles apart and separated by a deep saddle.

South Turner Mountain Trail (map 1: C3–D3)

This trail starts out across Roaring Brook at the Roaring Brook Campground and coincides with the Russell Pond Trail. (At 0.2 mi., the Russell Pond Trail goes left.) The Sandy Stream Pond Trail goes straight to Sandy Stream Pond. At 0.4 mi., it turns right, crosses the outlets, and continues around the southeastern shore of the pond. (This section is often wet and muddy during rainy seasons.) Along the trail near the southeastern shore of the pond, a number of side paths lead left to the shore. Wildlife frequent the pond. Please stay on the trails in this area around Sandy Stream Pond; off-trail areas are designated Wildlife Area Only.

The trail follows a right fork at 0.7 mi. (The left fork is the Sandy Stream Pond Trail, which leads northwest 0.9 mi. to Whidden Pond and a jct. with the Russell Pond Trail 1.1 mi. north of the Roaring Brook Campground.) The South Turner Mountain Trail enters a small boulder field at 0.9 mi. and follows cairns and paint blazes on the rocks as it climbs. At 1.1 mi., it turns left and rises steeply. At 1.5 mi., it passes a side trail right to a spring, bears left, and continues. At 1.8 mi., the trail leaves the scrub and starts over open ledges. It follows cairns and paint blazes to the summit at 2.0 mi.

Distances from Roaring Brook Campground

- *to* start (via Russell Pond Trail): 0.2 mi., 5 min.
- *to* Whidden Pond Trail junction: 0.7 mi., 20 min.
- *to* South Turner summit: 2.0 mi. (3.2 km.), 1 hr. 50 min.

Cranberry Pond Trail (map 1: D3–E3)

Near the Togue Pond Gate, several short day hikes provide excellent family walks through mixed-wood and evergreen forests. The Cranberry Pond Trail departs from just before the Tongue Pond gate on the left (east) side of the Park Tote Road and ambles 1.4 miles along the Togue, Cranberry, and Rocky ponds. Return via Park Tote Road 1.0 mi. to start to make a loop trip.

Distances from Togue Pond Beach Picnic Area

   to intersection with Park Tote Road: 1.4 mi., 45 min.

      Complete loop: 2.5 mi., 1 hr. 15 min.

Kettle Pond Trail (map 1: D2–D3)

Kettle Pond Trail is an easy 1.9 mi. trail that intersects the Park Tote Road. Kettle Pond Trail's southern junction with the Park Tote Road is 1 mi. from the Togue Pond Gate. The trailhead is on the right (north) side of the road. At 0.1 mi., the trail forks, with the right-hand fork leading to the Rum Pond Trail. Follow the left hand fork 1.3 mi. to the second intersection with the Park Tote Road. From here, it is an extra 0.4 mi. north to reach the Abol Pond parking and picnic area, or 2.5 road miles to return to Togue Pond Gate.

Rum Pond Trail (map 1: D3)

Rum Pond Trail forks right 0.1 mi. from the southerly entrance to the Kettle Pond Trail. This 2 mi. east/west trail travels past Round and Rum ponds to meet up with the Park Tote Road's eastern branch, approximately 0.1 mi. from the Rum Brook picnic area. The Togue Pond Gate is 1.0 mi. from both junctions with the Park Tote Road.

Distances from junction with Park Tote Road, 1.0 mi. (west) from Togue Pond Gate

   to junction of Kettle and Rum Pond Trails: 0.1 mi., 5 min.

   to Park Tote Road via Kettle Pond Trail: 1.8 mi., 1 hr.

   to Park Tote Road via Rum Pond Trail: 2.0 mi., 1 hr.

Blueberry Ledges Trail (map 1: D2)

From Katahdin Stream Campground, this trail travels 4.2 mi. through a variety of forest types and offers many interesting landscapes before meeting up with the Applachian Trail near the West Branch of the Penobscot. Much of the trail goes through young post-fire (1977) forest. The trail's namesake ledges are located about midway along the trail, along the tumbling waters of Katahdin Stream. The area features large expanses of exposed bedrock with views of Katahdin and other geologic features. "The Birches" long distance hiker shelters and tent platforms is at the northern trailhead of this trail.

Distance from Katahdin Stream Campground

   to junction with Applachian Trail: 4.2 mi.

Section 2

Aroostook County

RECOMMENDED HIKES

Easy

Quaggy Jo (rt: 1.6 mi., 1 hr. 20 min.) A short hike to the north summit of Quaggy Jo with views to the northwest and east.

Moderate

Deboullie Mountain (rt: 5.0 mi., 3 hr. 10 min.) An interesting hike to the open summit of Deboullie Mtn. with view from the fire tower.

Priestly Mountain (rt: 4.0 mi., 2 hr. 50 min.) This trail provides excellent views from the fire tower of the Allagash Wilderness Waterway.

Mount Chase (rt: 3.0 mi., 3 hr.) This trail provides extensive views from the summit.

LIST OF MOUNTAINS

A roostook County, with an area of 6453 square mi., sprawls along Maine's northern and northeastern boundary. It is larger in area than Connecticut and Rhode Island combined. Aroostook's greatest north-south dimension is about 120 mi., and its greatest east-west dimension is 104 mi.

The mountains of Aroostook County are widely scattered. There are no ranges or compact mountain areas except two small clusters of hills—the Deboullie Mtn. region west of Eagle Lake and east of the Allagash territory, and the hills west of Bridgewater and around Number Nine Lake. Solitary Mars Hill (1748 ft.), which rises from almost level country near the county's eastern boundary, is probably the best-known mountain. Peaked Mtn. (2260 ft.), a trailless summit in the wilderness west of Ashland, is the county's highest.

See the introduction to this guide for information on North Maine Woods and its control policies in the western part of Aroostook County.

Number Nine Mountain (1638 ft.)

This peak is west of Bridgewater in a small group of mountains around Number Nine Lake. The Lake has an interesting MFS campsite. Refer to the USGS Number Nine quadrangle, 7.5-min. series, and *The Maine Atlas* (DeLorme), map 59.

Entering Bridgewater from the south, turn left off US 1 onto Bootfoot Rd. and continue past the Bridgewater Grammar School on your right. The road runs west and at 3.1 mi. comes to a T, turn right (road turns to gravel), pass Whitney Brook Rd. on right at 4.5 mi., pass Harrington Rd. at 6.1 mi. on left. At 11 mi. road turns right, go straight; at 11.4 mi. bear left at fork and at 12.1 mi. come to parking/boat launching area on Number Nine Lake. Best parking is here, as parking beyond here is difficult on the edge of the old road.

From Number Nine Lake parking area/boat ramp the trail goes across a bridge and follows the old road (partially paved) around east side of lake. At 0.4 mi. pass gravel road on left, at 0.5 mi. take left fork and begin climb. At 1.1 mi. there is a yellow gate across road. Continue climb around gate and at 1.5 mi. reach a tower and small building. The tower is inaccessible but there is a fine almost 360-degree view.

Distance from parking area/boat ramp

   to Number Nine summit: 1.5 mi., 1 hr.

Mars Hill (1748 ft.)

This monadnock rises abruptly from an almost level area of farms and woodland in the eastern section of the town of the same name. Refer to the USGS Mars Hill quadrangle, 7.5-min. series, and *The Maine Atlas* (DeLorme), map 59.

The mountain runs north–south for about 3.0 mi. and parallels the Canadian border, which is about 1.0 mi. to the east. Big Rock Ski Area is on the west side of the mountain and there is ample space for parking. A proposal to place up to 33 389-ft. wind turbines along the Mars Hill Ridge received preliminary approval in 2004.

From the junction of routes US 1A and US 1 in Mars Hill village take US 1A north for 0.3 mi.; then turn right (east) onto Boynton Rd. and go 1.3 mi. to a T intersection. Turn right on Country Club Rd. (East Blaine Rd.) and take the first left (Graves Rd.) to Big Rock Ski Area.

The trail (unmarked) to the southern (highest) peak goes up the left side of the main ski slope and intersects the north–south trail. Turn right and follow the trail to the southern summit (highest peak). The views from the summit extend across the potato fields in all directions to other mountains in the county, and on to Katahdin to the southwest and across the St. John River Valley into New Brunswick to the east. This trail is now a portion of the International Appalachian Trail, which continues into Canada to the Forillon National Park in the Gaspé Peninsula.

Turning right (south) at the summit and passing by the radio towers will take the hiker to a lean-to (sleeps six) in about 0.6 mi. Water must be carried in. To continue along the International Appalachian Trail, turn left at the summit (north) and follow an abandoned road along the open ridge leading to a service road for the communication towers at the north summit. After following the service road for a short distance, the trail departs to the right, circles the north summit, and descends the northeast and north sides of the mountain to Knoxford Rd. From Knoxford Rd., it is 0.7 mi. to the International Boundary and approximately 5.0 mi. back to the Mars Hill village.

To climb the northern peak, take Country Club Rd. north 1.7 mi. from the end of Boynton Rd. to Tower Rd. on the right. There is a sign on the telephone pole: Private Drive. Also, there is a sign, "ATV access road to towers." If the wind turbines project receives final approval, this road will be developed and will become the access road for construction of the towers.

In the winter, Big Rock Ski Area, run by the nonprofit Maine Winter Sports Center, has more than six miles of cross-country ski trails and snowshoe trails that traverse up the mountain with spectacular views of the valley below.

Distance from start of access road

   to Mars Hill southern summit: est. 1.5 mi., 1hr. 15 min.

Distance from jct. of Boynton and Tower Roads

   to Mars Hill northern summit: est. 1.8 mi., 1 hr. 45 min.

Quaggy Jo (1213 ft.)

Quaggy Jo is the shortened form of its Indian name Qua Qua Jo, which trans-
lates to twin peaked. Quaggy Jo dominates Aroostook State Park from the
southwestern corner of Presque Isle. The 800-acre park offers hiking, swimming, boating, camping, and picnicking. Aroostook State Park became a real-
ity in 1939 and bears the honor of being Maine's first state park. From Presque
Isle go south on Route US 1 for 4.0 mi. and turn west (right) onto Spragueville
Rd. (state park sign) and in 1.0 mi., turn left on State Park Rd. and in 1.1 mi.
reach the park entrance and parking area. The park is open all year and there is
a fee charged. Refer to the USGS Echo Lake quadrangle, 7.5-min. series, and
The Maine Atlas (DeLorme), map 65.

   The mountain, which rises approximately 600 ft. above Echo Lake, has two
peaks. A North Peak Trail (1.25 mi.) starts at the day-use parking area. A
North–South Ridge Trail (1.0 mi.) connects the two peaks. A South Peak Trail
(0.75 mi.) starts from the campground. From both peaks there are fine views of
scenic Aroostook County.

Distance from day-use parking area

   to summit of northern peak: 1.25 mi., 1 hr.

Distance from campground

   to summit of southern peak: 0.75 mi., 45 min.

Deboullie Mountain (1981 ft.)

Deboullie is one of the most remote of all Maine's Public Reserve Lands. Its
22,000 acres include low rugged mountains and scenic remote trout ponds.
Deboullie Mountain is the highest of a small cluster of mountains in this
wilderness south of St. Francis and northwest of Portage. Refer to the USGS
Gardner Pond and Deboullie Pond quadrangles, 7.5-min. series, and *The
Maine Atlas* (DeLorme), map 63.

Deboullie is within the boundaries of the North Maine Woods, a large block of forest land, most of which is privately owned and cooperatively managed to provide recreational opportunities for the public. Visitors must register at a checkpoint and pay camping and day fees to enter the area.

The Bureau of Parks and Lands has designed the road from St. Francis Checkpoint (fee) as the primary access route. This road turns left off ME 161 about 6.5 mi. southwest of St. Francis and soon heads south and then east for some 20.0 mi., ending at Pushineer Pond.

There is an alternative access from Portage: Take West Rd. for 1 mi. and turn left on Fish Lake Rd. and continue to the Fish River Checkpoint (fee). After check-in continue on the Fish Lake Rd. and turn right on the Hewes Brook Rd. (mile marker 6). In about 3.4 mi. cross the Fish River bridge, and in another 2.3 mi. pass the road on left to Fish River Lake. Continue on Hewes Brook Rd. just past mile marker 12, turn left and follow signs to Red River Camps, and in about 6.5 mi., turn right at a T, and in 0.7 mi. enter Maine Public Reserve Lands. From here it's another 0.6 mi. to reach Pushineer Pond. Total distance from Portage to Pushineer Pond is about 27.8 mi. To reach the parking area and trailhead, cross the Red River and continue for about 0.25 mi. (*Note: A 4WD or high ground clearance vehicle is suggested for crossing the river.*)

The hiking trail starts west, skirts the northern edge of Deboullie Pond, crosses an intermittent rockslide, and at its western end, heads steeply up to the summit. Also there are trailheads at Denny Pond and at the boat access site at the base of Deboullie Mountain on Deboullie Pond. The inactive fire tower on the summit offers expansive views of the surrounding area.

Distance from end of auto road at Pushineer Pond

   to Deboullie summit: 2.5 mi., 1hr. 45 min.

Hedgehog Mountain (1594 ft.)

Hedgehog Mountain is in TR15 R6 just off the west side of ME 11, 3.5 mi. south of Winterville and 12.7 mi. north of Portage. T and R stand for "township" and "range." The state of Maine uses this system to designate unincorporated areas. Refer to the USGS Winterville quadrangle, 7.5-min. series, and *The Maine Atlas* (DeLorme), map 63.

There is parking, a picnic area, campsite, and a good spring on the west side of ME 11. The trail leaves from the southwest corner of the picnic area and in about 100 yd. passes an old warden's cabin and then climbs steadily to the top.

There are old steel footings remaining from an old tower. There are fine views to the south of Portage Lake and to the west of Lake St. Froid and the Fish River.

Distances from the picnic area

　to Hedgehog summit: 0.62 mi., 30 min.

Round Mountain (2147 ft.)

Round Mtn. is west of Ashland, south of American Realty Rd. and just north of Jack Mountain Rd. Round Mtn. is the northernmost peak of three adjacent peaks (Round, Middle, and Peaked) that run northeast to southwest. Peaked Mountain (2260 ft.) is the highest mountain in Aroostook County, but there is no trail to the summit. Refer to the USGS Round Mountain quadrangle, 7.5-min. series, and *The Maine Atlas* (DeLorme), maps 57 & 63.

Round Mountain is within the boundaries of the North Maine Woods, a large block of forest land, most of which is privately owned and cooperatively managed to provide recreational opportunities for the public. Visitors must register at a checkpoint and pay camping and day fees to enter the area. The 6 Mile Checkpoint is about 6.0 mi. from Ashland on the American Realty Rd. (*Note: In 2004, logging operations are ongoing in this area and may obscure access to trailheads and trails.*)

From the 6 Mile Checkpoint on the American Realty Rd. bear left onto Pinkham Rd. and continue southwest, crossing the Machias River in 8.7 mi. from the checkpoint, and turn right 0.1 mi. beyond the river onto Jack Mountain Rd. Continue on Jack Mountain Rd., and in 3.4 mi. pass road on right to Weeks Brook Campsite. In 0.8 mi. beyond this road, turn right onto unmarked logging road and continue on this logging road for 3.8 mi. to end in a gravel parking area. There are considerable signs of past logging operations in this area.

The unmarked trail leaves from where the road ends and follows an old tote road on the west side of Round Pond. Continue to follow the tote road to an intersection and bear left, passing camp off right side of road, and continuing straight up tote road. Trail to summit is supposed to be on left side of tote road before a log camp. In 2004, trail and signs were not visible, but one could bushwhack up to the summit from here on the overgrown trail.

Distances from parking area

　to Round Mountain summit: est. 1.5 mi., 1 hr. 30 min.

Horseshoe Mountain (2084 ft.)

Horseshoe Mountain is part of the Rocky Brook Range, which has some surprisingly rugged terrain for this part of the state. Refer to the USGS Mooseleuk Lake and Fifth Musquacook Lake quadrangles, 7.5-min. series, and *The Maine Atlas* (DeLorme), map 62.

Horseshoe Mountain is within the boundaries of the North Maine Woods, a large block of forest land, most of which is privately owned and cooperatively managed to provide recreational opportunities for the public. Visitors must register at a checkpoint and pay camping and day fees to enter the area. The 6 Mile Checkpoint is about six miles from Ashland on the American Realty Rd. (*Note: In 2004, logging operations are ongoing in this area and may obscure access to trailheads and trails.*)

The road to the trail leaves the left side of the American Realty Rd. 26.6 mi. from the 6 Mile Checkpoint and 1.8 mi. before the McNally Pond Campsite. In 1 mi. the road turns sharply left, park here, the trail begins straight ahead on this corner (no sign).

At first the trail is an obscure road that leads in about 0.3 mi. to an old firewarden's cabin. The trail then passes behind the cabin, and in about 200 yd., reaches a side trail on the right that goes 0.8 mi. to picturesque Horseshoe Pond. About 0.5 mi. from the cabin the main trail becomes steeper and in another 0.5 mi. reaches the flat summit.

Distance from parking at sharp bend in road

   to Horseshoe summit: 1.3 mi., 1 hr. 15 min.

Priestly Mountain (2084 ft.)

Priestly Mountain, in northern Piscataquis County, near the Aroostook boundary, rises west of the Allagash River about 60 mi. west of Ashland. Refer to the USGS Umsaskis Lake quadrangle, 7.5-min. series. and *The Maine Atlas* (DeLorme), maps 55 & 61.

Priestly Mountain is within the boundaries of the North Maine Woods, a large block of forest land, most of which is privately owned and cooperatively managed to provide recreational opportunities for the public. Visitors must register at a checkpoint and pay camping and day fees to enter the area. The 6 Mile Checkpoint is about six miles from Ashland on the American Realty Rd. (*Note: Logging operations in this area at the time of publication may obscure access to trailheads and trails.*)

From the 6 Mile Checkpoint on the American Realty Rd., continue west and go over the Umsaskis Thoroughfare in 49.0 mi. and in another 6.0 mi. turn left onto Churchill Dam Rd. Continue straight on Churchill Dam Rd. for about 7.5 mi. (road climbs uphill).

The trail (no sign) leaves the west side of Churchill Dam Rd. and, at first follows an old road and runs southwest for 1.5 mi. and crosses Drake Brook, the outlet of Priestly lake.

The trail turns south near the northwestern side of Priestly Lake. At 0.6 mi. from the brook, the trail passes an old firewarden's cabin and turns abruptly west uphill to the right of the cabin. It then climbs moderately for about 0.7 mi. to the summit. The firetower has excellent views, particularly of the Allagash Wilderness Waterway.

Distances from Churchill Dam Rd.

>   *to* firewarden's cabin: 2.1 mi.

>   *to* Priestly summit: 2.8 mi., est. 2 hr.

Mount Chase (2440 ft.)

This mountain, north of Patten and just west of the Aroostook County border, has an abandoned MFS fire tower. There are extensive views from the summit. Looking northeast of Katahdin, you can see Mt. Chase as the very prominent mountain in the distance. Refer to the USGS Mount Chase quadrangle, 7.5-min. series, and *The Maine Atlas* (DeLorme), map 52.

The approach road (Mountain Rd.) leaves the left side of ME 11 6.2 mi. north of the intersection of ME 11 and 159 in Patten, and 1.4 mi. north of the Penobscot/Aroostook county line, and about 9.5 mi. south of Knowles Corner. Follow Mountain Rd. west for 2.1 mi. to an unmarked parking area. This is a rough private road with several stream crossings and may not be accessible at times due to washouts. Hikers must respect the private property on both sides of the road.

The trail, marked at first (old signs with red painted arrows) leaves the right (northern) side of the parking area and proceeds first west, then almost due north, following an old jeep road to the abandoned warden's cabin, which it reaches in about 0.8 mi. Beyond the cabin the trail climbs steadily to the summit.

Distances from trailhead parking

>   *to* firewarden's cabin: est. 0.8 mi., 45 min.

>   *to* Mt. Chase summit: est. 1.5 mi., 1 hr. 30 min.

Section 3

Greater Moosehead Lake Region

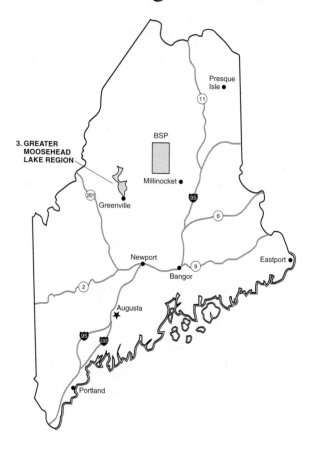

RECOMMENDED HIKES

Easy
Mount Kineo (lp: 3.6 mi., 3 hr. 30 min.) A loop trip around the Indian Trail and Bridal Trail, with views from the bare summit of Mt. Kineo of the surrounding areas.

Moderate
White Cap Mountain (rt: 4.2 mi., 3 hr.) A short, steep hike to the summit of White Cap Mtn., where the view is one of the finest in the state.

Big Moose Mountain (rt: 6.3 mi., 5 hr. 30 min.) A well-marked trail leads to the summit of Big Moose where there are views from the ledges.

Strenuous
Little Spencer Mountain (rt: 4.0 mi., 4 hr. 30 min.) A challenging hike that ascends through a narrow chimney and over steep terrain to the ledges of Little Spencer Mtn., with views of the area.

Big Spencer Mountain (rt: 4.0 mi., 5 hr.) The hike is steep and challenging at the top but the views are worth it.

LIST OF MOUNTAINS

The Lake, about 34.0 mi. long with an area of 117 square mi., is the state's largest lake. Lily Bay State Park is on the eastern shore of Moosehead Lake, 8.0 mi. north of Greenville on Greenville-Ripogenus Rd. This area of 576 acres offers picnicking, camping, boat launching, and swimming. (In 1974, the Scott Paper Company donated the Squaw Mountain ski area and considerable land on that mountain to the state for a park. In 1976, the state added the Little Moose unit by exchanging land with another paper company.) Big Squaw and Little Squaw mountains have been renamed to Big and Little Moose Mountains.

Big Moose Mtn. (3196 ft.) and Mt. Kineo (1806 ft.), reached by water through Rockwood, are the most frequently climbed and best-known peaks west of Greenville.An expanding network of private roads, open to the public, serves the wilderness country north of Rockwood. (See the section "Policies of Landowners in Northern Maine" in the front of this guide, which discusses the North Maine Woods association.)

Big Moose Mountain (3196 ft.)

Big Moose Mtn. dominates the country to the southwest of Moosehead Lake. It is located west of Greenville and is known for its exceptional views of the Moosehead Region and Mt. Katahdin. Remnants of the old fire tower marks the site of the first fire lookout in the state, established in 1905. Squaw Mountain ski area is on the mountain's eastern slope. This area is north of the hiking trail; refer to the USGS Greenville quadrangle, 15-min. series.

From the traffic light in downtown Greenville go north on ME 15, turn left (west) on the a dirt road just north of the bridge over Middle Squaw Brook and 5.2 mi. north of Greenville where there is a sign for Maine Public Reserve Lands Little Moose Unit. Drive up this road for about 1.5 mi. to where the fire warden's trail leaves the right side of the road and where there is parking on the right. The trail is well marked and leads 2.5 mi. to the old warden's cabin. From the cabin, the trail heads straight up the steep slope, with many rocks placed as stepping-stones. Reaching the narrow crest of the ridge, it turns right (north) and climbs another 0.5 mi. to the summit, which is cluttered by three small antennae and their buildings.

From the tower pad, a short trail leads north to a ledge with a view down over Mirror Lake, an isolated pond on the northeastern spur of the mountain.

A trail has been cut that goes north to the top of the Squaw Mountain ski area.

Distances from dirt road

   to cabin: 2.5 mi.

   to Moose summit: 3.3 mi., 2 hr. 45 min.

Little Moose Mountain (2126 ft.)

The hiking-trail system of Little Moose Mtn. focuses on the Loop Trail around Big and Little Moose ponds. Hiking it clockwise gives you the best view build-up and is easiest on the terrain. There are five camping areas in the Little Moose reserve, two at Big Moose Pond, and one each at Little Moose, Big Notch, and Little Notch Ponds. The area can be reached from the Mountain Rd. trailhead. To reach the trailhead, follow the directions for the Big Moose Mountain trailhead and go past the parking area. Take the left fork (Mountain Rd.) about 1.8 mi. from ME 15 and continuing for a total of 3.0 mi. to the trail-head at the point where the road ends. The trailhead is on the left.

Access to the Greenwood Trail may be had by going north from Greenville to the Greenwood Motel on the left, which is about 1.0 mi. after the railroad trestle in Greenville Junction. The trailhead begins in the south corner of the motel parking lot by the Maine Public Reserve Lands sign, where you may park.

From the Mountain Rd. trailhead, go southeast 0.5 mi. over log walks to Big Moose Pond and another 0.25 mi. to the intersection of the Loop Trail and the Greenwood Trail. The left fork goes to Little Moose Pond (0.25 mi.) and then to Papoose Pond (0.5 mi.) continuing up the ridge to the Greenwood Motel on ME 15. The right fork is the Loop Trail, which climbs to the next trail intersection in 0.5 mi. At this intersection the left fork is the Loop Trail, which returns to the Greenwood Trail between Little Moose and Papoose Pond (0.75 mi.). This loop presents varied terrain and several delightful outlooks over ponds and surrounding mountains, and provides a nice view of Little Moose Mountain.

At the final trail junction, the right fork follows the Notch Ponds Trail to Big and Little Notch Ponds (1.5 mi.) and proceeds pass Baker Falls to the Big Indian Pond trailhead at 1.25 mi.

Distances from the Mountain Rd. trailhead

   1.0 to 8.0 mi. round-trip depending on route for a 1 to 4 hr. round-trip hike

Mount Kineo (1806 ft.)

Mt. Kineo, with its sheer southeastern face, rises spectacularly 800 ft. above Moosehead Lake on a peninsula jutting from the eastern shore of the lake to within 1 mi. of the western shore at Rockwood. The view over the lake from the vacant refurbished MFS fire tower on the summit is quite remarkable. Refer to the USGS Moosehead Lake quadrangle, 15-min. series, or the Mt. Kineo quadrangle, 7.5-min. series.

To reach the mountain, from the railroad trestle in Greenville, go 18.1 mi. north on ME 15. Turn right on a road marked with signs for the Rockwood town landing and docks. From the landing it is about a 10 min. boat ride to Mt. Kineo. There are multiple shuttle services for a small fee in the village of Rockwood. The North Trail, Bridle Trail, or Indian Trail can be used to summit the mountain. All of the trails are blue-blazed; however, the Indian Trail trailhead isn't clearly marked. All three trails begin at the landing point and follow the shore along an old carriage road. The Indian Trail is the shortest route to the summit and fire tower, and it is also the trail that provides the most views. It diverges from the Bridle Trail at 0.8 mi. from the landing, and follows the edge of the cliffs. The trail then rises steeply to where it joins the Bridle Trail 0.4 mi. from the fire tower. The Bridle Trail is the original fire warden trail to the summit. It begins 0.3 mi. from the Indian Trail along the carriage road from the landing. It is longer and has no views, but it has easier grades. The longest trail is the North Trail, which includes the entire length of the carriage road. The trail initially follows the shore of Moosehead Lake all the way to Hardscrabble Point, where there are a few campsites. From here the trail continues along the shoreline over a rough trail consisting of rocks and roots, and then begins a strenuous climb through a stand of old hardwoods to the summit. There are limited views along this trail.

Distances from dock at Kineo Cove

to Bridle Trail and Indian Trail junction: 0.8 mi.

to Kineo summit (via Indian Trail): 1.6 mi., 1 hr. 10 min.

to Kineo summit (via Bridle Trail): 2.0 mi., 1 hr. 20 min.

to Kineo summit (via North Trail): 4.1 mi., 2 hr. 20 min.

Green Mountain (2395 ft.)

This mountain is northwest of Pittston Farm and northeast of Boundary Bald Mtn. in T3 R5 (T and R stand for "township" and "range," and identify unincorporated areas in Maine.) (Dolebrook TWP) in Somerset County. There is a MFS fire tower on the highest of its several summits. Refer to the USGS Penobscot Lake quadrangle, 15-min. series, or the Foley Pond quadrangle, 7.5-min. series.

Take the paper company gravel road (fee) for 20.0 mi. north from Rockwood to the tollgate. From the tollgate, take the right fork (Cut Off Rd.) to Seboomook Rd. Turn left (west) on Seboomook and go through Pittston Farm. Beyond Pittston Farm, Boundary Rd. to Green Mtn. forks left from North Branch Rd. The trail leaves the right (north) side of the road about 7.0 mi. beyond this fork.

The trail starts as a steep driveway to the warden's cabin, which it passes in 0.3 mi. It then rises gradually, with several short dips, to the summit. The trail is well worn and easy to follow.

Distances from North Branch Rd.

to cabin: 0.3 mi.

to Green Mtn. summit: 1.5 mi., 1 hr. 15 min.

Little Russell Mountain (2400 ft.)

Little Russell Mtn. is close to the Piscataquis county line in T5 R16, Somerset County. (T and R stand for "township" and "range," and identify unincorporated areas in Maine.) An abandoned MFS fire tower is on the summit. Refer to the USGS St. John Pond quadrangle, 15-min. series, and the Russell Mtn. quadrangle, 7.5-min. series.

Take the paper company gravel road (fee) for 20.0 mi. north from Rockwood to the tollgate. From the tollgate, take the right fork (Cut Off Rd.) to Seboomook Rd. Take the road right to the Seboomook Dam, and then drive north on the 490 Rd. toward Fifth St. Johns Pond, taking the right fork on to Russell Mountain Rd. The trail leaves the right (east) side of the road about 19 mi. north of the Seboomook Dam and about 1.3 mi. north of Lost Pond, which is in the saddle (about 1975 ft.) between Russell Mtn. and Little Russell Mtn. (There is a MFS campsite at Lost Pond, 0.3 mi. from the road.)

The trail ascends gradually. In its upper half, it gets steeper, with expanding views to the north. This trail is being reclaimed by the forest and requires bushwhacking to get to the top.

Distance from road

  to Little Russell summit: 1.3 mi., 1 hr.

Number Four Mountain (2890 ft.)

This summit, with an abandoned MFS fire tower, is at the northern end of the jumbled mountain mass lying between Kokadjo on the north, Lily Bay on the west, and Big Lyford and the West Branch ponds on the east. Baker Mtn. (3520 ft.) and Lily Bay Mtn. (3228 ft.), other major peaks in this mass, are higher but have no trails. (At time of publication, the AMC was in the planning phase of building a trail up Baker Mtn. For updates, see www.outdoors.org.) Refer to the USGS First Roach Pond quadrangle, 15-min. series, or the Number Four Mtn. quadrangle, 7.5-min. series.

From Greenville, drive north on the Lily Bay Rd. 18.2 mi. Turn right off Lily Bay Rd. about 0.4 mi. past the Frenchtown town line marker onto Frenchtown Rd., a dirt road. Go 2.3 mi. and take a right, then go another 1.4 mi. and take a left. At 0.9 mi. on this road you will cross a wooden bridge. Go another 0.1 mi. and look carefully on the left for a paper company sign that marks the trailhead for the trail. Parking is along side the road. In the beginning the trail is on an overgrown road for about 0.25 mi. and is blue blazed. The trail runs southwest, with little change in grade, for more than two miles. Then, 0.75 mi. after crossing Lagoon Brook, you will find a cairn on the left and a sign that reads No. 4 MT on a tree. From this point, the trail climbs, first gradually and finally more steeply, through white birch and spruce to the summit ridge. There are some rewarding views near the summit.

Distances from Frenchtown Rd.

  to fire tower: 3.8 mi., 2 hr. 30 min.

Soubunge Mountain (2104 ft.)

This mountain is north of the Ripogenus Dam and northwest of Doubletop Mtn. in T4 R11 (T and R stand for "township" and "range," and identify unincorporated areas in Maine.) in Piscataquis County. An abandoned MFS fire tower is on the summit. Refer to the USGS Harrington Lake quadrangle, 15-min. series, or the Doubletop Mtn. quadrangle, 7.5-min. series. Camping is available at Harrington Lake.

To get to the trailhead, from Kokadjo take Sias Hill Rd./Greenville Rd. north to the Golden Rd. Turn right (east) on the Golden Rd. and go the Ripogenus Dam. Turn left on Telos Rd. The trail leaves the northern side of Telos Rd. about 8 mi. north of the Ripogenus Dam. It runs generally northwest across level country for 1 mi., then climbs north to the tower. This trail is being reclaimed by the forest and requires bushwhacking to get to the tower.

Distance from road

   to Soubunge summit: est. 2.0 mi., 2 hr.

Big Spencer Mountain (3230 ft.)

Rising sharply from the countryside north of the tiny hamlet of Kokadjo, Big and Little Spencer mountains, near First Roach Pond, are prominent landmarks from many points in the Moosehead area. Big Spencer has an abandoned MFS fire tower on the northeastern end of its two-mile summit ridge (3230 ft.). The summit is about 0.3 mi. southwest of the tower. The unrestricted views in all directions are beautiful. Refer to the USGS Ragged Lake quadrangle, 15-min. series, or the Big Spencer Mtn. quadrangle, 7.5-min. series.

From Greenville, drive north on the Lily Bay Rd. 19 mi. to Kokadjo. Take the left fork 0.2 mi. north of Kokadjo onto Sias Hill Rd. Continue on Sias Hill Rd. about 8.0 mi. to a narrow, one-lane bridge, which crosses Bear Pond Brook (Bear Brook campsite is on right) and turn left after crossing the bridge. Take this road 6.1 mi. to the trailhead on the left. Park alongside the road. The trail leaves on the left (south) side of the road (sign) and climbs to the right (north) of the mountain's nose. At about 0.8 mi. up the trail is the old fire warden's cabin. In its upper part, beyond the warden's cabin, the trail is quite steep: It gains more than 1000 vertical feet in the last 0.7 mi. to the summit. There are short wooden ladders over some of the more slippery areas.

Distance from road

   to Big Spencer summit: 2.0 mi., 2 hr. 30 min.

Little Spencer Mountain (3040 ft.)

Like its partner, Big Spencer, the elongated mass of Little Spencer forms a prominent landmark in the Moosehead area. For years, its trail was just a flagged herd path used mostly by people staying at a local camp near Spencer Pond. The challenging trail starts out on a wooded easy grade but soon climbs steeply, crosses several sloping rock piles, and ascends through a narrow chimney. There are great views of the Moosehead Lake area from several rock outlooks and the summit. Refer to the USGS Lobster Mtn. quadrangle, 7.5-min. series, and *The Maine Atlas* (DeLorme), maps 41 & 49.

To reach the trail, from Greenville, drive north on the Lily Bay Rd. 19.0 mi. to Kokadjo. Take the left fork 0.2 mi. north of Kokadjo onto Sias Hill Rd. Continue for another 1.2 mi. then turn left again. Travel northwest on the gravel road and turn right at about 7.2 mi., where a sign reads Spencer Pond Camps. Little Spencer is now a very clear mountain profile ahead. Continue on the road for 2.1 mi. staying left and watch for a Little Spencer Mountain Trail sign on the right as it isn't well marked, about 80 yds. beyond a small brook culvert, near an old logging road. Park along side the road.

The trail, not blazed, rises through a hardwood forest, then becomes very steep as it enters a pine/balsam forest. There are spectacular views along the way. After crossing through an area with a few slides, the trail comes to a narrow chimney. *Caution: Use care when climbing through this chimney section. Hikers up ahead can dislodge loose rocks to injure climbers below. Send one person through at a time. There are ropes here to assist the hiker.* The trail then crosses a few more slides and is very close to the cliff edge in some parts. The trail climbs up to the ledges and from here it is a moderate hike to the summit where there are 360 degree views of Kathadin, Big Spencer, Moosehead Lake and Jackman area mountains.

Distance from road

    to Little Spencer summit: 2.0 mi., 2 hr. 15 min.

Section 4

100-Mile Wilderness

See AMC Maine Trail Map 3: Gulf Hagas.

RECOMMENDED HIKES

Easy

Little Wilson Falls (rt: 3.0 mi., 1 hr. 45 min.) A pleasant hike to a waterfall in a deep canyon.

River Trail (rt: 2.2 mi., 2 hr.) A pleasant woods walk along a former tote road to the West Branch of the Pleasant River and to the Gulf Hagas trail.

Moderate

Gulf Hagas (lp: 8.8 mi., 4 hr. 40 min.) A scenic circuit to a spectacular gorge with views of several waterfalls.

Borestone Mountain (Moore's Pond Route) to Eastern Peak (rt: 4.0 mi., 3 hr.) National Audubon Society has a sanctuary along this route. There are excellent views on the bare summit.

Laurie's Ledge Trail to overlooks (rt: 1.6 mi., 2 hr.) On a clear day, you can see as far as Mt. Katahdin from the easterly overlook.

Strenuous

Barren Mountain (rt: 11.2 mi., 7 hr.) A rewarding hike to the granite summit of Barren Mtn., passing the Barren Slide and Barren Ledges.

Chairback Mountain (rt: 8.2 mi., 5 hr. 10 min.) A hike along the AT to the summit with views to the north and west.

LIST OF MOUNTAINS

This section includes the mountains of Piscataquis County west and southwest of the Katahdin area, also known as the 100-Mile Wilderness. The approach to most of the mountains in this section is through Brownville in the east, or Greenville, a convenient and bustling "gateway" community at the southern end of Moosehead Lake.

The Appalachian Trail (AT) crosses White Cap Mtn. (3644 ft.), the highest peak in the section. The AT, in its northeast–southwest course, also passes over the Barren-Chairback Range and close to the interesting and striking Borestone Mtn. (1947 ft.).

A new trail built by the AMC on Indian Mountain provides views from the heart of the 100-Mile Wilderness to Katahdin. This trail and other trails near the AMC's Little Lyford Pond Camps connect to the AT via the River Trail (see page 83). The Club plan to expand mountain trails on its Katahdin Iron Works tract, which it purchased in 2003, as well as link to nearby trail networks. For more information about the Club's Maine Woods Initiative (MWI) and its purchase and management of land in Maine, go to www.outdoors.org/mwi.

Barren Mountain (2671 ft.)

At the western end of the Barren-Chairback Range, Barren Mtn. is the highest and most accessible peak. It is in Elliotsville Plantation (USGS Sebec Lake quadrangle, 15-min. series, and Barren Mtn. West and Barren Mtn. East quadrangles, 7.5-min. series). There are interesting outlooks from Barren Slide and Barren Ledges over Bodfish Intervale, Lake Onawa, and Borestone Mtn. The summit tower is now closed to hikers.

To climb Barren Mtn. via the Appalachian Trail, drive north on ME 15 from the center of Monson 0.5 mi. and turn right on Elliotsville Rd. Drive 7.3 mi. on Elliotsville Rd. to Big Wilson Stream and cross the bridge and turn left. Cross the railroad tracks and go past the trailhead for the Borestone Mountain Trail. At 11.8 mi. from Monson you will come to a wide open area known as Bodfish Farm. Stay on this road and descend down a steep hill where there are views of the Barren Slide. Bear left at the next fork before the bridge over Long Pond Stream. This road is not suited for driving and may be gated. Park along side the road.

Walk along the road for about 1.1 mi. to where the road crosses Vaughn Stream. The road goes uphill and reaches the AT 1.6 mi. from the parking area. Leave the road right (north) on the AT and descend 0.1 mi. Cross Long Pond Stream at the normally knee-deep ford. The trail turns east, passing Slugundy Gorge. At 0.9 mi., it reaches a blue-blazed side trail leading 150 yd. to the

Long Pond Stream Lean-to.

After the junction, the main trail climbs the northwestern slope of Barren Mtn. At 1.8 mi., another blue-blazed side trail leads south to the head of Barren Slide, an interesting mass of boulders with a view west. A little farther, the main trail crosses the head of Barren Ledges, from which there is a striking view. The route then bears left and winds along the northern slope of the range over rough terrain to the base of the cone. From there, it climbs steeply through boulders for a short distance to the summit.

(The AT continues northeast over the remaining peaks of the range to the valley of the West Branch of the Pleasant River. This hike is a camping trip of several days over rough terrain. See the MATC's *Appalachian Trail Guide to Maine* if you plan to take the trip across the range.)

Distances from parking area

> *to* side trail to Long Pond Stream Lean-to: 2.5 mi.

> *to* side trail to Barren Slide: 3.4 mi., 2 hr. 30 min.

> *to* Barren Mtn. summit: 5.6 mi., 4 hr.

Little Wilson Falls

A worthwhile side trip in this area is to Little Wilson Falls, a striking 57-ft. waterfall in the canyon gouged through slate by Little Wilson Stream. Drive north on ME 15 from the center of Monson 0.5 mi and turn right on Elliotsville Rd. Drive 7.3 mi. on Elliotsville Rd. to Big Wilson Stream and turn left crossing the bridge. Go for 0.7 mi. to the former Little Wilson Campsite which is maintained by the Maine Forest Service and park by the second campsite. Immediately cross the stream at the site of a washed-out bridge and turn left on a gravel road. Walk up the road uphill a little over a mile to where the AT comes in on the left before coming to a pond. Turn left onto the AT and at about 1.2 mi., cross Little Wilson Stream. At 1.5 mi., you will reach the rim of a ledge with an outstanding view of the 57-ft. falls and a deep slate canyon.

Distances from MFS Campsite

> *to* Little Wilson Falls: 1.5 mi., 1 hr.

Borestone Mountain (1947 ft.)

Spelled Boarstone on USGS and other maps, this small but rugged mountain, complete with two peaks and three small ponds well up on its southwestern slope, rises above Lake Onawa. The views from the bare summits are excellent. The National Audubon Society sanctuary established there welcomes hikers year-round on the Moore's Ponds Route. It is open dawn to dusk. From June 1 through October 31, nature programs, a self-guided tour, and a staffed interpretive center halfway up are available. A small fee may be charged. No dogs or guns are allowed in the sanctuary. Refer to the USGS Sebec Lake quadrangle, 15-min. series, or the Barren Mtn. West quadrangle, 7.5-min. series.

Moore's Ponds Route

Drive north on ME 15 from the center of Monson 0.5 mi. and turn right on Elliotsville Rd. Drive 7.3 mi. on Elliotsville Rd. to Big Wilson Stream and cross the bridge and turn left. Cross the railroad tracks and go approximately 0.1 mi. to the trailhead on the right. The parking area is on the left side of road. Follow a private road through a gate. The road climbs steadily through switchbacks and then runs along a shelf to Sunrise Pond, the lowest of the three Moore's ponds, where it ends. The other two ponds are known as Midday and Sunset. Follow the trail, blazed with green triangles, around the southeastern end of Sunrise Pond and cross the outlet. After that, the trail, turning north and then east, climbs steeply up the main cone to the open western peak. It descends slightly into the saddle and then rises to the higher eastern peak.

Distances from Elliotsville Rd.

- *to* Sunrise Pond: 1.0 mi., 40 min.
- *to* Borestone, western peak: 1.8 mi., 1 hr. 20 min.
- *to* Borestone, eastern peak: 2.0 mi., 1 hr. 30 min.

Nesuntabunt Mountain (1550 ft.)

This mountain, part of the Maine Public Reserve Land, is found in T1 R11. Its summit offers some of the best views of the Katahdin Range from the south as well as views over Nahmakanta Lake. The Wadleigh Stream Lean-to on the Appalachian Trail is about 2.0 mi. away. Refer to the USGS Rainbow Lake West quadrangle, 7.5-min. series, and map 1 of the MATC's *Appalachian Trail Guide to Maine*.

To get to the trailhead, take ME 11 about 16 miles northeast of Brownville Junction and turn left (north) on the Jo-Mary Rd. immediately after crossing Bear Brook. There is a checkpoint with fee just off ME 11 on the Jo-Mary Rd.

Follow the Jo-Mary Rd. for about 25 miles passing through another checkpoint toward the northwestern end of Nahmakanta Lake. Park where the AT crosses the road and follow the AT south to the northern summit. A 250-ft. side trail leads to splendid views.

Distance from Appalachian Trail crossing

   to   northern summit: 1.2 mi., 45 min.

White Cap Mountain (3644 ft.)

White Cap Mtn. is the highest point on the Appalachian Trail between Katahdin and Bigelow, and also the highest mountain in this section. There are outstanding views from its summit. Refer to the USGS First Roach Pond and Jo-Mary Mountain quadrangles, 15-min. series, the Big Shanty Mountain and Hay Mountain quadrangles, 7.5-min. series, or map 2 in the MATC's *Appalachian Trail Guide to Maine*.

White Brook Trail

To reach the White Brook Trail—the former route of the AT, and still maintained by the MATC—turn left (northwest) off ME 11 5.5 mi. north of Brownville Junction. The sign for the Katahdin Iron Works at the turnoff marks the start of a 6.8-mi. drive on a gravel road from ME 11 to a gate at the Iron Works, a very interesting state historical memorial with a blast furnace and a beehive charcoal burner. Register at the gate and pay a fee to the caretaker. Bear right after driving through the gate and cross the West Branch of the Pleasant River. At about three miles, fork right. About 5.8 mi. from the Iron Works, the road crosses the high, narrow bridge over White Brook. At the next junction, continue straight ahead up the western side of White Brook. (The left fork leads to Hay Brook and Gulf Hagas.) Follow the major gravel road for 3.8 mi., taking the main branch at each fork, and park well off the road where it crosses two brooks. The trail follows an old logging road for 1.0 mi. to a large wood yard. The White Cap–Hay Mountain sag is clearly visible from this yard. Depending on logging operations, this road may be impassable.

A blue-blazed trail leaves the left side of the road and climbs the southern slope toward the sag through a heavily logged area.

At 0.4 mi., the trail crosses White Brook near the ruins of the warden's cabin. From there, it climbs more steeply and reaches the junction with the AT at 1.0 mi.

Turn right and climb the last steep stretch to the summit at 2.1 mi. There are panoramic views from the open ledge. They take in Saddleback (2998 ft.), Little Spruce (3274 ft.), Baker (3520 ft.), Big Moose (3196 ft.), Hay (3244 ft.), and Big Spencer (3230 ft.) mountains, along with the vast lake country to the north, rising to the Katahdin Range. The view is one of the finest in the state.

Distances from road at wood yard

> *to* White Brook crossing: 0.5 mi.
>
> *to* AT junction: 1.0 mi.
>
> *to* White Cap summit (via the AT): 2.1 mi., 1 hr. 30 min.

Indian Mountain (2341 ft.)
Indian Mountain Circuit Trail (AMC) (map 3: C5–D5)

This summer hiking and winter cross-country ski trail primarily runs along the bottom third of Indian Mountain. Parking is located approximately one mile south of the trailhead at a jct. of an old forest road. The northern part of trail starts on the Upper Valley Road at the top of the driveway that leads to the AMC's Little Lyford Pond Camps. The southern access to the trail is located approximately half a mile south of the northern access. The trail is blazed with blue diamonds.

Note: As of December 2004, the northern section of Indian Mountain Circuit Trail is open. Construction on the southern section will proceed in summer 2005, with expectations that it will be open fall 2005.

The trail winds from the northern access through a primarily hardwood forest before passing through a stand of spruce. The trail gradually ascends the lower part of Indian Mountain where it intersects with the Laurie's Ledge Trail (blazed in yellow and signed). The Indian Mountain Circuit Trail then crosses over a bridge where a large rock outcropping can be seen left. The trail then flattens out for 0.1 mi. before starting to descend, at times following sections of old logging roads. At 1.8 mi., the trail crosses an access road before descending for 1.0 mi. to the Horseshoe Pond Access Trail. From Horseshoe Pond, the trail runs southwesterly, gaining elevation for about 0.3 mi. to where there is a branch trail that leads onto the access road. It is here that the trail will be continued to be constructed along the southern slopes of Indian Mountain.

Distances from north access across from AMC's Little Lyford Pond Camps

> *to* Laurie's Ledge Trail: 0.7 mi., 30 min.
>
> *to* Horseshoe Pond: 2.8 mi., 1 hr. 30 min.

Laurie's Ledge Trail (AMC) (map 3: C5–D5)

This summer hiking and winter snowshoeing trail leads off of the north leg of the Indian Mountain Circuit Trail. The trail was built by the AMC in 2003 and named for its then-president, Laurie Burt. The trail offers excellent views to the north at its easterly overlook of Whitecap and Gulf Hagus mountains and on a clear day offers a great view of Mt. Katahdin. At the Laurie's Ledge westerly outlook, excellent views of Elephant Mtn. and many of the areas ponds.

From the northern access, follow the newly constructed Indian Mountain Circuit Trail from where it begins across from the entrance to the AMC's Little Lyford Pond Camps. At 0.7 mi., the Laurie's Ledge Trail leaves left from the fork in the Indian Mountain Circuit Trial. The Laurie's Ledge trail is blazed in yellow. The trail moderately ascends the lower slopes of Indian Mtn., passing through a hardwood forest. The trail passes through an interesting rock formation about 0.1 mi. from the intersection with the Indian Mountain Circuit Trail. From here, the trail gradually ascends until you reach the bottom of a large cliff band. The trail runs along the lower parts of the cliff band for 100 yd. and then takes a turn to the right, in which it becomes steep before heading onto a narrow band of ledge and passing through a stand of small trees. A fine view to the east and south can be had from here. The trail continues for a few hundred yards before reaching the jct. of the trail to the easterly overlook on your right. This trail is 50 yd. long and dead-ends to a spot high on the ledges for a fine view to the north. The trail continues on, steeply for 100 yd. at first, then for another 0.4 mi. passing through stands of spruce and fir. The trail moderates and contours along the upper slopes of Indian Mtn. before reaching the westerly overlook, where the trail dead-ends.

Distances from junction of northern Indian Mountain Circuit Trail

   to   easterly overlook: 0.4 mi., 30 min.

   to   westerly overlook: 0.8 mi., 1 hr.

Gulf Hagas

Just off the Appalachian Trail between the Barren-Chairback Range and White Cap Mtn., Gulf Hagas is a unique scenic area consisting of a deep, narrow, slate canyon about four miles long on the West Branch of the Pleasant River in northern Piscataquis County. The West Branch falls about 400 ft. in the four miles, and in many places, the canyon's vertical slate walls force the river into very narrow channels that form a series of waterfalls, rapids, chutes, and pools.

The falls are particularly spectacular in late spring during peak runoff. During winter, ice builds up on the walls and, because the sun rarely reaches certain faces, often lasts into late June.

In 1968, the canyon was designated a registered natural landmark, and the owners agreed to set aside 500 acres, including the entire canyon, for the public's enjoyment. While retaining ownership, the paper companies agreed not to harvest wood on the reserved land as long as the area is designated a landmark. In 1986, the National Park Service obtained nearly 2000 acres, including the Gulf and the corridor along the Gulf Hagas Brook, to provide protection for the unique natural beauty of this area.

Loggers first harvested the area more than a century ago, when Pleasant River Tote Rd., the approach from both ends of the canyon, was built. Trails were cut to the rim of the canyon in the last century but fell into disuse. The last extensive logging took place during the 1930s, when new trails were cut. The trails are still well marked and well maintained. The trail system runs near the rim of the canyon, with frequent side trails to viewpoints and falls. By using the old Pleasant River Tote Rd., hikers can make a circuit from the south (see also River Trail on page 83). Refer to the AMC's Maine Trail Map 3, included with this guide, or the USGS First Roach Pond, Sebec Lake, and Sebec quadrangles, 15-min. series, the Barren Mountain East quadrangle, 7.5-min. series, or Map 2 in the MATC's *Appalachian Trail Guide to Maine*.

See the description of the approach to White Cap Mtn. (page 78). After crossing the high bridge 5.8 mi. from the Katahdin Iron Works, go left off the major gravel road at the first junction. Follow this logging road for about 1.8 mi. to Hay Brook, which is about 7.5 mi. from the Iron Works. The approach road is rocky and rough but generally passable. A campground with tent sites lies along the West Branch of the Pleasant River. Reservations can be made (fee) at the control gate at Katahdin Iron Works.

From the parking area, cross Hay Brook and follow Pleasant River Tote Rd., past Pugwash Pond, for 0.7 mi. There, the AT comes in from the left. Continue straight ahead. The trail shortly reaches the Hermitage, a beautiful stand of tall white pine now owned by The Nature Conservancy (a log cabin and other buildings have been removed). From the Hermitage area, follow the white-blazed AT northwest along Pleasant River Tote Rd. for 0.9 mi. to Gulf Hagas Brook, where the relocated AT turns sharply right to follow the brook. Continue straight ahead and cross Gulf Hagas Brook (*Note: No bridge and dangerous in high water*). Immediately after the crossing, the Rim Trail leaves left and descends steeply along the rim of the canyon to Gulf Hagas Brook, where it passes a series of spectacular waterfalls visible from viewpoints to the left of the falls trail.

The Rim Trail section continues west, and at 0.7 mi., a side trail leads left to Hammond Street Pitch, a point high above the canyon that offers a fine view of the gorge. Return to the rim trail and turn left (at 0.9 mi., a connector road leads 0.2 mi. back to Pleasant River Rd.). Continuing along the Rim Trail, at 1.2 mi. from Pleasant River Rd., is a series of side paths leading to views of the Jaws, where the river squeezes around a slate spur and narrows in many places. Back on the Rim Trail, at 1.8 mi. from Pleasant River Rd., a spur trail leads to a viewpoint below Buttermilk Falls. After that, the canyon gradually becomes shallower, and at times the trail approaches the banks of the West Branch. At 1.9 mi. from Pleasant River Rd., the trail passes Stair Falls; at 2.8 mi., it reaches the ledge above Billings Falls, where the narrowed river drops into a large pool. In another 0.1 mi., the trail bears sharply away from the river. (At this point, a short side trail leads left to the edge of the river near a rocky island called Head of the Gulf, where there are some interesting logging artifacts.) The trail rejoins Pleasant River Rd. in another 0.2 mi. Turn right (southeast) to follow the road along the side of the mountain high above Gulf Hagas back to Screw Auger Falls, the Hermitage, and Hay Brook. Although it is often very marshy and wet, the road offers a quicker return than the rim trail.

Distances from campground using Rim Trail and Pleasant River Rd.

> *to* AT junction: 0.7 mi., 20 min.
>
> *to* Screw Auger Falls Trail junction: 1.6 mi., 45 min.
>
> *to* rim-trail junction: 2.1 mi., 1 hr.
>
> *to* spur trail to Hammond Street Pitch (via Rim Trail): est. 2.4 mi., 1 hr. 10 min.
>
> *to* side paths to Jaws outlook: 2.9 mi., 1 hr. 30 min.
>
> *to* side trail to Buttermilk Falls: 3.5 mi., 1 hr. 45 min.
>
> *to* Stair Falls: 4.1 mi., 2 hr.
>
> *to* ledge above Billings Falls: 4.5 mi., 2 hr. 15 min.
>
> *to* side trail to Head of the Gulf: 4.6 mi., 2 hr. 20 min.
>
> *to* Pleasant River Rd.: 4.7 mi., 2 hr. 25 min.
>
> *to* rim-trail junction (via Pleasant River Rd.): 6.7 mi., 3 hr. 20 min.
>
> *to* Gulf Hagas Brook: 7.1 mi., 3 hr. 35 min.
>
> *to* campground: 8.8 mi., 4 hr. 40 min.

River Trail (AMC) (map 3: D5)

This trail runs from AMC's Little Lyford Pond Camps first along the west side, and eventually crossing the West Branch of the Pleasant River, to reach to the northern access trail to the Gulf Hagus Trail. The majority of this trail follows the route of the Pleasant River Tote Road that was used from the late 1800s to the mid-1900s. The trail is used primarily by fisherman and hikers in the summer and snowshoers and cross-country skiers in the winter.

The trail leaves from behind the main lodge at Little Lyford Pond Camps and next to the Mountain View Cabin. Start off by crossing a lowland area that has some old bog bridging and wet spots before coming to a jct. with a spur trail. (This spur leads to the river where there was an old dam.) The River Trail continues up a moderate grade, where it follows a ridge that parallels the river. The trail drops down, crosses a spot next to the West Branch of the Pleasant River, and then climbs gradually, crossing a minor drainage. From here the trail continues south, moving further away from the river. The jct. of the southerly terminus of the Indian Mountain Circuit trail comes in from the right at 0.9 miles. The trail continues for another 0.2 miles before coming out onto a forest road. The bridge crossing the West Branch of the Pleasant River can be seen on your left.

Distances from AMC's Little Lyford Pond Camps main lodge

   to Indian Mountain Circuit Trail (south terminus): 0.9 mi., 40 min.

   to bridge over the West Branch of the Pleasant River: 1.1 mi., 1 hr.

Chairback Mountain (2219 ft.)

This interesting, open peak is at the eastern end of the Barren-Chairback Range. It is a day hike from a logging road south of the West Branch of the Pleasant River. Refer to the USGS Sebec and Sebec Lake quadrangles, 15-min. series; the Silver Lake and Barren Mtn. East quadrangles, 7.5-min. series; or Map 3 in the MATC's *Appalachian Trail Guide to Maine*.

From Katahdin Iron Works, follow the gravel paper-company road. At about three miles., take the left fork at the LLPC (Little Lyford Pond Camps) sign. (The right fork leads to Gulf Hagas.)

Park at 6.7 mi. from the Iron Works, short of where the Appalachian Trail crosses the road. Then descend 0.2 mi. to the AT. Follow it south as it climbs a short way on a hauling road, then turns sharply left. At 1.7 mi., the AT reaches the top of a ridge, and a blue-blazed side trail leads right 0.2 mi. to East Chairback Pond. Continue over a series of ridges. The last half-mile of the climb rises over a very steep talus slope to reach the summit, with its outstanding views of the White Cap Range, Baker Mtn. and Elephant Mtn.

Distances from parking (via AT)

　to　side trail to East Chairback Pond: 1.7 mi., 1 hr. 20 min.

　to　Chairback summit (via AT): 4.1 mi., 2 hr. 35 min.

Section 5

East of the Penobscot

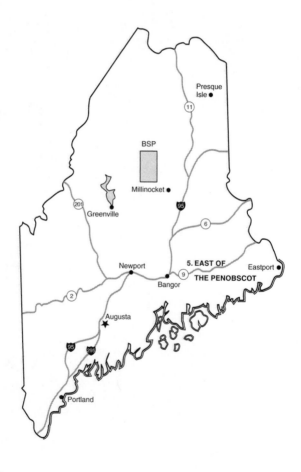

RECOMMENDED HIKES

Easy

Bald Mountain (rt: 1.0 mi., 1 hr. 45 min.) A short, easy climb to a fire tower that provides superb views to the north and east including Katahdin and Mt. Desert Island.

Blue Hill (rt: 2.0 mi., 1 hr. 30 min.) An easy-graded climb to the summit of Blue Hill, with extensive views of the Mt. Desert Island mountains and Blue Hill Bay.

Pocomoonshine Mountain (rt: 1.0 mi., 1 hr.) Take the blue-blazed loop trail for views of the surrounding area.

Moderate

Black Mountain Cliffs (lp: 2.7 mi., 3 hr.) A steep climb to the summit of Black Mtn., with good views of the surrounding lakes and mountains.

Lead Mountain (rt: 6.0 mi., 3 hr. 30 min.) Lead Mtn. is a small mountain with a flat, open summit that provides views to the south and west.

Schoodic Mountain from ME 200 (rt: 5.6 mi., 3 hr. 20 min.) The top of this popular mountain provides views of Mount Desert Island and Frenchman's Bay.

LIST OF MOUNTAINS

This section describes the mainland area east of the Penobscot River and south of Aroostook County, between the Penobscot river plain on the west and the coastal rivers, including the Union, Narraguagus, Machias, and St. Croix, on the south and east. In this region, the country rolls up into low, mostly widely scattered mountains. Lead Mtn. (1475 ft.) and Passadumkeag Mtn. (1463 ft.) are the highest, and several others are over 1000 feet. In general, extensive views characterize these mountains, some of which have attractive open summits and ledges. This section first describes the mountains to the south and west first, and then those to the north and east.

Tunk Mountain (1157 ft.)

This mountain is located in T10 SD (T stands for "township" and SD for "Southern Division"). It is northeast of Schoodic Mtn. There is no trail on Tunk's upper part, but bushwhacking is fairly easy. Refer to the USGS Tunk Lake quadrangle, 15-min. series, and the Tunk Mountain quadrangle, 7.5-min. series.

Take US 1 east from Ellsworth for 6 mi. and bear left on ME 182. At about 7.5 mi. east of ME 200 in Franklin, park at the entrance of a road on the left that is 0.2 mi. east of the eastern end of Fox Pond and 2.7 mi. west of the outlet of Tunk Lake.

The trail leads north through gentle terrain that rises gradually to Salmon Pond. It continues on to Mud Pond as a footpath, identifiable only by its worn treadway. Once the trail crosses by the western end of the pond, it rises sharply and becomes much less distinct as it passes through spruce forest. Eventually, it breaks onto open ledges on the slopes of the five-peaked summit ridge. The whole southern face of the mountain consists of cliffs and steep ledges. Views are limited but interesting, particularly those of Spring River Lake and the Black Hills.

Distance from entrance of road off ME 182

   to Tunk summit: 1.5 mi., 1 hr. 30 min.

Schoodic Mountain (1069 ft.)

Schoodic is one of a small group of mountains northeast of the head of Frenchman's Bay, and it is very popular for climbing. It is located in T9 SD. Refer to the USGS Tunk Lake quadrangle, 15-min. series, and the Sullivan quadrangle, 7.5-min. series.

A good trail to the abandoned firetower on the summit starts 2.2 mi. south of Franklin village and 4.0 mi. north of Sullivan. It leaves the eastern side of ME 200 between two bridges at the foot of a steep hill in East Franklin. Park in the space just north of the northern bridge. Take the paved road east and follow the right fork up a hill. At about 0.5 mi., the road (which can sometimes be driven to this point) crosses a large brook, the last sure source of water on the trail. At about 1 mi., the road crosses some railroad tracks. Turn right and follow the road beside the tracks for a short distance until it swings away to the left. Pass through a logged area, keeping straight at the next left fork. About 20 min. farther, take the well-worn path to the left (cairn). The trail then climbs steeply but presents no difficulties. The top of the mountain is bare and flat and offers views in all directions. Those of Mount Desert Island and Frenchman's Bay are very scenic.

Another easier approach to the mountain is by the trail that leaves from the southern (near) end of the Schoodic Beach parking lot. (See the directions to the parking lot in the Black Mtn. description, below.) Follow blue blazes through woods up the mountain until you reach open ledges where the trail from Schoodic Beach joins from the right at a large stone cairn. Continue following stone cairns up ledges to the top.

The trail from Schoodic Beach up Schoodic Mtn. leaves from the western end of the beach, following an old road for a short distance then ascending left. Schoodic Mountain

Distances from ME 200

> *to* large-brook crossing: est. 0.5 mi., 15 min.

> *to* railroad tracks: 1.0 mi., 30 min.

> *to* warden's cabin site: 2.0 mi., 1 hr.

> *to* Schoodic summit: 2.8 mi., 1 hr. 40 min.

Distances from Schoodic Beach parking lot

> *to* Schoodic summit: 0.8 mi., 45 min.

> *to* Schoodic Beach: 0.5 mi., 15 min.

> *to* Schoodic summit via beach: 0.6 mi., 45 min.

Black Mountain (1094 ft.)

The point from which most hikers access Black Mtn. is US 1 in East Sullivan. Turn onto ME 183 and proceed about 4.5 miles, following the main tarred road. About 150 yd. after you cross some abandoned railroad tracks, take the first gravel road to the left (look for a blue-and-white Public Lands sign). Follow the gravel road about 0.3 mi. to a Y. At this point, the Schoodic Beach Rd. bears to the left down a hill and another gravel road, known as Black Mtn. Rd., continues up the hill straight ahead. The left branch heads to Schoodic Mtn., Schoodic Beach, campsites on Donnell Pond, and Black Mtn. Cliffs. The right branch heads to the Black summit, Wizard Pond (Big Chief Trail), Rainbow Pond, and Caribou Mtn.

Black Mountain Cliffs Loop

To reach the Schoodic Mtn. and Black Mtn. Cliffs trailhead, bear left at the first Y and continue about 1 mi. to a second Y. Continue straight ahead, avoiding Flanders Pond Rd. to the left, for about 1 mi., to the Donnell Pond public parking lot at the end of the road. The trail up to Black Mtn. Cliffs leaves from the northern (far) end of the parking lot. Bear right just past the small brook and follow blue blazes through the woods, crossing several old logging roads up to the base of Black Mtn. Blazes and rock cairns continue up over interesting cliffs and ledges to the top of the ridge. At a jct. here, a trail bears right (northerly) toward Wizard Pond, Black Mtn. Bald, various other longer trail loops, and the trailhead on Black Mtn. Rd. To reach the cliffs, continue straight ahead along the ridgeline, through the spruce forest. The trail goes past several small overlooks to reach a jct. from which a side trail heads downslope over open ledges to the left to cliffs overlooking Donnell Pond. This overlook is a good spot for observing the large turkey vultures and eagles flying in the area. Continuing straight on the main trail, you will gradually descend through hardwood forest to Schoodic Beach. This hike is of moderate difficulty.

Distance from Schoodic Beach parking lot

- *to*   Black Mtn. base: 0.8 mi., 40 min.
- *to*   junction with Wizard Pond/Black Mountain Bald trail: 1.2 mi., 90 min.
- *to*   Donnell Pond overlook: 1.5 mi., 1 hr. 50 min.
- *to*   Schoodic Beach: 2.1 mi., 2 hr. 30 min.

    Complete Black Mtn. Cliffs loop: 2.7 mi., 3 hr.

Black Mountain Ridge

To reach the Black Mtn. Ridge trailhead, take Black Mtn. Rd. 2.0 mi. from its intersection with Schoodic Beach Rd. Just beyond a three-car parking area, currently marked with blue blazes and a stone cairn, the trail leaves left. It follows the approximate route of the old Big Chief Trail. It is well worn and easily followed as it passes beautiful granite cliff faces. It is marked with blue paint blazes until it breaks out onto the open granite ledges. At the jct. here, follow rock cairns around the southeastern face of the middle peak of Black Mtn. (continuing straight ahead would lead you to a Wizard Pond overlook). There are spectacular views across the adjacent lakes and the entire Downeast coast.

When you reach the cliff between the middle and eastern peaks of Black Mtn., you will find a trail jct. Bear right to drop down to Wizard Brook (Wizard Pond is just upstream), then proceed up the slopes of the easternmost and highest peak of Black Mtn. Known locally as Bald Peak, it has beautiful 360-degree views of Downeast Maine. From the junction, your first viewpoint (of Wizard Pond) lies about 200 yd. ahead. The trail continues, connecting with another trail on Black Mtn.'s ridgeline along with various long and short hikes including a loop around Caribou Mtn. This hike is easy to moderate.

Distance from trailhead

- *to* middle peak ledges: 0.4 mi., 35 min.
- *to* Wizard Pond overlook: 0.6 mi., 45 min.
- *to* Wizard Brook: 0.8 mi., 55 min.
- *to* Bald Peak: 1.0 mi., 1 hr. 5 min.

Blue Hill (934 ft.)

This isolated mountain rises just north of the town of the same name. There is a MFS firetower as well as a microwave tower on the summit. Refer to the USGS Blue Hill quadrangle, 15-min. series or 7.5-min. series.

Opposite the Blue Hill Fair Grounds, 13.0 mi. from Ellsworth on ME 172, go right onto a road that heads west. An excellent MFS trail leaves this road on the right (north), 0.8 mi. from ME 172. (You can also reach the start of the trail by turning east from ME 15, 1.0 mi. north of Blue Hill village and 11.0 mi. south of the jct. with US 1 between Orland and East Orland. The trail is on the left [north], 0.5 mi. from ME 15.) Not far from the start, it branches right and runs through a fine stand of spruce to the summit. Extensive views take in the

Mt. Desert Island mountains and Blue Hill Bay. See *A Hiker's Guide to Blue Hill Mountain*, by Alison Dibble, sponsored by the Blue Hill Heritage Trust. This pamphlet is available in local stores and inns for a $2.00 donation.

Distance from road between ME 172 and ME 15

to Blue Hill summit: 1.0 mi., 45 min.

Great Hill (1038 ft.)

Great Hill appears on the USGS Orland quadrangle, 7.5-min. series. It is also called Great Pond Mtn., and is known locally as Old Baldy. It is in the town of Orland, northeast of Alamoosook Lake.

Leave US 1 in East Orland 6.0 mi. east of Bucksport and 14.0 mi. west of Ellsworth at Toddy Pond Outlet (sign reading Craig Brook National Fish Hatchery). Take Hatchery Rd. to the north for 1.4 mi. Bear right onto the Don Fish Trail at brick gateposts. Park at 0.8 mi. Take the trail up to the left (sign reading Mt. Trail and tan register box). The trail climbs up and down through woods. Joining a ledgy jeep road up, it soon emerges onto spacious open ledges from which you can see from Mt. Desert Island to Penobscot Bay. The wooded summit, about 100 ft. higher with an open ledge, offers views to the northeast and east.

Be careful to note where the trail leaves the woods, so that you can find this spot again on the way down; there are no markers on the ledges.

Distance from parking area

to Great Hill summit: 1.8 mi., 1 hr. 15 min.

Bald Mountain (1234 ft.)

This interesting mountain (also known as Dedham Bald Mtn.) is in the town of Dedham, and a MFS trail in good condition leads to a tower and radio towers on the summit. The Bald Mtn. ski area used to occupy the western side of the mountain. After it closed, the lifts and other equipment were removed. Refer to the USGS Green Lake quadrangle, 7.5-min. series.

From US 1A in East Holden, 9.0 mi. from Bangor and 18.0 mi. from Ellsworth, turn south onto paved Upper Dedham Rd.; do not take ME 46. In 2.8 mi., take a left at the fire station. Then, 6.5 mi. from US 1A, where the road bears right, continue straight on FR 62 for 100 yd. and park on ledges to the left. The trail starts at the parking area and is easy to follow. It leads through open fields and over ledges to the tower, which the MFS maintains for communication. From the tower, you can see to the north and northwest from Katahdin to Bigelow, and the nearby ledges on the northern side of the mountain look out over beautiful Phillips Lake, now known as Lucerne-in-Maine. The eastern side offers views of the Mt. Desert Island mountains.

An alternative route follows the old ski trail, which is easy to see from the approach road. The ski trail intersects Upper Dedham Rd. 0.3 mi. before (north of) the firetower trail at the parking area.

Distance from parking area

   to Bald Mtn. firetower: 0.5 mi., 30 min.

Rider Bluff (813 ft.)

This bluff in Holden is in the first line of hills east of the Penobscot river plain. It makes a good outlook from which to view the Bangor-Brewer area and the mountains from Katahdin to Bigelow, Sugarloaf, and Abraham. Most people hike up the service road for the WLBZ-TV tower on the summit. (During dry weather, cars can usually make it up this road, too.) Refer to the USGS Brewer Lake quadrangle, 7.5-min. series.

From US 1A, turn southwest on paved South Rd., 8.0 mi. from Bangor and 1.4 mi. northwest of East Holden. The turn is just southeast of the Holden Town Hall and Grange. In 1.3 mi., the blacktop road makes a sharp left turn. Go straight ahead on the private access road. It descends slightly, crosses a small brook, then turns right (west) and climbs toward the col between Rider Bluff and Hog Hill. About 0.7 mi. from the blacktop road, it turns and climbs more steeply to the summit.

Distance from blacktop road

   to Rider summit: est. 1.0 mi., 40 min.

Blackcap Mountain (1022 ft.)

Five radio and TV masts top Blackcap Mountain, which is in Eddington. Vegetation blocks views, except to the east. Refer to the USGS Orono and Orland quadrangles, 15-min. series, and the Chemo Pond quadrangle, 7.5-min. series.

To reach the summit, take ME 46 northeast from US 1A at East Holden. Drive 4.3 mi. and turn right onto Blackcap Rd. (sign reading Katahdin Area Council Boy Scout Camp). The road to the scout camp goes left from the summit road, 0.5 mi. from ME 46. Stay right at that and all other junctions. Continue 1.9 mi. to the end of the road. If the road is washed out, a four-wheel-drive vehicle will be necessary.

Roberts Trail

Hikers can pick up the Roberts Trail either at the summit of Blackcap (at the southern end of the road), to the right of the southernmost tower, or on the scout camp road at the outlet of Fitts Pond, which is opposite a gravel bank near the entrance of the camp 1.5 mi. from the summit road. Other trails also diverge from this point and lead to Burnt Pond and Little Burnt Pond. Blue and white paint blazes and directional arrows mark the Roberts Trail, which crosses the pond outlet on a tripod bridge and climbs steeply to the cluster of radio and TV masts. It continues along the summit ridge over open ledges and through patches of trees to the southern end of the ridge. Then it drops steeply east and northeast to the southern end of Fitts Pond. It crosses a swampy patch to the eastern shore of the pond and runs along the shore. At first, it stays close to the shore. Then it goes up on the bluff and returns to the entrance of the Boy Scout camp. At the southern end of the pond, be careful not to take a wrong turn onto a jeep road that diverges east.

Distances from scout camp entrance

> *to* radio and TV masts: 0.6 mi., 45 min.
>
> *to* southern end of Blackcap summit ridge: 1.4 mi., 1 hr. 10 min.
>
> *to* southern end of Fitts Pond: 2.3 mi., 2 hr.
>
> *to* scout camp entrance: 3.8 mi., 3 hr.

Eagle Bluff (790 ft.)

With one of the more open and scenic views in eastern Maine, this sheer cliff overlooks Mountainy Pond and almost unbroken wilderness. A tote road rises gradually to within 0.8 mi. of the summit, which is bare. The sheer southern side is good for rappelling, friction climbing, and rock climbing. The granite is stable, but not many climbers take advantage of it. Refer to the USGS Orono and Orland quadrangles, 15-min. series, and the Green Lake quadrangle, 7.5-min. series.

The trail begins at the Katahdin Scout Camp. (See the preceding section for approach routes.) Park in the lot at the reservation.

From behind the mess hall (the largest building), the trail follows the road, which rises quickly at first. At about 2.8 mi., turn sharply right into a hunting camp. To the left of the camp, an orange-blazed trail climbs steeply, levels off, and then pitches quickly to the summit.

Distance from scout camp

to Eagle Bluff summit: 3.0 mi., 2 hr.

Woodchuck Hill (834 ft.)

An easy hike in the area northeast of Blackcap Mtn., Woodchuck Hill (also known as Snowshoe Mtn.) offers good campsites at both its summit and its base. Refer to the USGS Orono quadrangle, 15-min. series, and the Chemo Pond quadrangle, 7.5-min. series.

The approach by road is the same as for Blackcap Mtn. Park in the lot at Camp Roosevelt (a scout camp). Follow the unmarked road through the camp then turn left on the blue- and yellow-blazed trail. This passes through a campsite beyond Snowshoe Pond and comes out onto the Bangor Water District road (paved). Cross the road to utility pole 68, then follow well-marked blue and yellow blazes and arrows up over cliffs to the open summit with views.

Distance from scout camp

to Woodchuck summit: est. 1.3 mi., 45 min.

Peaked (1160 ft.) and Little Peaked Mountains

These two summits make a particularly rewarding snowshoeing trip in winter. It is easy to complete the circuit in an afternoon from many points in the surrounding area.

Peaked Mountain (Chick Hill)

Peaked Mtn., commonly called Chick Hill, straddles the Clifton–Amherst line. A well-marked and popular MFS trail leads to the summit. Refer to the USGS Great Pond quadrangle, 15-min. series, and the Hopkins Pond quadrangle, 7.5-min. series.

About 18.0 mi. from Bangor and 3.5 mi. east of the junction of ME 9 and ME 180, leave ME 9 on the northern (left) side onto a gravel road 1.1 mi. east of the Parks Pond Campground. In about 0.7 mi., after passing a small group of houses, park. Follow an old discontinued "Airline" road to the fire warden's campsite (0.2 mi.). There is a dependable spring behind the campsite. Continue on the old road and, at about 0.6 mi., as the road levels off, turn right onto a clearly blazed trail. At about 0.9 mi., the trail rises more steeply; from the lower ledge, you can see nearby Little Peaked Mtn. to the west. Occasional cairns mark the way to the summit, which offers vistas in all directions and is particularly colorful in fall. The view includes five lakes, the Penobscot River, the Mt. Desert Island mountains to the southeast, and Mt. Katahdin to the northwest.

Distance from parking area

>   *to* Peaked Mtn. summit: 1.3 mi., 50 min.

Little Peaked Mountain

The views from Little Peaked Mtn. (Little Chick Hill) are also good, except to the north. To reach Little Peaked Mtn., take the trail to the right at the parking area.

Another easy route is to take the trail up Peaked Mtn. Just before beginning the climb up the steeper part of the peak, turn right, descend briefly to the col, and bushwhack to Little Peaked.

For a third route, start up the Peaked Mtn. Trail. At 0.4 mi., go right onto a cairned road closed with a cable for 0.2 mi. Turn right at the cairn and climb directly to the summit.

Lead Mountain (Humpback) (1475 ft.)

Lead Mtn. is in T28 MD in Hancock County, just west of the Washington county line. (T for "township," MD for "middle Division.") The trail appears on the USGS Lead Mtn. quadrangle, 7.5-min. series.

Take the newly bulldozed road left at the rear of the yard of the MFS station (94 yd.) in Beddington. The station is 0.1 mi. west of the ME 9 bridge over the Narraguagus River and 1.1 mi. east of the ME 9 and ME 193 junction. Park at the turnaround 1.7 mi. from the station. The trail follows the gated road for 10 min., then turns right up into the woods just before the University of Maine acid-rain project structures and heads for the summit (blue-blazed). At 1.3 mi., a side path leads 200 yd. left to Bear Pond. At 1.5 mi., the trail divides. The left fork goes close to a reliable spring 100 ft. to the left of the main trail (sign).

Then it rejoins the main trail. At 2.5 mi., you will reach the warden's cabin in a col below the summit. The trail continues straight on past the cabin and then bears left (west) to the site of the firetower, which is on a flat summit several acres in area. The ledges 200 yd. southwest of the summit are a good lookout.

Descending, remember that where the trail divides, the right fork leads past the spring.

Distances from MFS station

> *to*   side trail to Bear Pond: 1.3 mi., 40 min.
>
> *to*   warden's cabin: 2.5 mi., 1 hr. 45 min.
>
> *to*   Lead summit: 3.0 mi., 2 hr.

Peaked Mountain (Wash. Co.) (938 ft.)

Peaked Mtn. is in T 30 in Washington County, north of ME 9 and less than 30 mi. east of the mountain near Clifton with the same name. Refer to the USGS Tug Mtn. quadrangle, 15-min. series, and the Peaked Mtn. quadrangle, 7.5-min. series.

A good MFS trail leaves the northern side of ME 9 at an MFS sign (09-67-0), found about 9.8 mi. east of the Narraguagus River and about 14.8 mi. west of Wesley. You will pass the cabin Mayor Haven at 0.2 mi. Take the right fork at 0.3 mi., and park at 0.6 mi. (hiker sign). Follow the tote road a short distance to the former fire warden's cabin (private, name of Pelton). Between buildings, take the trail, which rises gently to an open ledge with some views. The MFS firetower has been removed. Extensive wilderness spreads out below in all directions.

Distance from parking area on tote road

> *to*   Peaked Mtn. summit: 1.3 mi., 45 min.

Washington Bald Mountain (983 ft.)

This mountain's MFS firetower was abandoned in 1970. The mountain is in T42 MD. Refer to the USGS Fletcher Peak quadrangle, 7.5-min. series.

A paper company maintains the gravel road that leaves the northern side of ME 9, 14.0 mi. east of the Narraguagus River in Beddington and 10.5 mi. west of Wesley. Take the road north to its end (13.1 mi.), where there is room for four or five cars to park. From this point, logging operations have obscured the trail. A map-and-compass bushwhack is recommended. (See the section on Bushwhacking.) Climb the last steep pitch to a tower, which was erected in 1935. There is a well sunk in the granite near the warden's cabin (now privately leased).

Trails lead to Third, Fourth, and Fifth Machias lakes from the summit but are not recommended. You can see First, Second, Third, and Fourth Machias lakes and many mountains from the 65-ft. tower.

Distance from end of paper company road

   to Washington Bald firetower (via right fork): 2.2 mi., 1 hr. 30 min.

Passadumkeag Mountain (1463 ft.)

Passadumkeag Mtn. is southeast of Enfield. It runs in a gradual east–west arc for some 5 mi. and rises well above the surrounding countryside, which is particularly flat to the west and southwest. Until 1970, the MFS staffed the firetower on the highest summit and maintained a good logging road to it. Refer to the USGS Saponac quadrangle, 15-min. series, and the Burlington and Saponac quadrangles, 7.5-min. series.

Leave West Enfield on ME 155, heading east from its junction with US 2. After 2.5 mi., turn right onto ME 188, and follow it to the Saponac four corners (green buildings), about 19 mi. from US 2. Turn sharply right onto a gravel road and cross the Passadumkeag River. At 0.4 mi., turn right at the head of a gravel pit. Pass the blue house (a former ranger station) and continue on the increasingly rough road. From this road, where logging has obliterated the trail, the climb becomes a bushwhack to the 30-ft. firetower. The tower can also be reached by following Greenfield Rd. from the south, starting from US 2 in Costigan. This becomes a rough jeep trail. From the tower, you can see Brandy Pond to the southeast in T39 MD, Saponac Lake to the north, West lakes and Nicatous Lake to the east, and many mountains, including Katahdin.

Distances from parking area

   to private cabin: 4.0 mi., 2 hr.

   to Passadumkeag firetower: 4.5 mi., 2 hr. 30 min.

Pocomoonshine Mountain (605 ft.)

Located in Princeton, this mountain rises nearly 500 ft. above Pocomoonshine Lake. Before abandoning it in 1970, the MFS built a road on the back side of the mountain to the tower (the first trail described below). Refer to the USGS Big Lake quadrangle, 15-min. series, and the Princeton quadrangle, 7.5-min. series.

From US 1, 2.3 mi. south of Princeton, turn southwest onto South Princeton Rd. At 0.9 mi., turn right onto a gravel road (sign reading Pokey Mt. Scenic Area). Travel 4.1 mi. to a fork. The right fork leads to a parking area with view of Pocomoonshine Lake. A blue-blazed trail ascends to the summit and tower foundation following the old firewarden's road. The left fork leads 0.2 mi. to a second parking area. From there depart two blue-blazed trails, the left leading 0.1 mi. to a tent platform, the right meandering gradually up the mountain, joining the firewarden's road 0.1 mi. from the summit. There is no view from the site of the former firetower, but a blue-blazed trail loops around the summit area to some outcrops, which offer views in various directions.

Another trail to the summit leaves US 1 to the right at 3.8 mi.

Distance from parking area

   to Pocomoonshine summit: 0.5 mi., 30 min.

Section 6

Camden Hills

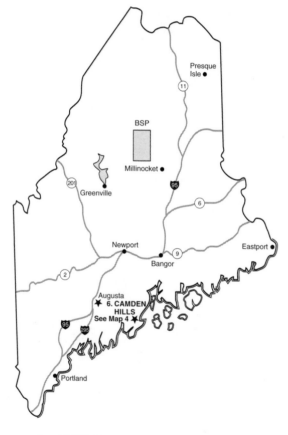

See AMC Maine Trail Map 4: Camden Hills.

RECOMMENDED HIKES

Easy

Mount Waldo (rt: 1.0 mi., 30 min.) A short hike to the granite ledges of Mt. Waldo where there are wonderful views to the east and north.

Bald Rock Mountain Trail via the Multi-Use Trail (rt: 4.2 mi., 2 hr. 40 min.) A pleasant hike to Bald Rock where there are sweeping views of the Midcoast islands, and on a clear day you can see Islesboro and Deer Isle.

Moderate

Mount Megunticook Loop (lp: 5.4 mi., 3 hr. 20 min.) A loop hike using the Mount Megunticook Trail, the Ridge Trail, the Slope Trail and the Multi-Use Trail. The highpoint of the hike is the spectacular views from Ocean Lookout.

Mount Battie Trail (rt: 1.0 mi., 1 hr.) Although a short hike, it is a steep hike gaining 600 ft. in 0.5 mi. The summit of Mt. Battie provides superb views of the Midcoast islands.

Strenuous

Monhegan Island Cliff Trail (lp: 3.5 mi., 3–4 hr.) A hike around the perimeter of Monhegan Island with spectacular views. Many sections are exposed and are difficult to traverse.

LIST OF MOUNTAINS

The Camden Hills, a compact and attractive group of mountains, rise above the western shore of Penobscot Bay in the towns of Camden, Lincolnville, and Rockport. They share many characteristics with the Mt. Desert Island mountains 40 mi. to the east—fine softwood forests, bold cliffs and ledges, and wide vistas of water and mountains. Mt. Megunticook (1385 ft.) is the highest of the group and, with the exception of Cadillac Mtn., is the highest point along the Atlantic seaboard in the United States. A chain of lower summits continues northeast for several miles; Bald Rock Mtn. (1100 ft.) is the most conspicuous. Cameron Mtn. (811 ft.) is west of Bald Rock and northeast of Maiden Cliff. The Cameron summit is private property, a commercial blueberry field. Mt. Battie (800 ft.) lies to the south of Megunticook and is only 0.5 mi. by trail from Megunticook St. in Camden. The Megunticook River and Lake separate the main peaks of the group from the hills running to the southwest, which are, from northeast to southwest, Bald Mtn. (1272 ft.), Ragged Mtn. (1300 ft.), Spruce Mtn. (960 ft.), Pleasant Mtn. (1064 ft.), and Meadow Mtn. (660 ft.). Refer to the USGS Camden, Lincolnville, and West Rockport quadrangles, 7.5-min. series, as well as the map included with this guide.

Camden Hills State Park (5500 acres) embraces much of the Mt. Megunticook Range, plus a large area to the north and northeast and a short stretch on Penobscot Bay north of Camden on US 1. Park facilities include picnic and camping areas. An automobile road (toll) runs to the summit of Mt. Battie from the park headquarters on US 1, 1.6 miles from the intersection with ME 52. The water supply is not reliable in many parts of the park, so carry water if you hike there. Most trails are blazed with white paint. All the trails in the Camden Hills are well-blazed and maintained.

Several outlying mountains to the west of the Penobscot River, south of US 2, and east of the Kennebec River, are included in this section of the guide though not in the Camden Hills. This section also covers the offshore island of Monhegan.

Mount Battie (800 ft.)

This mountain lies to the south of Mt. Megunticook. For climbing, it is the most popular of the Camden Hills, because its open ledges offer outstanding views, and it is close to Camden. For several years after 1897, there was a hotel on the summit. The stone viewing tower there now was erected as a war memorial in 1921.

A toll road for cars runs to the summit. Starting at the Camden Hills State Park Headquarters on US 1, it climbs gradually to the Battie-Megunticook col, turns southwest, and finally curves southeast to the top (1.4 mi.).

Mount Battie Trail (map 4: C2)

This trail, marked with white blazes and cairns, rises steeply over the rocky nose of Mt. Battie. Take ME 52 (Mountain St.) from its junction with US 1 in Camden. Then take the fourth right, and then the first left onto Megunticook St. Continue steeply uphill, where there is a small parking area. The trail first climbs northwest and then rises more steeply north through thinning woods. It soon emerges on the open ledges and runs to the summit tower.

Distance from parking area on Megunticook St.

   to Battie summit: 0.5 mi., 30 min.

Carriage Road Trail (map 4: C1–C2)

This generally easily-hiked trail climbs along the more gradual western and northwestern slopes of Mt. Battie, via the route of the old carriage road up the mountain, and leaves the right (northeastern) side of ME 52 about 1.3 mi. from the US 1 and ME 52 junction. At the trailhead, a very small wood sign says, Old Carriage Road – Mt. Battie Rd 1 mile. Park on the side of Route 52; the Old Carriage Road has no vehicular access. The Old Carriage Road runs north 0.3 mi. to where the Carriage Road Trail forks right, while the Carriage Trail, leading to the Tableland Trail, continues.

The Carriage Road Trail rises gently on the old carriage road, which is washed out in many places. The trail joins the toll road near the summit parking area.

Distance from ME 52

   to Battie summit: 1.1 mi., 35 min.

Carriage Trail (map 4: C1–C2)

In conjunction with the Tableland Trail, this trail provides a route up Mt. Megunticook from the southwest. To approach the trail, see the Carriage Road Trail, above.

The trail climbs very gradually. It reaches the Tableland Trail near the Battie-Megunticook col. To the right, the Tableland Trail leads to the Mt. Battie summit. (To the left, the Tableland Trail proceeds to Ocean Lookout and, beyond that, the true summit of Mt. Megunticook.)

Distances from ME 52

   to Tableland Trail junction: 1.0 mi., 30 min.

   to Ocean Lookout (via Tableland Trail): 1.7 mi., 1 hr. 20 min.

   to Megunticook summit (via Tableland and Ridge trails): 2.2 mi., 1 hr. 35 min.

Nature Trail (map 4: C2)

The Nature Trail is a 1.2-mi. link between the lower part of the Megunticook Trail and the Tableland Trail. It provides access to both Mt. Battie (via the Tableland Trail) and Mt. Megunticook (via either the Megunticook or Tableland Trail and the Ridge Trail).

The Nature Trail is accessed from the Mt. Battie hiker's parking lot, on right about 0.25 mi. up the Mt. Battie Rd. (state park entrance fee) from the intersection with ME 52. From the parking lot, turn left (northwest) to reach the Tableland Trail; turn right (north-northeast) to reach the Megunticook Trail. It is possible to make a nice loop of approximately 3.4 mi. over Ocean Lookout: Take the Nature Trail to the Megunticook Trail up to Ocean Lookout, then return via the Tableland Trail and the northwestern end of the Nature Trail.

Distances from Mt. Battie Rd. hiker's parking lot

   to Tableland Trail junction: 0.9 mi., 30 min.

   to Battie summit (via Tableland Trail): 1.7 mi., 45 min.

   to Ocean Lookout (via Megunticook Trail): 1.3 mi., 1 hr. 15 min.

   to Ocean Lookout (via Tableland Trail): 1.7 mi., 1 hr. 25 min.

Mount Megunticook (1385 ft.)

Mt. Megunticook is the highest of the Camden Hills. A ridge forms the mountain and runs northwest-southeast for approximately 3 mi. The true summit has no view, but Ocean Lookout, 0.4 mi. to the southeast, takes in the expanse of Penobscot Bay. Several outlooks on the Ridge Trail offer views to the northwest over Megunticook Lake. Maiden Cliff is a prominent bluff near the northwestern end of the mountain.

Mount Megunticook Trail (map 4: C2)

This trail climbs the eastern slope of the mountain from the northeastern end of the Nature Trail to Ocean Lookout. Parking is available at the Mt. Battie hiker's parking lot, on right about 0.25 mi. up the Mt. Battie Rd. (state park entrance fee) from the intersection with ME 52. Obtain a map of the state park at the entrance gate to identify the location of the trailhead. The trail starts from the northern end of the park camping area and climbs first gradually, then steeply. At 1.4 mi., it reaches Ocean Lookout, where the Tableland Trail from Mt. Battie comes up from the left (south). From Ocean Lookout, follow the Ridge Trail to the right about 0.4 mi. to the Mt. Megunticook summit.

The five-mile-long Multi-Use Trail has been cut along the eastern side of Mt. Megunticook. It leaves the right side of the Mt. Megunticook Trail just after camping area, leading around the eastern side of Mt. Megunticook before turning east to the Youngtown Rd. trailhead (found just northwest of the intersection of Youngtown Rd. and ME 173). Hikers can complete a loop trip over Mt. Megunticook via the Mount Megunticook Trail, the Ridge Trail, and the Multi-Use Trail, plus the Slope Trail (Bald Rock Mtn.).

Distances from park camping area

- *to* Ocean Lookout: 1.4 mi., 1 hr.
- *to* Megunticook summit and Slope Trail junction (via Ridge Trail): 1.9 mi., 1 hr. 20 min.
- *to* Multi-Use Trail (via Slope Trail): 3.4 mi., 2 hr. 10 min.
- *to* park camping area (via Slope and Multi-Use Trails): 5.4 mi., 3 hr. 20 min.

Tableland Trail (map 4: C2)

This trail starts from the summit of Mt. Battie. It crosses the parking area, runs to the northeast, and gradually descends—crossing the toll road at 0.5 mi.—to the Battie-Megunticook col. At 0.7 mi., you will pass the Nature Trail on the right and, at 0.8 mi., the Carriage Trail on the left. Starting the ascent of the Mt. Megunticook mass, the Tableland Trail keeps to the right (east) of two lines of cliffs and, again swinging to the northwest, climbs steeply to Ocean Lookout. The true summit is another 0.5 mi. to the northwest along the Ridge Trail.

Distance from Battie summit

- *to* Ocean Lookout: 1.5 mi., 1 hr.

Jack Williams Trail (map 4: B1–C2)

This woodland trail leaves the Tableland Trail below its intersection with the Ridge Trail and follows the plateau area below Megunticook Ridge before rising to meet the Ridge Trail approximately halfway between the junctions of the Ridge and Zeke's trails and the Ridge and Scenic trails. The Jack Williams Trail offers views of the rising cliffs along Megunticook Ridge, along with mature hardwood stands. The trail is named to honor a local trail volunteer.

Distance from Tableland Trail

   to Ridge Trail: 1.6 mi., 1 hr. 30 min.

Adam's Lookout Trail (map 4: C2)

This trail connects the Megunticook and Tableland trails while providing an excellent eastern-facing lookout over Penobscot Bay. An approximately 2.25-mi. loop can be made from the Mt. Battie Rd. hiker's parking lot by following the Nature Trail north to the Megunticook Trail, then taking the Adam's Lookout Trail to the Tableland Trail. Return to the parking lot via the western end of the Nature Trail.

Distance from Megunticook Trail

   to Tableland Trail: 0.3 mi., 10 min.

Maiden Cliff Trail (map 4: B1)

Maiden Cliff (800 ft.) rises abruptly above Megunticook Lake. A steel cross stands near the spot where Elenora French, a young girl, fell to her death in 1864. The trail starts from the northeastern side of ME 52 at a signed parking area about 2.7 mi. north of the junction of ME 52 and US 1 in Camden, where the highway approaches a cove of Megunticook Lake. The blue-and-white blazed trail climbs north and west, at first following a washed-out logging road along a small brook. At about 0.5 mi., the Ridge Trail to Mt. Megunticook continues ahead. The Maiden Cliff Trail branches left (west) then climbs more steeply to open ledges and the cross. The trail's steady gradual climb on a well-worn but not eroded trail makes it ideal for a winter snowshoe hike.

For a rewarding alternative route to Maiden Cliff, go straight on the Ridge Trail. Then, in about 0.25 mi., go left (north) on the Scenic Trail. After crossing several open ledges with fine views of the lake, the Scenic Trail reaches Maiden Cliff in another 0.5 mi.

Distances from ME 52

> *to*   Ridge Trail/Scenic Trail junction: est. 0.5 mi., 30 min.
>
> *to*   Maiden Cliff: 0.9 mi., 50 min.
>
> *to*   Maiden Cliff (via Ridge and Scenic trails): 1.2 mi., 1 hr. 10 min.

Scenic Trail (map 4: B1)

This blue-over-white blazed trail forks right (east) from the Maiden Cliff Trail near Maiden Cliff. It climbs over very open ledges with many views, then descends slightly to a jct. with the Ridge Trail (approx. 0.7 mi. from ME 52 via the Maiden Cliff and Ridge trails). Near the jct. with the Ridge Trail, an unused trail marked with cairns can be seen on left (north). Be sure to remain on the Ridge Trail, traveling either eastward toward Mt. Megunticook summit or south toward parking lot. The Scenic Trail can be traversed on snowshoes in winter, although skis are not advisable.

Distance from Maiden Cliff

> *to*   Ridge Trail junction: 0.5 mi., 30 min.

Ridge Trail (map 4: B1–C2)

The Ridge Trail leaves the Maiden Cliff Trail 0.5 mi. from ME 52 at a signed junction and runs along the main ridge of Mt. Megunticook, over the wooded summit (1385 ft.), and on to Ocean Lookout with its fine views of Penobscot Bay. From the Maiden Cliff Trail junction, hike up to the right (south) following a generally white-over-blue-blazed trail (some white blazes persist). In about 0.25 mi., the Scenic Trail to Maiden Cliff diverges left. The Ridge Trail continues to climb, after a brief descent, with occasional lookouts over Megunticook Lake. About 0.9 mi. from the jct. with the Scenic Trail, Zeke's Trail comes in from the left (sign). In another 0.2 mi., the Ridge Trail crosses over a subsidiary summit (1290 ft.), descends slightly, and then climbs gradually to the true summit, which is wooded. Just beyond the summit, the Slope Trail diverges left (north). In another 0.2 mi., the Ridge Trail descends to end at Ocean Lookout. The Ridge Trail is also a good winter hike with snowshoes.

Distances from ME 52

> *to*   start (via Maiden Cliff Trail): 0.5 mi., 30 min.
>
> *to*   Scenic Trail junction: 0.7 mi., 40 min.

   to Zeke's Trail junction: 1.6 mi., 1 hr. 5 min.

   to Megunticook summit and Slope Trail junction: 2.5 mi., 1 hr. 45 min.

   to Ocean Lookout: 2.9 mi., 2 hr.

Megunticook Traverse (map 4: B1–C2)

This traverse is probably the nicest walk in the Camden Hills area. It offers a series of marvelous views and a lot of ridge walking. Climb the Mount Battie Trail from Camden. Then follow the Tableland Trail to Ocean Lookout. Continue over Mt. Megunticook on the Ridge Trail to the Scenic Trail, which leads to Maiden Cliff. Then descend the Maiden Cliff Trail to ME 52. This route is equally good in the opposite direction. Either way, you will need a car spot.

Distance from parking area on Megunticook St. (Mt. Battie trailhead)

   to ME 52 (Maiden Cliff trailhead): 5.8 mi., 3 hr. 30 min.

Multi-Use Trail (former Snowmobile Trail) (map 4: A2–C2)

Hikers can approach Mt. Megunticook and its subsidiary summits from the north via a network of trails that for the most part branch from the Multi-Use Trail (formerly the Snowmobile Trail). On weekends the 20+ vehicle trailhead parking lot fills up early but there is always ample parking on the side of Route 173. The woods have suffered logging and extensive blowdowns in the past, so be particularly careful not to wander off the routes described. Since water supplies in the northern hills are not always dependable, always carry a supply of water.

    This trail serves as the chief approach to the trails up Mt. Megunticook from the north. It also is the approach for Frohock Mtn. (454 ft.), Cameron Mtn. (811 ft.), and Bald Rock Mtn. (1100 ft.). The southern end of the trail meets the lower end of the Megunticook Trail near the camping area. A summer bypass cuts out several low, wet areas of the trail. Trail use includes hiking, bicycling, horseback riding and snowmobiling only. This trail is an old fire road running from the Camden Hills Camping Area on US 1 to Route 173 in Lincolnville.

    To reach the Multi-Use Trail, take ME 173 from Lincolnville Beach. After 2.3 mi., turn left onto Youngtown Rd., and in 200 ft. turn left into a small parking area at the trailhead. The generally southwestern and blue-blazed trail starts here. At about 0.3 miles, the Frohock Mountain Trail goes left (southeast). In about 1.3 mi., the Bald Rock Trail goes up to left (southeast) and the Cameron Mountain Trail goes down to right (west). There are no signs. In another 0.3 mi., the Sky Blue Trail diverges right, leading to the Cameron Mountain Trail, which in turn provides access to the upper part of Zeke's Trail. At 2.5 mi. along the trail, Zeke's Trail diverges right and climbs to the Ridge Trail. At 3.0 mi., you will reach a jct. with the Slope Trail at the site of a former ski lodge. The Slope Trail climbs up to the Ridge Trail near the true summit of Mt. Megunticook. At 0.2 mi. beyond this jct. with the Ridge Trail, the Spring Brook Trail (not part of the park) bears left and down to US 1. At about 0.8 mi. from the Spring Brook Trail jct., the Multi-Use Trail takes a sharp right turn and ends at the Camden Hills Camping Area, completing the 5.0 mi. hike.

Distances from Youngtown Rd.

> *to* Frohock Mountain Trail junction: 0.3 mi., 15 min.

> *to* Bald Rock Mountain Trail and Cameron Mountain Trail: 1.3 mi., 50 min.

> *to* Sky Blue Trail junction: 1.6 mi., 1 hr.

> *to* Zeke's Trail junction: 2.5 mi., 1 hr. 30 min.

> *to* junction with lower end of Megunticook Trail: 5.0 mi., 3 hr.

Frohock Mountain Trail

This bicycle and hiking trail with a natural surface (rocks, roots) crosses an oak and spruce forest over three mountains (some steep slopes). This blue-blazed trail would be a pleasant winter snowshoe trail. There is no water available on the trail.

Frohock Mt. Trail begins approximately 0.3 mi. from the Multi-Use Trail's Youngtown Rd. trailhead. From the Multi-Use Trail, turn left on the Frohock Mtn. Trail heading southeast. There will be a trailhead sign on the left. In approximately 0.3 mi., the trail turns hard left (east). This is the (unmarked) junction of the Frohock Mtn. Trail and the Garey Mtn. Trail (also blue-blazed). The Frohock Mtn. Trail continues over Derry Mtn. (777 ft.) and ends at the Frohock Mtn. summit (454 ft.).

Garey Mountain Trail

The blue-blazed Garey Mountain Trail branches off from the Frohock Mountain Trail approximately 0.3 mi. from the Frohock Mountain Trail's junction with the Multi-Use Trail. This short (0.4 mi.) trail is strenuous, but the summit of Garey Mtn. (790 ft.) provides great views to the south of Seven Hundred Acre Island, Isleboro, and Deer Isle, as well as a great view of Lincolnville Beach to the northeast. There is a shelter near the summit of Garey Mtn.

Frohock Mtn. & Garey Mtn. Trails

Distances from the Youngtown Rd. trailhead

> *to* junction of Multi-Use and Frohock Mountain trails: 0.3 mi.
>
> *to* junction with Garey Mountain Trail: 0.6 mi.
>
> *to* Garey Mtn. summit (via Garey Mountain Trail): 2.0 mi.
>
> *to* Frohock Mtn. summit: 2.6 mi.

Bald Rock Mountain (1100 ft.)

About 2.5 mi. northeast of Mt. Megunticook, this mountain offers fine views from its ledgy summit. This would be a fine snowshoe trip in winter. There is no dependable water on the upper part of this route.

Bald Rock Mountain Trail (map 4: B2)

From the Multi-Use Trail, the Bald Rock Mountain Trail diverges left (southeast) 1.3 mi. from Youngtown Rd. The trail, a well-worn path, and an easy-to-moderate hike, climbs to the summit, passing a usable old shelter 50 ft. below the summit. From Bald Rock, there are excellent views of the Penobscot Bay.

Distance from Multi-Use Trail

> *to* Bald Rock summit: 0.5 mi., 30 min.

Cameron Mountain Trail (map 4: B1–B2)

This interesting trail diverges right (west) from the Multi-Use Trail about 1.3 mi. from the Youngtown Rd. trailhead opposite the Bald Rock Mountain Trail. At about 0.1 mi., it turns left (avoid the first left), following an old town road. It crosses Black Brook and rises gradually past abandoned farmland, old cellar holes, and apple trees. The trail then follows the boundary of Camden Hills State Park and passes the summit of Cameron Mtn. (811 ft.). This is private property; please do not trespass. The trail then descends a bit before turning left (south) and starting to climb (ignore Ski Lodge sign). About 0.8 mi. from the turn, the Sky Blue Trail diverges left. In another 67 yd. the Cameron Mountain Trail ends at Zeke's Trail.

Distances from Multi-Use Trail

> *to* Cameron Mtn., south of summit: est. 1.0 mi., 35 min.

> *to* Sky Blue Trail and Zeke's Trail junctions: 1.9 mi., 1 hr. 30 min.

> *to* Megunticook summit (via Zeke's and Ridge trails): 3.5 mi., 2 hr. 25 min.

Sky Blue Trail (map 4: B2)

This trail has been cleared and its cairns rebuilt. Although it offers few long views, it makes a very pretty walk in the woods, with mature beech and maple forest, some large black spruce trees, and open blueberry clearings. The Sky Blue Trail leaves the Multi-Use Trail about 0.3 mi. beyond the start of the Cameron Mountain Trail. It follows a course parallel to the Cameron Mtn. Trail. At about 1.5 mi., it reaches the Cameron Mountain Trail. At this jct., go left to reach Zeke's Trail or right to reach Cameron Mtn.

Distance from Multi-Use Trail

> *to* Cameron Mountain Trail junction: 1.5 mi., 1 hr. 30 min.

Zeke's Trail (map 4: B1–B2)

This trail diverges right (west) from the Multi-Use Trail about 2.5 mi. from the Youngtown Rd. trailhead. The Cameron Mountain Trail diverges right (north) at 0.8 mi., soon reaches a jct. with the Sky Blue Trail, and loops back east, past Cameron Mtn. to the Multi-Use Trail. At 1.3 mi., a trail (sign) leads right to Zeke's Lookout (1190 ft.) which, after a short, steep climb, offers good views of Bald Rock Mtn. and Upper Penobscot Bay. (This view is starting to disappear as tree growth increases.) Zeke's Trail ends at its junction with the Ridge Trail, about 1 mi. northwest of the summit of Mt. Megunticook.

Distances from Multi-Use Trail

> *to* Cameron Mountain Trail junction: 0.8 mi., 40 min.

> *to* Zeke's Lookout Trail: 1.3 mi., 1 hr.

> *to* Ridge Trail junction: 1.3 mi., 1 hr.

Slope Trail (map 4: B2)

This trail goes from the Multi-Use Trail east across the bridge (in disrepair) over Spring Brook to the summit of Mt. Megunticook. The trail climbs steeply and reaches the Ridge Trail close to the true summit of Mt. Megunticook, approximately 100 ft. up the Ridge Trail from this jct. The Slope Trail is a moderate to strenuous hike.

Distance from Multi-Use Trail

   to Megunticook summit: 1.5 mi., 1 hr. 30 min.

Camden Hills North Circuit (map 4: A2–B2)

This is an interesting and scenic circuit hike. Starting at Youngtown Rd., take the Multi-Use Trail to the Bald Rock Mountain Trail and climb Bald Rock Mtn. Return to Multi-Use Trail, then continue to the Sky Blue Trail, Zeke's Trail, and Zeke's Lookout. Backtrack to the Cameron Mountain Trail and return to the Multi-Use Trail and Youngtown Rd.

Ragged Mountain (1300 ft.)

This mountain, 4.0 mi. west of Camden, is the highest of the hills to the southwest of the Megunticook River and Lake. Its summit offers views comparable with those on the main Megunticook Range. There is a radio tower on the summit.

To approach from Camden, follow US 1 south to John St. on the right (sign reading Snow Bowl). Go left on Mechanic St. to Hosmer Pond Rd. Turn left on Hosmer Pond Rd. to the Ragged Mountain Recreation Area/Snow Bowl parking area by Hosmer Pond.

Follow the longest (T-bar) ski lift up the grassy slope as far as it goes. Then enter the woods, continuing in the same direction on a rocky trail that generally follows a power line, to climb to the summit.

Distance from Snow Bowl

   to Ragged summit: est. 1.1 mi., 1 hr. 10 min.

Frye Mountain (1139 ft.)

Frye Mtn. is in Montville. There is a MFS fire tower on its summit. Refer to the USGS Morrill quadrangle, 7.5-min. series.

A dirt road that is good enough for cars passes within 0.3 mi. of the top. From the south and west, take ME 220 north from ME 3 near Liberty for 6.0 mi. (You will pass the road to Center Montville at about five miles.) Turn right (east) onto a dirt road at the sign reading Frye Mountain, Game Management Area, State of Maine. At 0.6 mi., turn right (south). At 0.4 mi., you will cross a stream. After another 0.5 mi., turn left (east). Drive 1.1 mi. (total 2.6 mi.) to the start of the short trail (right) to the summit (sign reading Fire Tower and Scenic View). You can find an alternative route to the mountain about five miles south of Fosters Corner (in Knox) on ME 220.

The trail climbs southeast to the summit. The fire tower views are excellent.

Distance from dirt road

to Frye summit: 0.3 mi., 15 min.

Mount Harris (1233 ft.)

The highest of the cluster of hills in Dixmont, Mt. Harris has one of the few wooden fire towers in Maine on its heavily wooded summit. The fire tower is in disrepair and may be removed. This trail offers a pleasant woods-road walk, but no views in summer. The mountain is nearly halfway between Waterville and Bangor. Refer to the USGS Brooks quadrangle, 15-min. series, or the Dixmont quadrangle, 7.5-min. series.

The trail begins on the left side of ME 7, 1.6 mi. south of the jct. of ME 7 and US 202 in Dixmont at sign for Fire Tower Rd. There is limited parking by the left side of the road.

The lower portion of the trail is a well-graded jeep road rising gently in an almost straight line to the east. The road turns to the left above the first building it reaches, a hunting camp, but returns to the straight line. After it reaches a brown lean-to (enclosed and locked), the road rises more sharply to an intersection at the crest of the col. The trail to the tower leaves to the left. It rises steeply at first, and then more gently, to the large, wooden tower on the summit. The warden's cabin and another outbuilding (locked) are nearby.

Distance from ME 7

to fire tower: 1.3 mi., 1 hr.

Mount Waldo (1064 ft.)

This attractive mountain, with its many open ledges, is in Frankfort. It is best known for the granite quarries on its eastern side. Refer to the USGS Bucksport quadrangle, 15-min. series, or the Mt. Waldo quadrangle, 7.5-min. series.

The trail approach is via US 1A in Frankfort. Turn west onto Old Stage Rd. 0.15 mi. south of the Frankfort Town Office Building. Go under a railroad overpass and up the hill. At 0.2 mi., turn right onto Tyler Ln. and go to a fork (about 0.6 mi.); take the left branch (dirt road) for a total of about 2.1 mi. from the town office. Park your car at the right hand curve in the road. Follow the trail along the power line to the summit. There is a service road that is used by ATVs less than 0.1 mi. further on the road. Long views to the west are visible all the way up the trail, and on top, the view takes in an area from the Penobscot River Valley to Penobscot Bay.

Distance from parking place

    to Waldo summit: less than 0.5 mi., 20 min.

Monhegan Island

This rugged island, with its spectacular sea cliffs and pleasant hiking trails, is 12.0 mi. off the coast of Maine. In summer, visitors can get to the island either by excursion boat from Boothbay Harbor, by the Hardy Boat from New Harbor, or by mail boat from Port Clyde. The village of Monhegan clusters around the harbor, while the rest of the island is still in its natural state. The size of the island is about three-quarters of a mile by one and a half miles.

A hiking trail goes around the shore of the island, and many trails connect this shore path with the village. The southwestern section of the shore path gets more use and is easier to follow than the northeastern part. The most popular connecting trail goes from the end of the road in back of the lighthouse to Whitehead, the highest sea cliff on the island. Another popular trail goes through Cathedral Woods, a lovely stand of tall spruce.

Camping is not allowed on the island. There are several small hotels and guest houses where one can stay. An excellent trail map published by Monhegan Associates may be purchased on the ferries or at many sites on the island.

Section 7

Southwestern Maine/
Pleasant Mountain

7. SOUTHWESTERN MAINE/
PLEASANT MOUNTAIN

See AMC Maine Trail Map 5: Pleasant Mountain.

RECOMMENDED HIKES

Easy

Jockey Cap (rt: 0.4 mi., 25 min.) An interesting short trail with great views from the summit of the surrounding mountains. On the summit is a monument to Admiral Peary that shows the mountains seen in the view.

Ossipee Hill (rt: 1.2 mi., 1 hr.) A short hike to the ledges of Ossipee Hill where there are good views in all directions of the surrounding area.

Bradbury Mountain summit (rt: 0.6 mi., 30 min.) Although the trail is very easy, it is an excellent hike to take with the family especially in the spring when the hawk migration is occurring.

Moderate

Burnt Meadow Mountain (rt: 2.4 mi., 2 hr. 30 min.) A short, somewhat steep climb to the summit of Burnt Meadows Mtn. with views to the east and south.

Pleasant Mountain via the Southwest/MacKay Pasture Trail (rt: 5.8 mi., 4 hr.) A steady, moderate climb to the summit of Pleasant Mtn. where there are excellent views, particularly to the west.

Mount Agamenticus (Blueberry Bluff Trail) (rt: 3.6 mi., 2 hr.) A delightful stroll through blueberry patches to a great overlook with views of the White Mountains.

LIST OF MOUNTAINS

This section includes the mountains of York and Cumberland counties and those of Oxford County south of and near US 302. The mountains and hills of southwestern Maine are low, and woods cover many of them all the way to the top. Those summits that are open provide fine views of the surrounding country northwest toward the White Mountains and east and southeast to the coast. Because they are close to summer camps and population centers, many of the mountains in this section are popular hiking areas. Pleasant Mtn. (2006 ft.) is the highest. Most of the others are around 1000 ft. or lower.

Camping facilities are available at Bradbury Mountain and Sebago Lake state parks, as well as at many privately operated camping areas.

Bradbury Mountain (484 ft.)

This summit in Pownal is only partly wooded and offers good views of the countryside. Refer to the USGS Freeport quadrangle, 15-min. series, and the North Pownal quadrangle, 7.5-min. series.

To reach Bradbury Mtn., drive west from I-95 on ME 136 in Freeport and immediately turn left onto Pownal Rd. Drive 4.0 mi. to Pownal center and turn right (northeast) onto ME 9. Drive 0.8 mi. to Bradbury Mountain State Park, which has parking, picnic tables, playgrounds, and camping areas. A trail (sign reading Summit) leads 0.3 mi. from the northwestern corner of the picnic area to the ledgy southern summit of Bradbury. Near the top, another trail leads right to an outlook toward the north. From the summit, a series of short, well-marked trails interconnect to cover the whole park area. A pleasant loop, the Knight's Woods Trail, lies on the opposite side of ME 9. Like the Tote Road Trail on the mountain, it lends itself to cross-country skiing in winter. A map and information are available at the entrance from the ranger.

Distance from state park picnic area

to Bradbury, southern summit: 0.3 mi., 15 min.

Knight's Woods Trail loop: 1.3 mi.

Rattlesnake Mountain (1035 ft.)

This summit in the southwestern part of Casco is a favorite climb for camp groups in the vicinity. Refer to the USGS Gray quadrangle, 15-min. series, or the Raymond quadrangle, 7.5-min. series.

In 1992, flagrant incidents of public misuse of the area caused the Friends of Nubble Pond to shut off the southern access off Plains Rd. near Camp Hinds. The Northern Approach is overgrown and is difficult to follow. The mountain can still be enjoyed from the Bri-Mar Trail.

Bri-Mar Trail (Sheep Pasture)

This trail, near the northern end of Rattlesnake Mtn., is named for Brian and Marline Huntress by the family who owns the land and maintains the trails. Hikers are welcome, but please observe the rules shown on a sign. Park off ME 85 in a small space 0.9 mi. south of the jct. with ME 11 at Webb's Mills.

Distance from ME 85

> *to* Northern Approach Trail junction: 0.5 mi., 25 min.

> *to* Rattlesnake main summit: 1.0 mi., 40 min.

Mount Agamenticus (691 ft.)

This 691-ft. monadnock rises above the coastal plain of southern York County. Because it was so conspicuous, it was an important landmark for the early European explorers who sailed along the New England coast. According to legend, it was also the burial place of either St. Aspinquid or Passaconaway. There is a fire tower at the top, which was the site of a radar observation post during World War II. There is an unused ski development on the northern slope of the mountain. Refer to the USGS York Harbor quadrangle, 7.5-min. series.

The best approach route from the south is the Maine Turnpike. Take the York exit right just before the tollgate; turn left across the turnpike and take the second right, onto Chase Pond Rd. (Go past Chase Pond on the left.) Turn left onto Mountain Rd. and bear left at a small village. From this point, it is 1.6 mi. to the Big A Summit Road. From the north, follow US 1 through Ogunquit. Turn right onto Clay Hill Rd. Cross I-95 at 2.4 mi. from US 1, and at 4.1 mi., turn right onto Mountain Rd. At 5.7 mi., you will reach the summit road.

The blacktop summit road turns right and goes uphill 0.7 mi. to the summit. The dirt road straight ahead leads around the mountain to several trailheads and hiking and bicycle trails to the summit.

The road to the summit, which has two hairpin turns, should be driven with care. At the summit is a parking area, a closed ski lodge, and a riding stable. From the summit, the reservoirs that serve York and Kittery ME can be seen, and the York and Kittery water districts form part of the cooperative landowners group that has preserved Mt. Agamenticus.

Many paths, some maintained as bridle, bicycle, or ATV trails, lead through woods to the open summit.

Ring Trail Loop

From Mountain Road, park at the trailhead on the right just before the Big A Summit Road. At approximately 0.1 mi., the Ring Trail forks; take the right hand (east) fork. Follow the Ring Trail past the jct. with the Rocky Road/Hairpin Turn Trails at approximately 0.5 mi. At next jct. turn left onto the Witch Hazel Trail leading to the Mt. Agamenticus summit. Return via the Sweet Fern Trail (summit trailhead is slightly north of Witch Hazel Trail trailhead), which shortly reconnects to the Ring Trail. Turn left (west) onto Ring Trail, and continue to follow the Ring Trail across the Summit Road to return to the Mountain Road trailhead.

Distance from parking area

Complete loop: 1.5 mi., 1 hr.

Blueberry Bluff Trail

From Mountain Road, turn right on the Summit Road; park at 0.2 miles on the left in a small parking lot. Proceed on the Ring Trail through a hemlock forest on a white-blazed trail. At a Y-shaped junction, veer to the right (north) and begin climbing the hill. At the sign for the Blueberry Bluff Trail, turn right onto the red-blazed trail. Blueberry Bluff continues through blueberry patches and provides great overlooks. On a clear day, the White Mountains are readily seen from these ledges. To proceed to the summit, continue to the T-intersection with the Horse Trail, marked by a post. The summit is 50 yd. beyond this point.

Distance from parking area

to summit: 1.8 mi., 1 hr.

Ossipee Hill (1058 ft.)

Ossipee Hill (also called Ossipee Mtn.) is located in Waterboro. There are several radio towers, buildings, and a MFS firetower on its summit. From the firetower, there are good views of the Presidential Range in New Hampshire; to the east, you can see over the flat Saco River Valley and on to Portland Harbor and Casco Bay. A forest fire in 1947 burned off much of the mountain. Refer to the USGS Buxton quadrangle, 15-min. series, or the Waterboro quadrangle, 7.5-min. series.

From ME 5 at Waterboro Center, take the crossroad (Ossipee Hill Rd.) southwest and immediately turn sharply right onto paved McLucas Road beyond the fire station. This road changes to dirt and, in winter, is plowed for only about 0.4 mi. It is starting to see residential development. During winter, Ossipee Hill can be climbed using snowshoes or crosscountry skis, although snowmobiles do use the unplowed McLucas Road.

McLucas Road rises gradually west-northwest about 1.7 mi. to a saddle. In dry conditions, most cars find it passable to this saddle, where limited parking (unsigned) is available at the roadside. At the saddle, turn left (south) off McLucas Road, park, and climb by foot steeply on access road for about 0.25 mi. before the road levels out. Along this stretch there are several old stone foundations and a small spring on the eastern side of the road. Turn right at a large metal gate to climb toward the summit. The towers are just southeast of the true summit, which does not have a trail but can be reached by a short bushwhack.

Distances from ME 5

   to saddle (may be driven or walked): 1.7 mi., 1 hr.

   to Ossipee summit: 2.3 mi., 1 hr. 30 min.

Douglas Mountain (1416 ft.)

This small mountain in Douglas Hill, west of Sebago Lake, offers excellent views of the Presidentials, Pleasant Mtn., and the Atlantic Ocean. It is the highest of the Saddleback Hills. Douglas Mtn. was purchased by The Nature Conservancy, which donated it to the Town of Sebago in 1997. The town maintains the area and charges a fee ($3 at time of publication) for parking to support these costs. Refer to the USGS Sebago Lake quadrangle, 15-min. series, or the Steep Falls quadrangle, 7.5-min. series.

Turn west from ME 107 onto Dyke Mtn. Rd. There is no street sign, but the intersection is 0.5 mi. north of the jct. of ME 107 and Long Hill Rd., and 1 mi. south of Sebago. Just before the turn, there is a small hiker sign reading Douglas Mountain—1 mile. Turn left on Douglas Mountain Road and left on Ledge Road and into parking lot. To reach the trailhead, walk back out of parking lot for 0.2 miles to the paved Douglas Mountain Road and hike another 0.2 miles on that road to the trailhead. The yellow-blazed path starts between two stone pillars and is easy to follow straight up ledges to the top. A second, even easier path through the woods splits off right soon after the trailhead. The two trails meet at the top, where there is a stone observation tower and a large rock inscribed *Non sibi sed omnibus* (Not just for myself, but for all). An orange-blazed nature trail makes a 0.75-mi. loop from the summit.

Distance from parking area

    to the trailhead: 0.4 mi., 10 min.

    to Douglas summit: 0.7 mi., 25 min.

Mount Cutler (1232 ft.)

The open ledges of this summit in Hiram offer good views of the White Mountains to the northwest. Refer to the USGS Cornish and Hiram quadrangles, 7.5-min. series.

At the jct. of ME 5 and ME 117 in Hiram, cross the cement bridge to the western bank of the Saco River. Drive to the left of a former store and continue west on Mountain View Ave. to the site of a former railroad station, where there is ample parking. The red-blazed trail starts across the tracks. In 100 yd., it turns right into a picnic area that holds some abandoned ells once used by the railroad. The trail up the mountain continues straight ahead from the upper left end of the picnic area. It climbs the first ledge, and soon it turns sharply left. At this turn, a faint trail to the right leads 60 yd. to an overlook above the ledges facing the bridge. The main trail soon reaches the long, open ridge of Mt. Cutler, where south-facing ledges look down on the Saco River. The trail turns right (west) to the eastern summit, descends to cross a woods road, then climbs to the main summit as an open bushwhack. There are ledges and good views.

Distances from railroad station site

    to overlook: 0.4 mi., 20 min.

    to Cutler, eastern summit: 0.7 mi., 40 min.

    to Cutler, main summit: 1.3 mi., 1 hr. 5 min.

Pleasant Mountain (2006 ft.)

This mountain on the Denmark–Bridgton town line rises abruptly from the comparatively flat surrounding countryside. It is an isolated mountain mass that stretches about 4 mi. on a north-south line. The ledgy, open main summit, where there is a MFS firetower, was once known as House Peak because there was a hotel there from 1873 to 1907. At least six other summits along the ridge also have names. The mountain was burned over in about 1860, and the forest and ledges are open enough for many views. The views from the main summit and from Big Bald Peak are outstanding. The southeastern face of Mt. Washington, 29 mi. to the northwest, is particularly noticeable. The Shawnee Peak ski area is on the northern slope of the northern peak. Loon Echo Land Trust in partnership with The Nature Conservancy, landowners on Pleasant Mtn., and other environmental organizations are working to protect Pleasant Mtn. Refer to the USGS Pleasant Mtn. quadrangle, 7.5-min. series, as well as the map included with this guide.

Firewarden's Trail (Fire Tower Trail, Old Carriage Road) (map 5: B4–B5)

Although not the most scenic route up Pleasant Mtn., this trail is the most popular one. It climbs to the main summit from the west. From US 302, turn south onto Wilton Warren Rd. 2.3 mi. west of the access road to the ski area and 7 mi. east of Fryeburg. Stay right at all road junctions. There is a farmhouse on the left and a large barn on the right 1.2 mi. from US 302 with parking on the left. The trail starts at the right end of the parking area.

For its first half, the trail is actually a truck road. In recent years this road has been used for logging and it is deeply rutted in places. It crosses a brook and climbs easily along the north bank. It recrosses the brook at the warden's cabin. The trail then narrows to a rough jeep road (not open to private cars), swings right (southeast), and climbs steadily to the summit ridge. In the final 0.2 mi., the Bald Peak Trail (blue-blazed) comes in on the left (sign); there is a storm shelter to the right.

Distances from parking area at farmhouse

- *to* warden's cabin and campsite: 1.3 mi., 50 min.
- *to* Bald Peak Trail junction: 2.3 mi., 1 hr. 50 min.
- *to* Pleasant Mtn. main summit: 2.5 mi., 2 hr.

MacKay Pasture Trail (Southwest Ridge Trail) (map 5: B5–C4)

This attractive scenic trail is being used by hikers, local camp groups, and snowmobilers. From the jct. of ME 117 and ME 160 in Denmark take ME 160

0.3 mi. to the Moose Pond Dam. Turn right on Denmark Road and drive 3.5 mi. to the parking area on the right. The parking area is opposite the sign for Spiked Ridge Road (FR 78). The parking area may also be approached from US 302 in East Fryeburg by taking the Denmark Rd. 3.4 mi. The trail follows a woods road, marked by cairns and yellow blazes, generally northeast through mixed hardwoods; it then becomes steeper through pine forest. At approximately 0.4 mi., the trail turns sharply right (southeast), slabs across the hill, turns left, and reaches the open ledges at 0.6 mi. The trail ascends the mostly open ridge, northeasterly, marked by cairns to the southwestern summit (1900 ft.) at 1.6 mi., with almost constant views over Moose and Beaver ponds, as well as back to Long Pond. The trail, keeping to the ridge, descends over a short saddle where it slabs across and down the hillside to a deep gully and then slabs back up to the ridge to the pine forest. There the trail grade becomes more gradual following the edge of the ridge through hardwoods until it ends at the Ledges Trail (blue-blazed) at 2.7 mi. This route is not a winter route. The recommended winter route is to follow the cell tower access road to where the trail re-enters the forest at 2.4 mi.

Distances from Denmark Rd.

   to southwestern summit: 1.6 mi., 1 hr. 20 min.

   to Ledges Trail: 2.7 mi., 2 hr.

   to Pleasant Mtn. main summit: 2.9 mi., 2 hr. 15 min.

Ledges Trail (map 5: B5)

The trail leaves the western side of the Mountain Road along the western side of Moose Pond 3.3 mi. south of US 302, 1.5 mi. south of the Bald Peak Trail, and 0.6 mi. north of the Walker's (narrows) Bridge, which separates the two sections of Moose Pond. There is a small parking area on the left side of the road next to FR 54.

   The trail, blue-blazed, begins on a logging road (sign) and gradually climbs through a recently logged, marshy area. At 0.5 mi., cross two often dry streambeds. Climb steeply for 0.3 mi. to open ledges with views south and southeast.

   The trail follows the ledges, with the southwestern summit visible ahead on the left. At 1.6 mi., the Southwest Trail comes in on the left. It climbs through oak scrub and blueberry bushes to the main summit tower. Views to the west, including Fryeburg and the Saco River Basin and ponds, are good.

Descending, the trail enters the woods on a southeasterly bearing from the tower.

Distances from Mountain Rd.

> *to* streambeds: est. 0.5 mi., 25 min.

> *to* lower end of ledges: 1 mi., 1 hr.

> *to* Southwest Trail junction: 1.6 mi., 1 hr. 30 min.

> *to* Pleasant Mtn. main summit: 1.8 mi., 1 hr. 40 min.

Bald Peak Trail (map 5: A5–B5)

This trail climbs the eastern side of Pleasant Mtn. to Big Bald Peak, and then runs south along the ridge to join the Firewarden's Trail just below the main summit.

When combined with the Ledges Trail and a 1.5-mi. walk on the road, the Bald Peak Trail forms an enjoyable circuit. The ski trail described below also allows a circuit. There is no sure water on this trail during dry periods.

To reach the trail, follow the Mountain Road along the western shore of Moose Pond to a point about 1.8 mi. south of the road's jct. with US 302, and about 1.3 mi. south of the Shawnee Peak ski area. Just south of Shawnee Peak East, and 0.1 mi. south of the entrance to East Pinnacle Condominiums, you will find the trailhead on the right between utility poles 49 and 50 (sign). Limited parking is available. The trail starts westward, crosses a brook, and climbs steeply. At 0.2 mi., turn left and follow the northern bank of the brook. At 0.4 mi., a short spur trail (sign) leads left to the Needle's Eye, a brook cascading through a cleft in the ledge. At 0.7 mi., just before the second of two small brooks, turn left (Sue's Way turns right). Climb steeply through a stand of hemlock, then come out of some scrub onto the ledges (cairn); turn left to reach, in 100 yd., Big Bald Peak (1940 ft.) at 1.1 mi. There are excellent views in all directions.

At the sign, the blue-blazed North Ridge Trail comes in on the right from the top of the ski area via the northern peak. Descending, note that the trail to the ski area continues straight ahead (north); the Bald Peak Trail bears right (east-northeast).

From Big Bald Peak, the Bald Peak Trail follows the crest of the ridge, first south and then southwest over two humps toward the main summit. At 2.2 mi. from the start, the trail joins the Firewarden's Trail, which leads left (south) past the storm shelter to the Pleasant Mtn. main summit and the fire tower.

Descending, the Bald Peak Trail diverges right from the Firewarden's Trail (sign) about 0.2 mi. north of the tower.

Distances from Mountain Rd.

> *to* Needle's Eye Trail: 0.4 mi., 35 min.
>
> *to* brook crossing and Sue's Way junction: 0.7 mi., 50 min.
>
> *to* Big Bald summit: 1.1 mi., 1 hr. 20 min.
>
> *to* Firewarden's Trail junction: 2.2 mi., 1 hr. 50 min.
>
> *to* Pleasant Mtn. main summit (via Firewarden's Trail): 2.4 mi., 1 hr. 55 min.

Sue's Way (map 5: A5)

This blue-blazed trail, named in memory of Sue W. Blood, runs from a point 0.7 mi. up the Bald Peak Trail to the North Ridge Trail near the North Peak. It allows an interesting loop hike over these two peaks. There is a spring one-third of the way up the trail.

Distance from Bald Peak Trail

> *to* North Ridge Trail: est. 0.5 mi., 25 min.

North Ridge Trail (map 5: A5–B5)

This trail begins at the base of the Shawnee Peak ski area. From the base lodge (which is open all year), the trail follows the chairlift directly up the mountain for 1.0 mi. to the warming hut at the North Peak. The views are extensive. The North Ridge Trail leads south from the warming hut past the chairlift from Shawnee Peak East. Descend 100 yd. on the upper edge of the southernmost ski trail. At the first turn, enter the woods on the right. Sue's Way (blue-blazed) enters from the gully on the left. The trail turns due west, stays level for a bit, and then goes slightly downhill. At 1.2 mi., it turns left and slabs around the western side of the North Peak through open red pine to a low peak about 0.5 mi. from the warming hut. The trail bears right to cross an open ledge with a view of Big Bald Peak and Pleasant Mtn.'s main summit, then drops steeply into a col before heading up to Big Bald Peak. Just before the final climb up the cone, the Bald Peak Trail comes in from the left.

Distances from ski area base lodge

> *to* warming hut: 1.0 mi., 1 hr.
>
> *to* Sue's Way junction: 1.1 mi., 1 hr. 5 min.
>
> *to* Big Bald summit (via Bald Peak Trail): 2.0 mi., 1 hr. 45 min.

Burnt Meadow Mountain (northern peak 1575 ft.)

Located in Brownfield, this mass consists of three summits of nearly equal height. Deep cols separate the middle peak, Stone Mtn. (1624 ft.), from the northern and southern peaks (1575 ft. and 1592 ft., respectively). Fire swept the entire mountain in 1947, and the trails that existed then disappeared. Trail development by snowmobilers and the construction of a ski area, now abandoned, have opened up new routes. Refer to the USGS Kezar Falls quadrangle, 15-min. series, and the Brownfield quadrangle, 7.5-min. series.

One approach is the eastern spur of the northern peak. This trail was reopened in 1984. From the jct. of ME 113/5 and ME 160 in East Brownfield, drive west and south on ME 160 through Brownfield and past Burnt Meadow Pond. The trailhead is 3.1 mi. from the jct. with ME 113/5 and 160 and 0.4 mi. past Burnt Meadow Pond. The trailhead is unmarked and easy to miss. It is on the right hand side of the road at the top of a slight rise. If you pass a horse farm on your left, you have gone too far. You will see the blue-blazed trail at the north side of the parking area, which can hold approximately five to six vehicles.

The trail heads west up the slope, staying on the southern edge of the ridge. At 0.4 mi., it passes over a small hump and drops slightly into a shallow col. Beyond the col, continue west up the crest of the spur, which becomes steeper and more open, with a sharp drop-off on the left, as it rises to the summit. In places, cairns as well as blazes are used to mark the trail. There is no water on the trail.

A snowmobile trail leads north from the summit along the ridge to the top of the old ski area, with partial views. The mountain is a good winter snowshoe trail.

Distance from ME 160 (via eastern spur)

to northern peak summit: 1.2 mi., 1 hr. 30 min.

Peary Mountain (958 ft.)

The open ledges of this little mountain in Brownfield afford good views of the White Mountains and the mountains of western Maine. Refer to the USGS Brownfield quadrangle, 7.5-min. series.

At the jct. of ME 160 and ME 113 in East Brownfield, proceed north on ME 113 for 2.2 mi. to Farnsworth Rd. (5 mi. south of the US 302 and ME 113 junction in Fryeburg). Turn west onto Farnsworth Rd. and drive 1.4 mi. to the bridge crossing the Little Saco River. There is parking at the trailhead for three or four vehicles.

The trail (snowmobile trail), not marked, begins at the east side of the stream. It heads south first on the level, and then at a gradual grade, to a col in a small clearing at 0.8 mi., with an old foundation and a fireplace on the right. Turn left (southeast) off the trail and go through open woods and ledges (following cairns) 0.2 mi. to the southern summit. There are good views in all directions. The main summit is 0.4 mi. northeast across open ledges and scrub without a trail. Views are to the east and north. This trail is suitable for winter use by snowshoes and cross-country skis. Be aware that there may be winter snowmobile use on this trail as well.

Distances from trailhead

   to col: 0.8 mi., 35 min.

   to Peary, southern summit: 1.0 mi., 45 min.

   to Peary, main summit: 1.4 mi., 1 hr.

Jockey Cap (600 ft.)

This ledge near Fryeburg ME rises perpendicular about 200 ft. above the valley. Although this is a very short hike, the view from the summit is excellent. At the top, there is a wonderful bronze profile of the surrounding summits, a monument to Robert E. Peary, who lived in Fryeburg in 1878–1979. The profile affords a great way to identify neighboring mountains, including Mt. Washington. Refer to the USGS Fryeburg quadrangle, 7.5-min. series.

A trail leaves the northern side of US 302, 1.0 mi. east of the intersection of 302 and 113 (traffic light) in the center of Fryeburg. The trail begins through a gateway between a store and the Jockey Cap Cabins. Walking to the right, it soon reaches Molly Lockett's cave, named for the last of the Pequawket Indians; she is said to have used it for a shelter. The trail then divides. The left branch continues ahead, circling to the west; the right branch turns abruptly right and climbs steeply, hugging the eastern side of the ledge. Descending, be alert, since there are many side paths that do not lead back to the cabins. (Round-trip by either route: 25 min.)

Distance from US 302

   to Jockey Cap summit: 0.2 mi., 15 min.

Section 8

Oxford Hills/Evans Notch

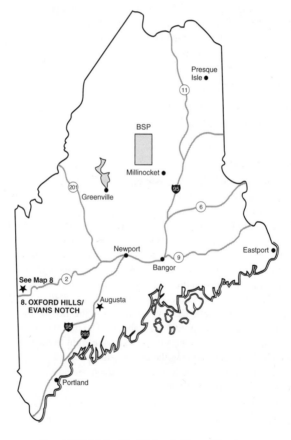

See AMC Maine Trail Map 8: Evans Notch.

RECOMMENDED HIKES

Easy

Singepole Ridge (rt: 2.6 mi., 1 hr. 20 min.) An easy trip to the spectacular views from the ledges of Singepole Ridge, particularly at sunset.

Sabattus Mountain (lp: 1.6 mi., 1 hr.) A loop hike to the summit of Sabattus Mtn., with impressive views southeast to northwest.

Moderate

Bald Mountain/Speckled Mountain (Peru) (rt: 4.6 mi., 4 hr.) An interesting traverse in a little-known area to two small peaks. The sheer cliffs of Speckled Mtn. provide extensive views in all directions.

Blueberry Mountain Loop (lp: 4.2 mi., 3 hr.) A loop hike using the Shell Pond, Stone House, White Cairn, and loop trails. This hike has everything: waterfalls, a swimming hole, views, blueberries, and beavers.

Strenuous

Speckled Mountain (Evans Notch) (lp: 8.6 mi., 5 hr. 30 min.) An interesting loop hike that uses the Bickford Brook and Blueberry Ridge trails to access the summit of Speckled Mtn., where there are views from the northwest to the southeast.

Caribou Mountain (lp: 6.9 mi., 5 hr. 10 min.) A pleasant loop hike to the summit of Caribou Mtn., where there are excellent views using the Caribou Mtn. and Mud Brook Trails.

LIST OF MOUNTAINS

This section describes the part of Oxford County that lies between US 302 on the south and the Androscoggin River on the north. The summits in the eastern part of the Oxford Hills are scattered. They include, among others, Streaked Mtn. (1770 ft.) near South Paris; Speckled Mtn. (2183 ft.) in the secluded Shagg Pond area; Mt. Zircon (2240 ft.) south of Rumford; Mt. Abram (1960 ft.), with its ski slope, near Locke Mills; and Mt. Tire'm (1104 ft.), a good viewpoint in Waterford.

Farther west, the hills build up into the continuous mountainous areas of the Evans Notch–Chatham region, which is along the Maine–New Hampshire border. Most of these mountains lie within the White Mountain National Forest (WMNF), where the network of trails is more complete and signs and maintenance are usually better. This guide describes those summits that lie in Maine, plus West Royce, just over the line in New Hampshire. For a description of the other New Hampshire summits, see the AMC White Mountain Guide. Most of the western Oxford Hills appear on the Evans Notch and Mahoosuc Range map in this guide.

The minerals of the Oxford Hills are interesting, especially in the Mt. Mica Mine near Paris Hill and the Bumpus Mine between Bethel and Lynchville.

There are four small WMNF campgrounds in the region covered here. One is Crocker Pond, which you can reach from US 2 at West Bethel or from ME 5 south of Bethel. Hastings Campground is on Evans Notch Rd. just south of its junction with Wild River Rd. The Cold River and Basin campgrounds are 0.3 mi. west of the Maine–New Hampshire border and just south of Evans Notch.

Streaked Mountain (1770 ft.)

Streaked Mtn., in Hebron and Buckfield, is a conspicuous, rounded summit with open ledges commanding fine views in all directions. It is easy to reach, and there is a closed MFS firetower on the summit as well as several antenna arrays. Refer to the USGS West Sumner quadrangle, 7.5-min. series.

Turn southeast from ME 117 onto paved Streaked Mtn. Rd. about 2.9 mi. from the jct. of ME 117 and ME 119 in South Paris and 5.3 mi. southwest of Buckfield. At 0.5 mi., the trail starts left by the brook where there is limited parking on the right. The trail soon enters the woods, and climbs steeply onto the ledges. After that, it is an open climb to the top, as the trail slabs along the ledges to the left and joins the power line. Descending, leave the power line at the second pole, and slab left down the ledges. Be careful not to go too far south and miss the point where the trail enters the woods.

Distance from Streaked Mtn. Rd. on South Paris side

   to   Streaked Mtn. summit: 0.5 mi., 40 min.

Singepole Ridge (1420 ft.)

Across the valley southwest of Streaked Mtn. is Singepole Ridge. This open ridge offers broad views to the west and southwest and wonderful sunset views. Brett Hill Rd. leaves south off ME 117, about 2.1 mi. from the jct. of ME 117 and ME 119 in South Paris. At the point Brett Hill Road turns west the trail begins straight ahead (south) on a gravel road that is gated. Park by the gate. The trail is not open to motorized vehicles. Go up the road approximately 0.2 mi. (5 min.) and take the left fork at a storage area for old vehicles. Follow the rough, rocky road to an old quarry at 0.9 mi. Just beyond the quarry, there is an open area where the tailings from the quarry are stacked. Bear right on the rocks where the snowmobile trail/road goes to the left. Follow the trail to the south end of the ledges. This trail is excellent for snowshoeing.

   To access the north end of the ledges from the main trail from the gate, at about 0.7 mi. bear right on an old road/trail and climb steeply to the ledges.

Distance from gate

   to   Singepole summit: 1.3 mi., 40 min.

Crocker Hill (1374 ft.)

Crocker Hill, locally called Brown Mtn., in Paris, site of George L. Vose's 1868 panorama of the White Mountains, also offers views of the surrounding countryside and other mountains. Refer to the USGS West Sumner quadrangle, 7.5-min. series.

   Leave Paris Hill Rd. in Paris Hill just north of the Paris Hill Country Club on Lincoln St. and continue east (Mt. Mica Rd.) for 1.1 mi. Take Thayer Rd. a gravel road, 0.7 mi. to where the road turns left and park. There is limited parking and no motorized vehicles are allowed on trail. The Old Crocker Hill carriage road leaves straight ahead. Take the left fork where the old carriage road divides. Look for an old stamping mill on the left soon after the trail forks. The trail ascends gradually, then veers sharply right just above the mill. A few yards after the switchback, on the left, is the old mine shaft. After a view off to left, turn right at a rocky area and climb steadily about 0.25 mi. up to western viewpoint. Faded yellow blazes mark the trail. To reach the eastern viewpoint follow the trail 0.1 mi. past cairn on left.

Distance from parking place

to Crocker summit: 0.8 mi., 30 min.

Bear Mountain (1208 ft.)

Southerly access to Bear Mtn. in Hartford is via Old County Rd. This road used to serve a fire tower (now dismantled) and logging operations. It is no longer good enough for passenger cars. Refer to the USGS Buckfield quadrangle, 7.5-min. series. From the north, access is from ME 108 in Livermore; see the description below.

From ME 4 at North Turner, turn west onto ME 219. At 0.4 mi., turn right onto Bean St. across the outlet of Bear Pond. Then take an immediate (0.1 mi.) left on Berry Rd. along the northern shore of the pond. Follow the blacktop road 2.3 mi. to a crossroad, turn right on Bear Mountain Rd. There is a marked hiker parking area immediately on the right. Follow the road past a brook (often dry) and gradually climb the ridge. As the road levels out a trail to the right leads to the western summit of Bear Mtn. (Stay to the right at all intersecting logging roads.) There is a good view to the southwest.

The main road continues straight ahead toward the height-of-land. At about 1.1 mi. the trail from the north comes in on the left, and the road swings around to the right (south). There are good views to the west, south and southeast from the summit.

Distances from parking area

to side trail to western summit: est. 0.9 mi., 35 min.

to Bear main summit: 1.9 mi., 1 hr. 25 min.

Bear Mountain from the North

Refer to the USGS Canton quadrangle, 7.5-min. series. From ME 108 in Livermore, 0.4 mi. from ME 4, turn south onto Bear Mtn. Rd. just past a gravel operation. There is minimal parking at 0.6 mi. The trail is the old road, which dips to a brook then climbs steadily, eventually leveling off. Turn left at the junction with the road from the south, and climb steadily up to the open summit ledges and views. This trail/road has heavy ATV use.

Distances from trailhead

> *to* jct.: est. 1.3 mi.
>
> *to* Bear main summit: est. 2.0 mi., 1 hr. 25 min.

Black Mountain (2133 ft.)

A broad, flat mass, this mountain lies in Sumner and Peru, east of adjacent Speckled Mtn. There are about five more or less definite summits, running roughly east–west. A trail with no signs climbs to the easternmost summit (2080 ft.) from the Sumner side. Refer to the USGS Worthley Pond quadrangle, 7.5-min. series.

From jct. of ME 26 and ME 219 in West Paris, go 8 mi. east to Greenwood Rd. and turn left. There is a sign indicating to ME 108. Follow Greenwood Rd. 1.5 mi. to Black Mountain Rd. and turn left. Bear right at fork and go straight on Black Mountain Rd. for a total of 2.3 mi. from the Greenwood Rd. Park where a woods/jeep road goes to left and farm road goes right. The trailhead isn't currently marked.

Follow this dirt road for 0.4 mi., turning right onto a woods road. Just before a logging yard, fork left across a brook on a stone culvert and take the right trail up the mountain (approximately 20-degrees mag.). The road levels out in 0.5 mi. and crosses the brook. Beyond the brook, pass a cairn soon thereafter and bear left (northeast) onto the trail at the next turn. The trail leaves right, partly eroded, narrow, and poorly marked. It climbs steadily northeast to ledges and the eastern summit. The view to the east and south is only partly open. Woods cover the main summit, 0.5 mi. to the west-northwest, and there is no trail. Exploration of the ledges will reveal a small but beautiful pond as well as additional views.

Distance from parking place

> *to* Black Mtn., eastern summit: 1.3 mi., 1 hr. 20 min.

Bald Mountain (1692 ft.)

This mountain is in the northeastern corner of Woodstock near Shagg Pond. Together with neighboring Speckled Mtn., just to the east, it offers interesting hiking in a little-known, secluded area. Refer to the USGS Mt. Zircon quadrangle, 7.5-min. series.

From the jct. of ME 26 and ME 219 in West Paris, go east on ME 219 about 4.1 mi. To Tuell Hill Rd. and turn left. Take Tuell Hill Rd. to where it dead ends at Redding Rd. and turn left. Follow Redding Rd. past Shagg Pond and continue along the road for 0.5 mi. to a parking area left at the top of the hill. There are good views of Bald and Speckled mountains from the public landing at Shagg Pond. Redding Rd. past Shagg Pond isn't maintained in the winter. The trail begins across the road from the parking area on an old road. The trail leads to Little Concord Pond, which comes into sight in 0.4 mi. and is heavily used by ATVs. It is worth the time to see Little Concord Pond. The trail up Bald Mtn. leads right just before the road reaches the pond and is blazed with blue blazes. The trail starts at the top of a 20-ft. ledge (cairn). To reach it, climb the crack of the ledge to the right. At the top, locate the cairn; from there, hike up the ridge to the summit. From the ledges south of the summit is a fine view of the Shagg Pond area. See below for a description of how to reach Speckled Mtn. from the Bald Mtn. ledges.

Distances from parking area

   to Little Concord Pond: 0.4 mi.

   to Bald Mtn. summit: 1.0 mi., 1 hr.

Speckled Mountain (2183 ft.)

Speckled Mtn. is to the east of Bald Mtn. in Peru. The route to it from the summit of Bald Mtn. drops into a col and follows the ridge to the Speckled summit. This mountain's outstanding feature is its rugged southern face—a line of nearly sheer cliffs. The views from the summit are extensive in all directions. Refer to the USGS Mt. Zircon quadrangle, 7.5-min. series.

Route from Bald Mountain

From the ledge viewpoint on Bald Mountain, follow the open ledge southeast to find a steep blue-blazed trail north to the col. Cross a snowmobile trail, then climb generally east to the ridge and summit of Speckled Mtn. The trail has been obscure in some areas.

Distance from Bald Mtn. ledges

   to Speckled Mtn. summit: 1.3 mi., 1 hr. 10 min.

Speckled Mountain Pasture Trail

The Speckled Mountain Pasture Trail offers a direct approach to the mountain instead of the traverse from Bald Mtn. Views are open to the north.

From ME 108 in West Peru, turn on Main St. Go through West Peru staying on Main St. which becomes Dickvale Rd. at about 4.3 mi. There is limited parking on right along the road along side a brook. The trail starts as a very rough gated logging road to the left (south).

From the main road, go 1.0 mi. to an old wood yard and a fork in the road. Take the right fork (the left fork is a snowmobile trail, which crosses the brook) and follow the road, passing an old camp on the right, for another mile to a large and obvious stone wall. Turn left and follow the line of the wall. After the wall ends in about 0.3 mi., cross a gravel logging road and follow the trail more steeply up the mountain. ATVs use the trail up to this point. From this point, you can follow the blazes, cairns, and flagging to the summit. The trail is intermittently marked; be careful of the confusing cairns near the summit, where several routes leave in different directions.

Distance from paved road

   to Speckled summit (via ridge): 3.0 mi., 2 hr.

Mount Zircon (2240 ft.)

This mountain is in the towns of Milton and Peru. The view is well worth the climb. To reach Mt. Zircon, from ME 26 take ME 232 6.8 mi. to the South Rumford Rd. Turn right on South Rumford Rd and go 6.4 mi. to a gated dirt road on the right where a Rumford Water District tree farm sign is located. Park in the grassy area along side the South Rumford Rd. From US 2 at the west edge of Rumford, take the South Rumford Rd. 3.2 mi. to the parking area. Refer to the USGS Mt. Zircon quadrangle, 7.5-min. series.

Following the gated dirt road, take the left fork at 1.0 mi., passing a springhouse on the left at 1.5 mi. The trail leaves the eastern side of the road about 2.0 mi. south of the highway. It climbs steadily, with a short scramble just below the rocky summit. There has been extensive logging in the area, and the trail has been disrupted in recent years. You can get water just south of the foot of the trail, near the site of the former warden's cabin.

Distances from South Rumford Rd.

   to start of trail (via truck road): 2.0 mi., 1 hr. 10 min.

Mount Tire'm (1104 ft.)

Mt. Tire'm in the town of Waterford yields a good view, with little effort, of the Long Lake region. Refer to the USGS Norway quadrangle, 15-min. series, or the Waterford Flat quadrangle, 7.5 min. series.

Daniel Brown Trail (Old Squire Brown Trail)

Follow ME 35 to the center of Waterford, then turn northwest onto Plummer Hill Rd. The trail starts 100 yd. beyond and up the road from the Wilkins Community House (next to the church). Park there or at the trailhead. A 1979 plaque on the left, reading Daniel Brown Trail, marks the start. Visitors are requested to stay on the trail, because it is on private property.

The trail emerges from the woods with widening views of the hills and lakes of Waterford and Norway. Along with views, the summit has woods and boulders to explore.

Distance from Plummer Hill Rd.

 to Mt. Tire'm summit: 0.7 mi., 40 min.

Sabattus Mountain (1253 ft.)

The chief feature of this summit in Center Lovell is the immense, nearly vertical cliff that forms its southwestern face. From the top of the cliff, impressive views of the countryside spread from Pleasant Mtn. to the Baldfaces. Refer to the USGS Center Lovell quadrangle, 7.5-min. series.

You can reach the trail by following ME 5 north from Lovell to Center Lovell. Take Sabattus Mountain Rd. right (east) at 0.7 mi. past the Center Lovell General Store and continue to a fork at 1.5 mi. from ME 5. Bear right onto Sabattus Trail Rd. at the fork and drive 0.7 mi. on this dirt road, to a new, marked parking lot on the right. The trail and protection of the mountain is a joint partnership with the Maine Bureau of Parks and the Greater Lovell Land Trust. The trail is a loop and is yellow blazed. From the parking area, keep to the left and climb steadily to a rocky area and then bear right to a large quartz outcrop and a viewpoint at about 0.7 mi. Continue along trail to the main viewpoint at 0.8 mi. The trail provides many viewpoints to the south and west. At the main viewpoint bear right past a memorial and follow trail back to parking area.

Distance from parking area

    to Sabattus summit: 0.8 mi., 30 min.

        Complete loop trail 1.6 mi., 1 hr.

Evans Notch–Chatham Region

The Cold River runs south from Evans Notch and flows into an extensive valley 3.0 mi. to the south. The valley floor is no more than 600 ft. above sea level. It is divided between Stow ME and Chatham NH; the line runs almost directly up the valley. The principal summits in Maine are East Royce (3116 ft.), Ames Mtn. (2686 ft.), Speckled Mtn. (2906 ft.), and, to the north of Evans Notch, Mt. Caribou (2828 ft.).

Two WMNF campgrounds, Basin and Cold River, are at the northern end of the valley, on the western side of NH/ME 113 about 0.3 mi. west of the Maine–New Hampshire border. The WMNF Hastings Campground entrance is 0.2 mi. south of the junction of NH/ME 113 and Wild River Rd. The Wild River Campground (WMNF) is reached by Wild River Rd. It is about 5.7 mi. southwest of the jct. of Wild River Rd. and NH/ME 113. The Kimball Lakes, South Chatham, and Fryeburg offer opportunities for fishing.

The AMC Cold River Camp is in North Chatham. For more information, go to www.outdoors.org/lodging, or contact the AMC at 603-466-2721 to find out the current camp manager's contact information.

Caribou–Speckled Mountain Wilderness

Wilderness regulations, intended to protect wilderness resources and promote opportunities for challenge and solitude, prohibit use of motorized equipment or mechanical means of transportation of any sort. Camping and wood or charcoal fires are not allowed within 200 ft. of any trail except at designated campsites. Hiking and camping group size must be no larger than 10 people. Camping and fires are also prohibited above the treeline (where trees are less than 8 ft. tall) except in winter, when camping is permitted above the treeline in places where snow cover is at least 2 ft. deep, but not on any frozen body of water. Caribou Shelter has been dismantled.

Forest Protection Areas

The WMNF has established a number of Forest Protection Areas (FPAs)—formerly known as Restricted Use Areas—where camping and wood or charcoal fires are prohibited throughout the year. The specific areas are under continual review, and areas are added to or subtracted from the list in order to provide the greatest amount of protection to areas subject to damage by excessive camping, while imposing the lowest level of restrictions possible. A general list of FPAs in this section follows, but since there are often major changes from year to year, one should obtain current information on FPAs from the WMNF.

1. No camping is permitted above treeline (where trees are less than 8 ft. tall), except in winter, and then only in places where there is at least 2 ft. of snow cover on the ground—but not on any frozen body of water. The point where the restricted area begins is marked on most trails with small signs, but the absence of such signs should not be construed as proof of the legality of a site.

2. No camping is permitted within a quarter mile of any trailhead, picnic area, or any facility for overnight accommodation such as a hut, cabin, shelter, tent site, or campground, except as designated at the facility itself. In this section, camping is also forbidden within a quarter-mile of ME/NH 113 for one-half mile in either direction from Hastings Campground.

Established Trailside Campsites

Caribou Shelter (WMNF), formerly located on the Caribou Trail northeast of the summit of Caribou Mtn., has been removed. The spring near the shelter site is not reliable.

To obtain more current information about the condition of trails in the Evans Notch–North Chatham area, contact the WMNF Evans Notch Ranger District, Bridge St., Bethel ME 04217 (207-824-2134).

The 7.5-min. USGS maps are a very valuable addition to the map that comes with this guide. Trails are named on the 7.5-min. quadrangles. See especially those for Wild River in New Hampshire, and for Speckled Mtn., East Stoneham, Bethel, Center Lovell, and Gilead in Maine. In the older 15-min.

series, see the Bethel and Fryeburg quadrangles for Maine, and the Gorham and North Conway quadrangles for New Hampshire.

The Chatham Trails Association, Inc. (CTA), has published a 1998 update of its map of the Cold River Valley and Evans Notch. Copies may be obtained from Al Cressy, P.O. Box 74, Bethel ME 04217 (207-824-0508), or in season at the AMC Cold River Campground or Brickett Place. The price is $6.00 per map.

Evans Notch Road (NH/ME 113)

This scenic auto road, NH/ME 113, continues the Valley Rd. of North Chatham northward past Brickett Place, under the impressive cliffs of East Royce, and through Evans Notch to Hastings. It crosses Evans Brook twice and ends 3.4 mi. farther at US 2, just east of the bridge over the Wild River in Gilead.
Evans Notch Road (NH/ME 113)

Distances from Brickett Place

> *to* Royce Trail (west): 25 yd.
>
> *to* service road to Speckled Mtn. (east): 0.3 mi.
>
> *to* Laughing Lion trailhead: 2.1 mi.
>
> *to* East Royce (west) and Spruce Hill (east) trailheads: 3.1 mi.
>
> *to* Haystack Notch (east) trailhead: 4.6 mi.
>
> *to* Mud Brook/Caribou (east) trailhead: 6.0 mi.
>
> *to* Wheeler Brook Trail (Little Lary Brook Rd.) (east): 7.0 mi.
>
> *to* Hastings (west) trailhead: 7.5 mi.
>
> *to* Roost (east) trailheads: est. 7.1 mi. and 7.8 mi.
>
> *to* US 2/Gilead: 10.9 mi.

Roost Trail (WMNF) (map 8: B4)

This trail ascends to the Roost, a small mountain with fine views, from two trailheads about 0.7 mi. apart on the east side of ME 113. The north trailhead is located just north of a bridge over Evans Brook, 0.1 mi. north of the jct. of ME 113 with Wild River Rd. at Hastings ME; the south trailhead is just south of another bridge over Evans Brook.

Leaving the north trailhead, the trail ascends a steep bank for 30 yd., then bears right (east) and ascends gradually along a wooded ridge. It crosses a small brook at 0.3 mi., then rises somewhat more steeply and emerges on a small rock ledge at the summit at 0.5 mi. Here a side trail descends 0.1 mi. west through woods to spacious open ledges, where the views are excellent. The main trail descends generally southeast from the summit at a moderate grade and crosses a small brook, then turns right (west) on an old road (no sign) and follows it past a cellar hole and an old clearing back to ME 113.

Distances from ME 113, north trailhead (820 ft.)

> *to* the Roost (1374 ft.): 0.5 mi., 550 ft., 30 min.

> *to* ME 113, south trailhead (850 ft.): 1.2 mi., 550 ft. (rev. 500 ft.), 55 min.

Wheeler Brook Trail (WMNF) (map 8: B4)

The trailheads for this trail are on the south side of US 2, 2.3 mi. east of the jct. of US 2 and ME 113, and on Little Lary Brook Rd. (FR 8) 1.6 mi. from its jct. with ME 113, which is 9.2 mi. north of the road to Cold River Campground and 3.7 mi. south of the jct. of US 2 and ME 113.

From US 2, the trail joins and follows the west side of Wheeler Brook, generally following old logging roads and crossing the brook four times. It turns left (arrow) at a logging road fork at 1.0 mi., just before the third crossing of the brook. The trail rises to its highest point, just over 2000 ft., at the crest of the northwest ridge of Peabody Mtn. (2462 ft.) at 2.1 mi. (There is no trail to the wooded summit of Peabody Mtn.) The trail then descends generally southwest, merges onto an old logging road that comes down from the left, and reaches Little Lary Brook Rd. Turn left on Little Lary Brook Rd. and continue about 100 yd. to a locked gate near the bridge over Little Lary Brook, 1.6 mi. from ME 113.

In the reverse direction, proceed along Little Lary Brook Rd. about 100 yd. from the locked gate, then turn right at the junction where FR 185 continues straight ahead. The trail leaves the left side of the road in another 0.3 mi.

Distance from US 2 (680 ft.)

> *to* gate on Little Lary Brook Rd. (1100 ft.): 3.5 mi. 1350 ft. (rev. 900 ft.), 2 hr. 25 min.

Mount Caribou (2828 ft.)

This mountain, called Calabo in the 1853 Walling map of Oxford County, is in the town of Mason. The bare, ledgy summit affords excellent views. The Caribou and Mud Brook trails make a pleasant loop. The Caribou summit and much of the surrounding area are part of the Caribou–Speckled Mountain Wilderness Area. Its west trailhead, which it now shares with the Mud Brook Trail, is located on the east side of ME 113 about 6 mi. north of the road to WMNF Cold River Campground and 4.6 mi. south of US 2. The east trailhead is on Bog Rd. (FR 6), which leaves the south side of US 2 1.3 mi. west of the West Bethel Post Office (there is currently a sign for Pooh Corner Farm as well as a road sign at this jct.) and leads 2.8 mi. to the trailhead where a gate ends public travel on the road.

From ME 113 the trail runs north. It crosses Morrison Brook at 0.4 mi. and turns east to follow the brook, crossing it several more times. The third crossing, at 2.0 mi., is at the head of Kees Falls, a 25-ft. waterfall. The trail levels off at the height-of-land as it crosses the col between Gammon Mtn. and Caribou Mtn. at 2.9 mi. Soon the Mud Brook Trail leaves right to return to ME 113 via the summit of Caribou Mtn., passing the site of the former Caribou Shelter and Caribou Spring (unreliable) in 0.3 mi. The Caribou Trail continues ahead at the jct., descends more rapidly, then turns northeast toward the valley of Bog Brook, which lies east of Peabody Mtn. It then follows a succession of logging roads down this valley. At 4.8 mi. it bears left in a clearing, then bears left again on the extension of Bog Rd. (FR 6) and continues to the gate.

Distances from ME 113 (960 ft.)

  to Mud Brook Trail (2420 ft.): 3.0 mi., 1450 ft., 2 hr. 15 min.

  to Bog Rd. (860 ft.): 5.5 mi., 1450 ft. (rev. 1550 ft.), 3 hr. 30 min.

  to Caribou Mtn. summit (2850 ft.) via Mud Brook Trail: 3.6 mi., 1900 ft., 2 hr. 45 min.

Mud Brook Trail (WMNF) (map 8: B4)

This trail begins on ME 113 at the same point as the Caribou Trail, about 6 mi. north of the road to WMNF Cold River Campground, then passes over the summit of Caribou Mtn. and ends at the Caribou Trail in the pass between Caribou Mtn. and Gammon Mountain Despite the ominous name, the footing on the trail is generally dry and good. The eastern section of this trail is in the Caribou–Speckled Mtn. Wilderness.

From ME 113 the trail runs generally south, then turns east along the north side of Mud Brook, rising gradually. It crosses the headwaters of Mud Brook at 1.9 mi. and swings left (north) uphill, climbing more steeply. The trail crosses several smaller brooks and at 3.0 mi. comes out on a small bare knob with excellent views east. It turns left into the woods and makes a short descent into a small ravine, then emerges above timberline and crosses ledges to the summit of Caribou Mtn. at 3.4 mi. It then descends north, passes Caribou Spring (unreliable) left at 3.6 mi. and the site of the former Caribou Shelter right 70 yd. farther, and meets the Caribou Trail in the pass.

Distances from ME 113 (960 ft.)

> *to* Caribou Mtn. summit (2850 ft.): 3.4 mi., 1900 ft., 2 hr. 40 min.

> *to* Caribou Trail (2420 ft.): 3.9 mi., 1900 ft. (rev. 400 ft.), 2 hr. 55 min.

Haystack Notch Trail (WMNF) (map 8: B5–C4)

This trail, with good footing and easy grades but some potentially difficult brook crossings, runs through Haystack Notch. The middle section of this trail is in the Caribou–Speckled Mountain Wilderness. Its western trailhead lies on the east side of ME 113, 4.8 mi. north of the road to the WMNF Cold River Campground. The east trailhead is located on the Miles Notch Trail 0.2 mi. from the trail's northern terminus. From the post office in West Bethel, go south on Flat Road; turn right at 2.6 mi. at a fork, or continue another 0.5 mi. and turn right at a crossroads. These routes merge just after a bridge and cemetery, respectively, and the road continues up the east bank of the West Branch. Just over a mile from the merger, the pavement ends, and the road becomes gradually worse. About 0.8 mi. from the end of pavement, turn right at a Forest Service sign; in another 0.3 mi., the road reaches a clearing (former log yard). The left fork here is the Miles Notch Trail and the right fork is the Haystack Notch Trail, with no sign and with blazes only to the right. Leaving right, the trail ascends the valley of the West Branch of the Pleasant River, making several crossings of that brook, some of which may be difficult at high water. At 3.3 mi., it crosses through Haystack Notch and descends generally west along the East Branch of Evans Brook, crossing it several times before reaching ME 113. The last crossing, in particular, may be difficult at high water.

In the reverse direction, follow the right fork of the logging road, then follow the trail as it soon leaves right on a woods road and descends to the river. The trail crosses the West Branch and a major tributary four times in the next half-mile, then ascends south and crosses a woods road at 1.2 mi. from the clearing (high-water access). It then ascends along the edge of the valley, with several more minor brook crossings, to Miles Notch.

Distances from Miles Notch Trail

   to Haystack Notch: 3.3 mi., 1 hr. 35 min.

   to ME 113: 5.4 mi., 3 hr. 5 min.

Albany Mountain (1910 ft.)

Views from the open summit ledges are excellent in all directions. Refer to the USGS Bethel quadrangle, 15-min. series, and the East Stoneham quadrangle, 7.5-min. series.

Albany Notch Trail (WMNF) (map 8: C5)

This trail passes through the notch west of Albany Mtn. Parts of its northern section still suffer from invasion by berry bushes as a result of the loss of mature forest in the windstorm of 1980, and are wet from beaver-dam flooding. The southern section, which is located mostly on old, overgrown logging roads and is disrupted by recent logging, is poorly marked, is wet, and requires much care to follow. Most hikers use the northern section, which makes possible a loop hike over Albany Mtn. in combination with the Albany Mountain Trail and the branch trail that runs from the height-of-land in Albany Notch to the base of the ledges on the Albany Mountain Trail.

To reach the north trailhead, follow Flat Road south from US 2 opposite the West Bethel Post Office, which becomes FR 7 when it enters the WMNF at 4.5 mi. At 5.8 mi., turn right onto FR 18, following signs for the Crocker Pond Campground. The trailhead is located in a parking area on the right in another 0.6 mi., just past the end of an extensive beaver swamp. To reach the trailhead from Bethel, take ME 5 south about five miles passing Songo Pond on the left. Turn right on Patte Brook Road, which becomes FR 7 as you enter the WMNF. Turn left at 2.9 mi. from ME 5 on FR 18, which ends at the Crocker Pond Campground.

To reach the southern trailhead, leave ME 5 at the western end of Keewaydin Lake, 2.4 mi. west of the East Stoneham Post Office and 0.7 mi. east of the Lovell–Stoneham town line, and follow Birch Rd. north. Bear right at the fork staying on Birch Rd. at 0.4 mi. from ME 5. Continue on Birch Rd for 0.6 mi. Park carefully along side of road, avoiding blocking any roads at a point where the road narrows and turns to gravel. There is a sign for the trail that isn't easily seen on the right hand side of the road just beyond the point the road narrows.

Leaving the parking area on FR 18, the trail follows an old logging road that becomes well defined after the first few yards. At 0.6 mi., the Albany Notch Trail bears right at the jct. where the Albany Mountain Trail diverges left (south). At 1.2 mi., it enters the region damaged by blow down, where berry bushes may be a nuisance, though the trail becomes markedly drier underfoot. Returning to mature woods at 1.4 mi., it climbs at a moderate grade to the left of a small brook. In this area there has been a great amount of beaver activity. Due to this activity, the trail may be impassable particularly during wet weather. At 1.7 mi., the trail reaches the jct. where a branch trail leads left (east) 0.4 mi. to the Albany Mountain Trail at the base of the ledges.

The trail now descends moderately with a few steeper pitches just below the pass, and crosses a small brook several times. It then runs mostly on a very old road until it reaches a much newer logging road at 2.4 mi. and turns left on this road; if ascending from the south, turn sharp right off the road. This road is fairly easy to follow, but is rather wet and overgrown with tall grasses and other vegetation that permit little evidence of a footway. It passes junctions with a snowmobile trail on the left at 2.8 mi. and 3.1 mi.; at the second jct. the road bears right and improves greatly, then crosses Meadow Brook on a snowmobile bridge at 3.6 mi. and continues to the trailhead.

Distances from FR 18

> *to* Albany Mountain Trail: 0.6 mi., 25 min.
>
> *to* branch trail junction in Albany Notch: 1.7 mi., 1 hr. 15 min.
>
> *to* trailhead on Birch Ave.: 4.2 mi., 2 hr. 30 min.

Albany Mountain Trail (WMNF) (map 8: C5)

This trail ascends the northern slope of Albany Mtn. to an open ledge near its summit that affords good views east and north. It begins on the Albany Notch Trail 0.6 mi. from FR 18.

Leaving the Albany Notch Trail, it soon turns left onto a skidder road that it follows for 20 yd., then leaves to the right. It continues to ascend moderately through woods that have seen some light to moderate wind damage. At 0.6 mi., the trail turns right at the foot of a small, mossy rock face, and climbs to a jct. at 0.9 mi. where a branch trail leads right (west) 0.4 mi. to the Albany Notch Trail at the height-of-land in Albany Notch. Soon the trail passes a ledge with a good view of the Baldfaces and Mt. Washington and continues to the northeastern outlook, where regular marking ends. The true summit, wooded and not reached by any well-defined trail, is located about 100 yd. south. The summit area has other viewpoints not reached by the trail that repay efforts devoted to cautious exploration by experienced hikers. The best viewpoint, somewhat overgrown, lies about 0.1 mi. southwest of the true summit; a sketchy and incomplete line of cairns leads to it.

Distance from Albany Notch Trail

to Albany upper outlook: 1.3 mi., 1 hr. 5 min.

Albany Brook Trail (WMNF) (map 8: C5)

This short, easy trail follows the shore of Crocker Pond and then leads to attractive, secluded Round Pond. It begins at the turnaround at the end of the main road at the Crocker Pond Campground (do not enter the actual camping area). You can reach this by following the road that runs south from US 2 opposite the West Bethel Post Office, which becomes FR 7 when it enters the WMNF at 4.5 mi. At 5.8 mi., turn right onto FR 18, following signs 1.5 mi. to the campground entrance.

Leaving the turnaround, the trail descends to a small brook and follows the western shore of Crocker Pond for 0.2 mi., then joins and follows Albany Brook with gentle ups and downs. At 0.9 mi., it goes straight through a logging-road intersection with a clearing visible on the right, and soon reaches the northern end of Round Pond.

Distance from Crocker Pond Campground

to Round Pond: 1 mi., 30 min.

Speckled Mountain (2906 ft.)

This mountain lies east of Evans Notch, in Batchelder's Grant and Stoneham. It is one of at least three mountains in Maine that have been known by this name. The summit's open ledges have excellent views in all directions. There is a spring about 0.1 mi. northeast of the summit, off the Red Rock Trail.

Miles Notch Trail (WMNF) (map 8: B5–C4)

This trail runs through Miles Notch, giving access to the east end of the ledgy ridge that culminates in Speckled Mtn. To reach its south terminus, near which the Great Brook Trail also begins, leave ME 5 in North Lovell ME on West

Stoneham Road and follow that road northwest for 1.8 mi., then turn right onto Hut Rd. just before the bridge over Great Brook and continue 1.5 mi. to the trailhead. To reach the north terminus, follow the road that leads south from US 2 opposite the West Bethel Post Office to a crossroads at 3.1 mi., then take the road that runs right (west) and continue straight ahead at a junction just beyond a small cemetery. The road becomes rather rough after about 1 mi. from the crossroads, and it may not be possible for some cars to drive all the way to the trailhead, which is about 2.5 mi. from the crossroads.

From the south terminus, the trail follows an old logging road generally north. At 0.3 mi. it bears left off the road (arrow), then climbs over a small ridge and descends steadily into the valley of Beaver Brook. At 1.2 mi. it enters another old logging road, which it follows it to the left for 0.2 mi., then bears to the right off the old road and soon crosses a branch of Beaver Brook. At 2.3 mi. it crosses Beaver Brook, passes over a steeper section, runs in the gully of a small brook, then turns left away from the brook and reaches Miles Notch at 2.9 mi. The trail now descends gradually, and at 3.2 mi. the Red Rock Trail leaves on the left for the summit of Speckled Mtn. The Miles Notch Trail then descends moderately, crossing Miles Brook repeatedly. At 5.4 mi. the Haystack Notch Trail enters on the left, and the Miles Notch Trail soon reaches its northern end.

Distances from south terminus (470 ft.)

to Red Rock Trail (1800 ft.): 3.2 mi., 1700 ft. (rev. 400 ft.), 2 hr. 25 min.

to north terminus (800 ft.): 5.6 mi., 1700 ft. (rev. 950 ft.), 3 hr. 40 min.

Bickford Brook Trail (WMNF) (map 8: C4)

This trail ascends Speckled Mtn. from the Brickett Place on ME 113, 0.2 mi. north of the road to WMNF Cold River Campground. Most of this trail is in the Caribou–Speckled Mountain Wilderness. The trail enters the woods near the garage, then at 0.3 mi. turns to the right onto an old WMNF service road built for access to the former fire tower on Speckled Mtn. and follows this road for the next 2.5 mi.

The trail soon enters the Wilderness, and at 0.7 mi. the Blueberry Ridge Trail leaves on the right (east) for the lower end of the Bickford Slides and Blueberry Mtn.; this trail rejoins the Bickford Brook Trail 0.5 mi. below the summit of Speckled Mtn., affording the opportunity for a loop hike. At 0.9 mi. the Bickford Slides Loop enters on the right from the lower end of the Upper Slides, and at 1.1 mi. the spur path along the Upper Slides enters on the right.

The Bickford Brook Trail soon swings away from the brook and winds up a southwest spur to the crest of the main west ridge of the Speckled Mtn. range, where the Spruce Hill Trail enters left at 3.1 mi. The Bickford Brook Trail then passes west and north of the summit of Ames Mtn. into the col between Ames Mtn. and Speckled Mtn., where the Blueberry Ridge Trail rejoins (right) at 3.8 mi. The Bickford Brook Trail then continues upward to the summit.

Distances from ME 113 (600 ft.)

> *to* Blueberry Ridge Trail, lower junction (950 ft.): 0.7 mi., 350 ft., 30 min.

> *to* Spruce Hill Trail (2420 ft.): 3.1 mi., 1800 ft., 2 hr. 25 min.

> *to* Blueberry Ridge Trail, upper junction (2590 ft.): 3.8 mi., 2000 ft., 2 hr. 55 min.

> *to* Speckled Mtn. summit (2906 ft.): 4.3 mi., 2300 ft., 3 hr. 20 min.

Blueberry Ridge Trail (CTA) (map 8: C4)

This trail begins and ends on the Bickford Brook Trail, leaving at a sign 0.7 mi. from its trailhead at the Brickett Place on ME 113 and rejoining 0.5 mi. below the summit of Speckled Mtn. (The upper part of the Blueberry Ridge Trail may also be reached from Stone House Rd.—formerly Shell Pond Rd.—via the Stone House or White Cairn trails.) This entire trail is in the Caribou–Speckled Mountain Wilderness.

Leaving the Bickford Brook Trail, the Blueberry Ridge Trail descends toward Bickford Brook, and at 0.1 mi. the trail passes the lower end of the Bickford Slides Loop, which diverges to the left just before the main trail crosses Bickford Brook. Care should be taken to avoid (or else deliberately explore) numerous unofficial side paths from the Bickford Slides and over to the Bickford Brook Trail.

Bickford Slides Loop. This side path, 0.5 mi. long, leaves the Blueberry Ridge Trail just before it crosses Bickford Brook, at a point 0.1 mi. from its lower jct. with the Bickford Brook Trail. At the same point a spur path descends along Bickford Brook 50 yd. to the Lower Slides.

At a point 20 yd. from its beginning, the Bickford Slides Loop crosses Bickford Brook (may be difficult at high water) and climbs along it for 0.3 mi. to another jct. near the base of the Upper Slides. Here the main path bears left across the brook at the base of the Upper Slides and in another 0.2 mi. rejoins the Bickford Brook Trail at a point 0.2 mi. above the lowest jct. of these paths, while a spur path 0.3 mi. long continues up along the brook and the Upper

Slides, then crosses the brook above the slides and rejoins the Bickford Brook Trail 0.3 mi. above the lowest jct. of the paths.

From the jct. with the Bickford Slides Loop and the spur path to the Lower Slides, the Blueberry Ridge Trail crosses Bickford Brook (may be difficult at high water) and ascends steeply southeast past a good western outlook to an open area just over the crest of Blueberry Ridge, where the White Cairn Trail enters right at 0.7 mi. An overlook loop 0.5 mi. long, with excellent views to the south, leaves the Blueberry Ridge Trail shortly after this jct. and rejoins it shortly before the Stone House Trail enters on the right at 0.9 mi., a few steps past the high point of the trail on Blueberry Mtn.

From the jct. with the Stone House Trail, marked by signs and a large cairn, the Blueberry Ridge Trail bears left and descends to a spring (unreliable) a short distance from the trail on the left (north). Here it turns sharp right, and ascends over ledges with fine views, marked by cairns, and through patches of woods, passing over several humps. The trail ends at the Bickford Brook Trail in the shallow pass at the head of the Rattlesnake Brook ravine, about 0.5 mi. below the summit of Speckled Mtn.

Distances from Bickford Brook Trail, lower junction (950 ft.)

> *to* Stone House Trail (1750 ft.): 0.9 mi., 900 ft., 55 min.

> *to* Bickford Brook Trail, upper junction (2590 ft.): 3.1 mi., 1850 ft., 2 hr. 30 min.

Spruce Hill Trail (map 8: C4; AMC WMNF map 5: F13)

This trail begins on the east side of ME 113 3.0 mi. north of the road to WMNF Cold River Campground, opposite the start of the East Royce Trail, and ascends to the Bickford Brook Trail, with which it forms the shortest route to the summit of Speckled Mtn. Most of this trail is in the Caribou–Speckled Mountain Wilderness. It ascends moderately through woods, passing the Wilderness boundary sign at 0.6 mi., to the summit of Spruce Hill at 1.5 mi. It then descends into a sag and climbs to meet the Bickford Brook Trail on the ridgecrest west of Ames Mtn.

Distances from ME 113 (1450 ft.)

> *to* Bickford Brook Trail (2420 ft.): 1.9 mi., 1050 ft. (rev. 200 ft.), 1 hr. 30 min.

> *to* Speckled Mtn. summit (2906 ft.) via Bickford Brook Trail: 3.1 mi., 1650 ft., 2 hr. 25 min.

Cold Brook Trail *(map 8: C4; AMC WMNF map 5: F13–F14)*

This trail ascends Speckled Mtn. and affords fine views from numerous open ledges in its upper part, which is in the Caribou–Speckled Mountain Wilderness. Its trailhead is reached from ME 5 in North Lovell ME, 2.0 mi. south of Keewaydin Lake, by following West Stoneham Rd. (signs for Evergreen Valley Ski Area) for 1.9 mi. Take the first right (Adams Rd., with an Evergreen Valley sign) just after the bridge over Great Brook, then continue to a gravel road on the right 2.2 mi. from ME 5. The WMNF sign is on the paved road, but it may be possible to drive 0.5 mi. on the rough gravel road to a parking area. It can also be approached via the Evergreen Link Trail, a shorter and more attractive alternative to the lower section of this trail.

Beyond here the road becomes rougher, and in 0.7 mi. from the paved road it bears left past a gate. The next 1.0 mi. is on a muddy road that circles on contour to a cabin, the Duncan McIntosh House. Continuing ahead on the road, take the left fork, then the right. The trail descends to Cold Brook and crosses it at 1.9 mi., just above a fork. It then climbs and circles along the farther branch, passes west of Sugarloaf Mtn., and ascends the south side of Speckled Mtn., passing a jct. left at 2.7 mi. with the Evergreen Link Trail from the Evergreen Valley Ski Area. It emerges on semi-open ledges at 3.5 mi., passes two excellent south outlooks, and bears right to re-enter the woods at 4.4 mi. At 4.9 mi. it emerges on semi-open ledges again and soon reaches the jct. with the Red Rock Trail right and the Bickford Brook Trail left, where it follows the latter trail left 30 yd. to the summit of Speckled Mtn.

Distance from paved road (500 ft.)

   to   Speckled Mtn. summit (2906 ft.): 4.9 mi., 2500 ft., 3 hr. 40 min.

Evergreen Link Trail *(map 8: C4; AMC WMNF map 5: F13)*

This trail provides the easiest access to Speckled Mtn. via the scenic ledges on the upper Cold Brook Trail. It is lightly used but easily followed by experienced hikers. To reach the trailhead, leave ME 5 in North Lovell, 2.0 mi. south of Keewaydin Lake, and follow West Stoneham Rd. for 1.9 mi. Just beyond the bridge over Great Brook, turn right onto Adams Rd. (sign for Evergreen Valley) and follow it for 1.5 mi., passing the trailhead for Cold Brook Trail. Then turn right onto Mountain Rd. (sign for Evergreen Valley Inn), drive 0.4 mi. up this road to the inn, and park in the lot just above or in a sandy area just below. On foot, follow the paved road uphill for about 100 yd. Where it turns left, take the dirt road (soon gated) straight ahead and continue climbing steeply. At 0.4 mi. turn left onto a grassy logging road (a sign reads, LINK), then right onto the Link Trail proper at 0.7 mi. (a sign reads, Speckled Mountain via Cold Brook Trail). The trail, blazed in yellow, leads off at a bearing of 70°. It crosses a woods road at 1.0 mi. and reaches the Cold Brook Trail at 1.2 mi.; turn left for the ledges and Speckled Mtn.

Distances from inn at Evergreen Valley (530 ft.)

> *to* Cold Brook Trail (1130 ft.): 1.2 mi., 600 ft., 55 min.
>
> *to* Speckled Mtn. summit (2906 ft.) via Cold Brook Trail: 3.4 mi., 2400 ft., 2 hr. 55 min.

Red Rock Trail (map 8: C4–C5; AMC WMNF map 5: F13–F14)

This trail ascends to Speckled Mtn. from the Miles Notch Trail 0.3 mi. north of Miles Notch, 3.2 mi. from its southern trailhead and 2.4 mi. from its northern trailhead. It traverses the long eastern ridge of the Speckled Mtn. range, affording fine views of the surrounding mountains. All of this trail is in the Caribou–Speckled Mountain Wilderness.

It leaves the Miles Notch Trail, descends to cross Miles Brook in its deep ravine, then angles up the north slope of Miles Knob and gains the ridgecrest northwest of that summit. It descends to a col, then ascends, passing an obscure side path that leads left downhill to a spectacular viewpoint (dangerous if wet or icy) at the top of the sheer south cliff of Red Rock Mtn. The main trail continues to the ledgy summit of Red Rock Mtn. at 1.2 mi., where there is a view to the north, and follows the ridge, with several ups and downs, over Butters Mtn. at 2.5 mi. and then on to the next col to the west. Here, at 3.4 mi., the Great Brook Trail diverges left (east) and descends southeast to its trailhead, which is very close to the southern trailhead of the Miles Notch Trail. The Red Rock Trail swings southwest and crosses the summit of Durgin Mtn.—which is ledgy with some outlooks—at 4.4 mi. It then descends easily to a notch, climbs sharply, then runs generally southwest to the jct. with the Cold Brook Trail and Bickford Brook Trail 30 yd. east of the summit of Speckled Mtn. There is a spring near the trail about 0.1 mi. east of the summit.

Distances from Miles Notch Trail (1750 ft.)

> *to* Great Brook Trail (2000 ft.): 3.4 mi., 1000 ft. (rev. 750 ft.), 2 hr. 10 min.
>
> *to* Speckled Mtn. summit (2906 ft.): 5.6 mi., 2100 ft. (rev. 200 ft.), 3 hr. 50 min.

Great Brook Trail (map 8: C4; AMC WMNF map 5: F13–F14)

This trail ascends to the Red Rock Trail east of Speckled Mtn. The upper part of this trail is in the Caribou–Speckled Mountain Wilderness. To reach its trailhead, leave ME 5 in North Lovell ME on West Stoneham Rd. and follow that road northwest for 1.8 mi. Turn right here just before the bridge over Great Brook onto Hut Rd., and continue 1.5 mi. to the trailhead, which is about 100 yd. past the southern trailhead for the Miles Notch Trail.

The trail continues up the gravel road and bears right onto FR 4 at 0.8 mi., just after crossing Great Brook on a bridge with a gate. At 1.8 mi. it turns left onto a grassy older road and follows Great Brook. At 3.0 mi. it crosses Great Brook, with some interesting cascades just above the crossing. The trail then bears left (arrow), becomes steeper, and continues along Great Brook to the ridgecrest, where it joins the Red Rock Trail in the col between Butters Mtn. and Durgin Mtn.

Distances from trailhead (500 ft.)

- *to* Red Rock Trail (2000 ft.): 3.7 mi., 1500 ft., 2 hr. 35 min.
- *to* Speckled Mtn. summit (2906 ft.) via Red Rock Trail: 5.8 mi., 2600 ft. (rev. 200 ft.), 4 hr. 10 min.

Stone House Trail (CTA) (map 8: C4)

This trail ascends to the scenic ledges of Blueberry Mtn. from Stone House Rd. (formerly Shell Pond Rd.) The upper part of this trail is in the Caribou–Speckled Mountain Wilderness. To reach the trailhead, leave NH 113 on the east side 1.3 mi. north of AMC Cold River Camp and follow Stone House Rd. 1.1 mi. to a padlocked steel gate; park here.

The trail leaves the road on the left (north) 0.5 mi. beyond the gate, east of an open shed. It follows a logging road and approaches Rattlesnake Brook. At 0.2 mi. from Stone House Rd. it merges with a private road (descending, bear right at arrow) and immediately reaches the jct. with a spur path that leads right 30 yd. to a bridge overlooking Rattlesnake Flume, a small, attractive gorge. The main trail soon swings right (arrow), and at 0.5 mi. another spur leads right 0.1 mi. to the exquisite Rattlesnake Pool, which lies at the foot of a small cascade. The main trail soon enters the WMNF, and at 1.2 mi. it swings left and begins to climb rather steeply straight up the slope, running generally northwest to the top of the ridge, where it ends at the Blueberry Ridge Trail only a few steps from the top of Blueberry Mtn. For Speckled Mtn., turn right on the Blueberry Ridge Trail.

Distance from Stone House Rd. (formerly Shell Pond Rd.) (600 ft.)

   to Blueberry Ridge Trail (1750 ft.): 1.5 mi., 1150 ft., 1 hr. 20 min.

White Cairn Trail (CTA) (map 8: C4)

This trail provides access to the open ledges on Blueberry Mtn. and, with the Stone House Trail, makes an easy half-day circuit. The upper part of this trail is in the Caribou–Speckled Mountain Wilderness. It begins on Stone House Rd. (formerly Shell Pond Rd.), which leaves NH 113 on the east side 1.3 mi. north of AMC Cold River Camp and runs 1.1 mi. to a padlocked steel gate; park here.

The trail leaves Stone House Rd. at a small clearing 0.3 mi. beyond the gate. It follows old logging roads north and west to an upland meadow, where it may be affected by beaver activity, and passes into the WMNF at 0.3 mi. At 0.8 mi. it begins to climb steeply up the right (east) margin of the cliffs that are visible from the road, then turns sharp left and begins to climb on ledges. The grade soon moderates as the trail runs northwest along the crest of the cliffs to the west, with views to the south. At 1.2 mi. it passes a spring, then swings right (north) and passes another spring just before ending at the junction with the Blueberry Ridge Trail, 0.2 mi. west of the upper terminus of the Stone House Trail. A loop trail that leaves the Blueberry Ridge Trail near its jct. with this trail provides a scenic alternate route to the Stone House Trail.

Distance from Stone House Rd. (formerly Shell Pond Rd.) (600 ft.)

   to Blueberry Ridge Trail (1750 ft.): 1.4 mi., 1150 ft., 1 hr. 15 min.

Shell Pond Trail (map 8: C4–D4; AMC WMNF map 5: G13)

This trail runs between Stone House Rd. (formerly Shell Pond Rd.), at the locked gate 1.1 mi. from NH 113, and Deer Hill Rd. (FR 9), 3.5 mi. from NH 113. Stone House Rd. leaves NH 113 on the east side 1.3 mi. north of AMC Cold River Camp. Much of this trail is on private property, and hikers are requested to stay on the marked trails, especially in the vicinity of the Stone House. The trail itself does not come within sight of the pond, but the Shell Pond Loop provides access to a viewpoint on the shore.

From the gate on Stone House Rd., continue east on the road on foot. The Shell Pond Loop leaves right at 0.2 mi., and in another 80 yd. the White Cairn

Trail leaves left. At 0.4 mi. the trail emerges on a grassy airplane landing strip and soon bears right at a fork where the Stone House Trail diverges left. The Shell Pond Trail heads east across the field with good views of the surrounding mountains, passing to the right of the Stone House at 0.6 mi.

The trail leaves the landing strip at 0.8 mi., entering a patch of woods to the left, and follows a grassy old road through an orchard. The trail is not clearly marked in this area; in the reverse direction, bear left at a fork to reach the landing strip. The trail crosses Rattlesnake Brook on a bridge at 1.1 mi., passes through a wet area, and turns left off the road at 1.2 mi., where the Shell Pond Loop bears right. From here the Shell Pond Trail ascends gradually to Deer Hill Rd.

Distance from gate on Stone House Rd. (600 ft.)

   to Deer Hill Rd. (850 ft.): 1.8 mi., 250 ft., 1 hr.

Shell Pond Loop (CTA) (map 8: C4–D4)

This trail skirts the south side of Shell Pond, making possible a pleasant loop hike in combination with the Shell Pond Trail. It is located almost entirely on private property and also serves as an ATV trail. It leaves the south side of the Shell Pond Trail 0.2 mi. east of the gate on Stone House Rd. (formerly Shell Pond Rd.) and leads through woods near the edge of a field, making several turns marked by yellow blazes.

At 0.2 mi. it turns right onto a grassy road, crosses a bridge over Shell Pond Brook, and soon swings left (east) on a well-worn woods road. It traverses the slope well above the south shore of Shell Pond, with several minor ups and downs. At 1.3 mi. the trail turns left off the road and descends, then meanders through the woods behind the east shore of the pond, crossing several small brooks. At 1.7 mi. a spur path leads 25 yd. left to a clearing and a bench with a fine view across the pond to the Baldfaces and Mt. Meader. The main trail bears right here and continues at easy grades to the Shell Pond Trail, 0.6 mi. west of the latter's eastern trailhead on Deer Hill Rd. and 1.2 mi. from the gate on Stone House Rd.

Distance from western junction with Shell Pond Trail (600 ft.)

   to eastern junction with Shell Pond Trail (630 ft.): 1.9 mi., 150 ft. (rev. 100 ft.), 1 hr.

Horseshoe Pond Trail (CTA) (map 8: D4)

This trail, blazed with bright yellow paint, starts from Deer Hill Rd. (FR 9) 4.7 mi. from NH 113 at a small parking area at a curve in the road, where the pond is visible; it ends on the Conant Trail. The former Horseshoe Pond Loop is now closed to public use, so there is no public access to the shore of this pond.

From Deer Hill Rd., it descends moderately past the Styles grave, which is on the right of the trail and enclosed by a stone wall, then enters a recent gravel logging road and turns right onto it. The trail follows this road, keeping straight at a jct. in 100 yd. At 0.3 mi., just before the gravel road ends, the trail turns right onto a grassy road that leads up into a brushy area, and ascends through the clear-cut resulting from the timber salvage operations after the 1980 windstorm. It follows cairns and overgrown skid roads back into the woods to the old trail, which continues to the Conant Trail between Lord Hill and Harndon Hill.

Distance from Deer Hill Rd. (700 ft.)

   to Conant Trail (1100 ft.): 1.1 mi., 500 ft. (rev. 100 ft), 50 min.

Conant Trail (CTA) (map 8: D4)

This loop path to Pine Hill and Lord Hill is an interesting and fairly easy walk with a number of good outlooks. It is frequently referred to (and may be signed as) the Pine-Lord-Harndon Trail, though it does not go particularly close to the summit of Harndon Hill; it should not be confused with the Conant Path, a short trail (not open to the public) near AMC Cold River Camp. It is reached by following Deer Hill Rd. (FR 9) and making a right turn 1.5 mi. from NH 113, then turning left in 0.1 mi. onto Harndon Hill Rd. and parking near a dike.

The trail runs straight ahead along the dike across swampy Colton Brook—Colton Dam is located several hundred yards to the right from here—and continues on a gravel road to the loop jct. at 0.4 mi., where the path divides. From here the path is described in a counterclockwise direction. The south branch turns right and follows a logging road (Hemp Hill Rd.) to a level spot at 1.0 mi. near the old Johnson cellar hole. Here it turns left on a logging road, then left again in a few steps. The trail turns left again at 1.2 mi. and ascends Pine Hill, rather steeply at times, passing a ledge with a fine view to the west at 1.4 mi. It reaches the west end of the summit ridge and continues to the most easterly knob, which has a good view north, at 2.0 mi. The trail zigzags down past logged areas, crosses Bradley Brook at 2.3 mi., and then climbs, crossing the logging road that provides access to the mine on Lord Hill and passing an outlook over Horseshoe Pond. It reaches ledges near the summit of Lord Hill at 3.0 mi., where the Mine Loop leaves on the left.

Mine Loop (map 8: D4)

This path is 1.0 mi. long, 0.1 mi. shorter than the section of Conant Trail it bypasses. Except for the one critical turn mentioned below, it is fairly easy to follow. From the jct. with the Conant Trail near the summit of Lord Hill, it climbs briefly to the ledge at the top of the old mica mine and then descends on a woods road, and at 0.1 mi. it passes a spur path that leads right 30 yd. to the mine. At 0.5 mi. it turns sharp left on a good logging road, then at 0.7 mi. it reaches a fork and turns sharp right back on the other branch of the road, which shows much less evidence of use. This turn is easily missed because it is difficult to mark adequately and the correct side road is less obvious than the main road. (The main road, continuing straight at this fork, crosses the Conant Trail between Pine Hill and Lord Hill and continues south toward Kezar Lake.) At a clearing the Mine Loop leaves the road on the right and descends 50 yd. to rejoin the Conant Trail 1.1 mi. from its trailhead.

From Lord Hill the Conant Trail descends to the jct. with the Horseshoe Pond Trail on the right at 3.2 mi., where it bears left, then soon turns left and runs at a fairly level grade along the south side of Harndon Hill. It passes a cellar hole, and the Mine Loop rejoins on the left at 4.1 mi. At 4.5 mi. the road passes a gate, becomes wider, reaches the loop jct., and continues straight ahead across the dike to the trailhead.

Distance from trailhead off Deer Hill Rd. (550 ft.)

Complete loop: 5.2 mi., 1000 ft., 3 hr. 5 min.

Deer Hills Trail (CTA) (map 8: D4)

This trail ascends Little Deer Hill and Big Deer Hill, providing a relatively easy trip that offers interesting views. Several trail sections in this area have been renamed to provide a more rational nomenclature. The trail proper runs from the AMC Cold River Camp to Deer Hill Rd. (FR 9) 1.4 mi. from NH 113. Members of the public who wish to use this trail starting at the north end are requested to park at the Baldface Circle Trail trailhead parking area and follow a path called the Deer Hill Connector, which runs south of Charles Brook for 0.3 mi. to a jct. on the right with the Tea House Path (not open to the public) from Cold River Camp, then runs another 0.1 mi. to the dam on the Cold River near Cold River Camp. Here the trail from the AMC camp enters on the right; its jct. with the Conant Path is a few steps to the right (neither of these trails is open to the public). Distances given below include those traveled on the Deer Hill Connector.

The Deer Hills Trail crosses Cold River on the dam, soon passing the jct. on the left with the Leach Link Trail and then the jct. on the right with the Deer Hills Bypass. The Deer Hill Trail continues straight ahead and climbs moderately past an outlook west, then bears left onto ledges and reaches the summit of Little Deer Hill at 1.3 mi. Here the Frost Trail enters on the right, having ascended from the Deer Hills Bypass. The main trail descends into a sag, then climbs to the summit of Big Deer Hill at 2.0 mi. It then descends the south ridge with several fine outlooks, turning left at 2.5 mi. where the Deer Hills Bypass leaves on the right. Soon the Deer Hills Trail turns left again, then turns right onto an old logging road at 2.7 mi. Here a spur path follows the logging road left for a few steps, then descends in 0.2 mi. to Deer Hill Spring (also called Bubbling Spring), a shallow pool with air bubbles rising through a small area of light-colored sand. The main trail descends from the jct. to Deer Hill Rd.

Distances from ME 113 at the Baldface Circle Trail parking area (520 ft.) via Deer Hill Connector

- *to* Little Deer Hill summit (1090 ft.): 1.3 mi., 550 ft., 55 min.
- *to* Big Deer Hill summit (1367 ft.): 2.0 mi., 1000 ft. (rev. 200 ft.), 1 hr. 30 min.
- *to* Deer Hill Rd. (500 ft.): 3.3 mi., 1000 ft. (rev. 850 ft.), 2 hr.

Deer Hills Bypass (CTA) (map 8: D4)

This trail skirts the south slopes of the Deer Hills, making possible various loop hikes over the summits. It leaves the Deer Hills Trail just east of Cold River Dam and follows a level grassy road south along the river. (This section of trail was formerly part of the Leach Link Trail.) At 0.4 mi it turns left off the road and ascends past a ledge with a view west. At 0.6 mi. the Ledges Trail leaves left, and the Deer Hills Bypass climbs steadily alongside a stone wall. At 0.8 mi. a spur path called the Frost Trail leaves left, climbing 0.2 mi. to the summit of Little Deer Hill. The Deer Hills Bypass descends into a shallow ravine, then ascends easily to rejoin the Deer Hills Trail on the south ridge of Deer Hill, 0.5 mi. below the summit.

Distance from western junction with Deer Hills Trail (500 ft.)

> *to*   eastern junction with Deer Hills Trail (1000 ft.): 1.4 mi., 550 ft (rev. 50 ft.), 1 hr.

Ledges Trail (CTA) (map 8: D4)

This trail passes interesting ledges and a cave but is very steep and rough, dangerous in wet or icy conditions, and not recommended for descent. It leaves the Deer Hills Bypass, 0.6 mi. from the Cold River Dam, and climbs rather steeply with numerous outlooks. At 0.2 mi. the Ledges Trail divides; the right branch, which is slightly longer, rejoins in about 100 yd. Just above the point where these branches rejoin, the Ledges Trail meets the Frost Trail, a short spur from the Deer Hills Bypass. The summit of Little Deer Hill is 70 yd. left on the Frost Trail.

Distance from Deer Hills Bypass (700 ft.)

> *to*   Little Deer Hill summit (1090 ft.): 0.3 mi., 400 ft., 20 min.

Leach Link Trail (CTA) (map 8: D4)

This trail gives access to Little Deer Hill and Big Deer Hill from Stone House Rd. (formerly Shell Pond Rd.), which leaves NH 113 on the east side 1.3 mi. north of AMC Cold River Camp. The trail starts at a gated road on the right side of Stone House Rd. 0.3 mi. from NH 113. The northern part of the trail uses the former Shell Pond Brook Trail.

Beyond the gate the trail follows a grassy road across a snowmobile bridge over Shell Pond Brook. At 0.2 mi. the trail turns right off the road (sign), then in another 50 yd. bears left and runs through hemlock woods along a bank high above the brook. It then descends and at 0.5 mi. turns left at a point where the former route of the trail came across the brook from the right. The trail continues south at easy grades and ends at the Deer Hills Trail a few steps east of Cold River Dam. To ascend the Deer Hills, turn left on the Deer Hills Trail.

Distance from Stone House Rd. (600 ft.)

> *to*   Deer Hills Trail (500 ft.): 1.2 mi., 0 ft. (rev. 100 ft.), 35 min.

Section 9

Grafton Notch/ Mahoosuc Range Region

See AMC Maine Trail Map 7: Mahoosuc Range.

RECOMMENDED HIKES

Easy

Mount Will (lp: 3.25 mi., 2 hr., 15 min.) The first part of the loop is a nature trail with markers identifying trees and providing history of the area. The North and South Ledges provide views of the Androscoggin River Valley.

Table Rock Trail (lp: 2.4 mi., 1 hr. 45 min.) A short, moderately steep, but spectacular climb via the Baldpate Mtn. Trail (AT) to a prominent rock ledge on Baldpate Mtn. An extensive slab-cave system is seen on this trail.

Moderate

South Puzzle Mountain via the Grafton Loop Trail (rt: 6.4 mi., 5 hr.) An interesting hike over a newly created trail to the summit of South Puzzle Mtn. where there are extensive views in all directions.

Old Blue Mountain via the AT (rt: 5.6 mi., 5 hr.) A steep but steady climb to the krummholz covered summit of Old Blue Mtn. where there are outstanding views of the surrounding area.

Strenuous

Old Speck Trail (rt: 7.6 mi, 5 hr. 15 min.) The Old Speck Trail which is part of the AT ascends to the summit of Old Speck, the third highest mountain in Maine, where there is an observation tower that affords a tremendous 360 degree view of the western Maine mountains.

Mount Goose Eye via the Wright Trail (lp: 9.5 mi., 6 hr. 10 min.) This is a scenic route through rugged, varied terrain, which provides a loop trail to the East and West peaks of Mt. Goose Eye. The peaks offer views of the Mahoosucs, White Mtns., and the Androscoggin River Valley.

LIST OF MOUNTAINS

This section covers the area bounded on the south and west by the Androscoggin River; on the north by Umbagog, Richardson, and Mooselookmeguntic lakes of the Rangeley Lakes chain; and on the east by ME 17. Grafton Notch, in the heart of this area, lies between Old Speck (4180 ft.) on the west and Baldpate Mountain (3780 ft.) on the east. It is traversed by ME 26.

The Mahoosuc Range, which appears on the Mahoosuc Range map that comes with this guide, extends southwest from Old Speck across the Maine/New Hampshire line to Mt. Hayes near Gorham NH. As the crow fly, the range is about 17 mi. long, but it is nearly 30 mi. long by trail. Mt. Goose Eye (3870 ft.) and Mahoosuc Notch are among the many interesting features of the Mahoosuc Range. Both lie on the Maine side of the border, but the usual access is via the Mahoosuc Trail, which involves overnight camping, or via trails from Success Pond Rd., which leads east from Berlin NH to ME 26 north of Grafton Notch.

Rumford Whitecap (2200 ft.) is the most popular of the low range of mountains lying between Andover and Rumford.

To provide detailed descriptions of alternative approaches from the west to the trails in the Mahoosuc Range, this guide incorporates relevant trail descriptions from the Mahoosuc Range Area section of the latest edition of the AMC White Mountain Guide. In addition to the map in this guide, refer to the USGS Old Speck and Gorham NH/ME quadrangles, 15-min. series; Old Speck Mtn., Puzzle Mtn., Shelburne, and Success Pond quadrangles, 7.5-min. series; or map 7 in the MATC's *Appalachian Trail Guide to Maine.*

Grafton Notch State Park

Grafton Notch State Park contains 3132 acres extending on both sides of ME 26, west and north, from the Newry–Grafton town line to about 1.5 mi. north of the Appalachian Trail crossing. It includes the summit and northeastern slopes of Old Speck and the lowest western and southwestern slopes of Baldpate, including Table Rock.

The area is now a major hiking center. In addition to the mountain trails, short, graded trails and paths lead from some parking areas to points of interest nearby. Water and toilet facilities are available at Screw Auger Falls and Spruce Meadow Picnic area from May 15 to October 15. *Note: There is no camping in the park.*

Scenic Areas and Short Walks

Step Falls. At the lower (southern) end of Grafton Notch, a short trail from the east side of the road leads 0.6 mi. to Step Falls, a series of cascades, with a total drop of 250 ft. The falls are on Wight Brook, which drains the southeastern slope of Baldpate Mtn. The area is a Nature Conservancy reservation. The parking area is 7.9 mi. north on ME 26 from the junction of US 2 and ME 26 and is on the right side of ME 26. A small sign indicates Wight Brook; the parking area is on the right just before ME 26 crosses Wight Brook.

Screw Auger Falls and the Jail. A mile north of the road sign marking the park entrance and on the left side is the parking area and picnic tables for Screw Auger Falls. Screw Auger Falls plunges 20 ft. over a granite ledge. Below the ledge, the Bear River travels through a series of cascades, past large potholes, shallow pools, and grottoes. There is a natural bridge where the side of a large pothole has been breached. There is a well defined path with guard rails of about 0.1 mi. that may be taken to see the falls. A small access fee is charged. The Jail, a large pothole, is not visible from the road, and nothing marks its location, but you can find it easily by entering the woods to the south (left) of the highway about 100 yd. east of the first highway bridge above Screw Auger Falls. To reach the Jail from below, enter the woods about 150–200 yd. farther east of the bridge and go south to the brook. Follow the brook upstream to a falls. The Jail is on the right (north) bank.

Mother Walker Falls and Moose Cave. Mother Walker Falls are 1.1 mi. north of Screw Auger Falls. There is a parking area on the right side of ME 26. Mother Walker Falls, a series of cascades with a total drop of 100 ft., located in a gorge. There is a short trail that leads to an overlook at the lower end of the falls. Moose Cave, a narrow and deep flume, is about 0.8 mi. farther north and 0.7 mi. south of the Old Speck Trail (Appalachian Trail). From the parking lot, a trail goes down about 0.1 mi. through the woods to the gorge that is 600 ft long and 50 ft. deep. Large slabs of rock have fallen from the hillside and are in the gorge, and in places the stream completely disappears under them. There is an excellent view of Table Rock from the highway at this point.

Grafton Notch Parking Area. Near the height-of-land 2.7 mi. northwest of Screw Auger Falls and about 12 mi. north of US 2, there is a Maine Department of Parks and Recreation parking area (sign reading Hiking Trails) on the left (west) side of ME 26. All trails on Old Speck and Baldpate Mtn. leave from this point. The Appalachian Trail crosses ME 26 at this point.

Spruce Meadow Picnic Area. The Spruce Meadow Picnic Area is approximately 1 mi. farther north on ME 26 and offers outstanding views down the Notch. It also provides excellent facilities for picnicking.

Old Speck (4180 ft.)

Old Speck, so named to distinguish it from the Speckled mountains in Stoneham and Peru, dominates the western side of Grafton Notch. Long thought to be the second-highest peak in the state, after Hamlin Peak on Katahdin, Old Speck has now yielded that honor to Sugarloaf Mtn. and ranks third. There is an open observation tower on the wooded summit. Refer to the Mahoosuc Range map with this guide; the USGS Old Speck quadrangle, 15-min. series; or the Old Speck Mtn. quadrangle, 7.5-min. series.

Old Speck Trail (map 7: C3)

This trail, part of the Appalachian Trail and blazed in white, ascends Old Speck Mtn. from a well-signed parking area on ME 26 at the height-of-land in Grafton Notch. From the northern side of the parking lot, follow the left trail (the right trail goes to Baldpate Mtn.). In 0.1 mi., the Eyebrow Trail leaves right to circle over the top of an 800-ft. cliff shaped like an eyebrow and rejoins the Old Speck Trail. The Old Speck Trail crosses a brook and soon begins to climb, following a series of switchbacks, to approach the falls on Cascade Brook. Above the falls, the trail, now heading more north, crosses the brook for the last time (last available water). At 1.1 mi., it passes the upper terminus of the Eyebrow Trail on the right. The main trail bears left and ascends gradually to the northern ridge, where it bears more left and follows the ridge, which has occasional views southwest. High up, the trail turns southeast toward the summit, and at 3.1 mi., the Link Trail, which is no longer maintained, diverges left. The Old Speck Trail turns more south and ascends to the Mahoosuc Trail, where it ends. The flat, wooded summit of Old Speck, where an observation tower affords fine views and a recently cleared summit plateau affords views in all directions, is 0.3 mi. left (east); the Speck Pond Shelter is located 1.1 mi. to the right.

Distances from ME 26

> *to* Eyebrow Trail, upper junction: 1.1 mi., 1 hr. 5 min.
>
> *to* Link Trail (not maintained): 3.1 mi., 2 hr. 40 min.
>
> *to* Mahoosuc Trail: 3.5 mi., 3 hr. 10 min.
>
> *to* Old Speck summit (via Mahoosuc Trail): 3.8 mi., 3 hr. 20 min.

Eyebrow Trail (map 7: C3)

The Eyebrow Trail provides an alternative route to the lower part of the Old Speck Trail, passing along the edge of the cliff called the Eyebrow that overlooks Grafton Notch. The trail leaves the Old Speck Trail on the right 0.1 mi. from the parking area off ME 26. It turns right at the base of a rock face, crosses a rockslide (potentially dangerous if icy), then turns sharply left and ascends steadily, bearing right where a side path leaves straight ahead for an outlook. Soon the trail runs at a moderate grade along the top of the cliff, with good views, then descends to an outlook and runs mostly level until it ends at the Old Speck Trail.

Distance from Old Speck Trail, lower junction

> *to* Old Speck Trail, upper junction: 1.2 mi., 1 hr. 10 min.

Speck Pond Trail (AMC) (map 7: C3)

This trail ascends to Speck Pond from Success Pond Rd.; take the right fork of the road 11.4 mi. from Hutchins St. and continue 0.8 mi. to the trailhead. The trail leaves the road, enters the woods, and follows the northern side of a small brook for 1.4 mi. It then swings left away from the brook, climbing steeply at times; passes a relatively level section; then climbs steeply to a junction at 3.1 mi. with the May Cutoff, which diverges right and leads over the true summit of Mahoosuc Arm to the Mahoosuc Trail. The Speck Pond Trail passes an excellent outlook over the pond and up to Old Speck, then descends steeply to the pond and reaches the campsite and the Mahoosuc Trail.

Distance from branch of Success Pond Rd.

> *to* Speck Pond Campsite: 3.6 mi., 3 hr.

May Cutoff (AMC) (map 7: C3)

This short trail runs 0.3 mi. (10 min.) from the Speck Pond Trail to the Mahoosuc Trail, across the probable true summit of Mahoosuc Arm, with only minor ups and downs.

Mount Goose Eye (3870 ft.)

Mt. Goose Eye in Riley shares a common trailhead with Mt. Carlo (see below) and makes possible a very interesting loop hike.

Notch Trail (AMC) (map 7: C2)

This trail ascends to the southwestern end of Mahoosuc Notch, providing the easiest access to this wild and beautiful place. It begins on a spur road that leaves Success Pond Rd. 10.9 mi. from Hutchins St. and runs 0.3 mi. to a small parking area. The trail continues on the spur road across two bridges, then turns left (sign) onto an old logging road at 0.3 mi. It ascends easily along a slow-running brook with many signs of beaver activity, following logging roads much of the way with bypasses at some of the wetter spots. At the height-of-land, it meets the Mahoosuc Trail; turn left to traverse the notch. Very soon after entering the Mahoosuc Trail, the valley, which has been ordinary, changes sharply to a chamber formation, and the high cliffs of the notch, not visible earlier on the Notch Trail, come into sight.

Distance from spur road off Success Pond Rd.

   to Mahoosuc Trail: 2.2 mi., 1 hr. 30 min.

Wright Trail (MBPL) (map 7: C2)

This Maine Bureau of Public Lands trail, rated strenuous or difficult, provides access to Goose Eye Mtn. and the Mahoosuc Range via a scenic route from the east that begins in a place known as Ketchum, located on a branch of the Sunday River. The upper part of the trail has two separate branches that make possible a loop hike; the north branch passes through old-growth forest and a small glacial cirque, while the south branch follows a scenic ridge. To reach the trailhead, leave US 2 2.8 mi. north of Bethel ME and follow Sunday River Rd. At a fork at 2.2 mi. bear right onto Ketchum Rd. (no sign), and follow it past Artist Covered Bridge (left) at 3.8 mi. from US 2. At 6.5 mi. the road becomes gravel.

At 7.8 mi. turn left across the two steel bridges, then take the first right, which is Bull Branch Rd. (no sign). At 9.3 mi. Goose Eye Brook is crossed on a bridge, and at 9.5 mi. from US 2 there is a small parking area on the left with signs.

The blue-blazed trail leaves the south side of the parking area and runs toward Goose Eye Brook, then follows its north side upstream past several large pools and a 30-ft. gorge. At 0.5 mi. it makes a left turn onto a woods road and follows it for 0.2 mi., then makes a right turn onto an older road. At 0.9 mi. it bears left off the road and descends gradually 100 yd. to Goose Eye Brook at its confluence with a tributary, where it bears right and follows the tributary for 0.1 mi., then turns sharp left and crosses it. From this point the trail roughly follows the north side of Goose Eye Brook until it reaches the junction of the two parts of the loop at 2.5 mi.

North Branch. The north branch continues a gradual ascent on an old logging road along Goose Eye Brook for 0.2 mi., crossing it twice, then bears right and climbs moderately up away from the floor of the small glacial cirque in which Goose Eye Brook originates. It passes beneath several large rock slabs, then at 3.0 mi. comes out on an open ledge from which the whole cirque is visible. The trail descends from this ledge, crosses Goose Eye Brook, and climbs a steep and rough slope with a number of wooden steps along Goose Eye Brook, crossing the stream six more times. Finally it reaches the ridgecrest and descends gradually for 100 yd. to the jct. with the Mahoosuc Trail at 4.0 mi. For the south branch of the Wright Trail, follow the Mahoosuc Trail south for 0.3 mi., switchbacking up the ledgy East Peak of Mt. Goose Eye and descending the other side of the peak to the jct. in the col. From this point the West Peak (main summit) of Mt. Goose Eye can be reached in 0.4 mi. by following the Mahoosuc Trail (southbound) and the Goose Eye Trail.

South Branch. The south branch immediately crosses Goose Eye Brook and starts its climb, gradually at first and then moderately by switchbacks with rough sections and wooden steps, to the ridgecrest at 3.1 mi. At 3.4 mi., after a rough ascent, it reaches an open spot, then descends slightly back into the woods. It then resumes a rough ascent on ledges to an open knob with beautiful views at 3.6 mi. The trail continues along the ridge with several open areas and occasional minor descents to cross small sags, then finally climbs moderately to the Mahoosuc Trail in the small gap between the East Peak and the West Peak (main summit) of Mt. Goose Eye at 4.4 mi. The main summit can be reached in 0.4 mi. by following the Mahoosuc Trail to the left (southbound) and then the Goose Eye Trail. The upper end of the north branch of the Wright Trail is on the far side of the steep, ledgy East Peak, 0.3 mi. to the right (northbound) via the Mahoosuc Trail.

Distances from parking area on Bull Branch Rd.

   to loop junction: 2.5 mi., 1 hr. 35 min.

   to Mahoosuc Trail via north branch: 4.0 mi., 3 hr. 5 min.

   to Mahoosuc Trail via south branch: 4.4 mi., 3 hr. 25 min.

   Complete loop with side trip to West Peak of Mt. Goose Eye via Mahoosuc Trail and Goose Eye Trail: 9.5 mi., 6 hr. 10 min.

Goose Eye Trail (AMC) (map 7: C2)

This trail ascends Goose Eye Mtn. from Success Pond Rd., starting in common with the Carlo Col Trail 8.1 mi. from Hutchins St., and reaches the Mahoosuc Trail 0.1 mi. beyond the summit. This is a generally easy trail to a very scenic summit. The lower part of the trail must be followed with care through logged areas. From the road, the two trails follow a broad logging road, and in 100 yd., where the Carlo Col Trail continues straight ahead the Goose Eye Trail diverges sharply left down an embankment. It then turns sharply right onto another logging road. The Goose Eye Trail follows the logging road, crosses two brooks, and enters a more recent gravel road that comes in from the right (descending, bear right). In 100 yd., it diverges right (watch carefully for sign) from the gravel road, passes through a clear-cut area, crosses a wet section, and, at 1.4 mi., reaches the yellow-blazed Maine–New Hampshire state line. The trail angles up the southern side of a ridge at a moderate grade through hardwoods, climbs more steeply uphill, then becomes gradual at the crest of the ridge; at 2.6 mi., there is a glimpse of the peak of Goose Eye ahead. The trail ascends moderately along the northern side of the ridge, then steeply: the main path now bypasses the scramble up a difficult ledge and soon comes out on the open ledges below the summit. From the summit, which has magnificent views in all directions, the trail descends steeply and roughly over ledges 0.1 mi. to the Mahoosuc Trail, which turns right (southbound) and runs straight ahead (northbound).

Distances from Success Pond Rd.

   to Goose Eye summit: 3.1 mi., 2 hr. 40 min.

   to Mahoosuc Trail: 3.2 mi., 2 hr. 45 min.

Mount Carlo (3562 ft.)

Mt. Carlo, in Riley, can be climbed from a common trailhead with the Goose
Eye Trail on Success Pond Rd., 8.5 mi. from Berlin NH and 11.5 mi. from
ME 26.

Carlo Col Trail (AMC) (map 7: C2)

This trail ascends to the Mahoosuc Trail at the small box ravine called Carlo
Col; it leaves Success Pond Rd. in common with the Goose Eye Trail 8.1 mi.
from Hutchins St. The lower part of the trail must be followed with care
through logged areas. From the road, the two trails follow a broad logging
road. In 100 yd., the Goose Eye Trail diverges sharply left down an embankment, while the Carlo Col Trail continues straight ahead on the road, which it
follows east for 0.8 mi. with little gain in elevation. Turning left off the road at
a log yard, the trail immediately crosses the main brook (may be difficult at
high water), continues near it for about 0.3 mi., then turns left away from the
brook and follows a branch road with a steeper grade. It swings back to the
south, crossing over the north and south branches of the main brook, and bends
east up the rather steep southern bank of the south branch. Avoiding several
false crossings of the brook, it climbs to the Carlo Col Shelter at 2.4 mi. (last
water, perhaps, for several miles). The trail continues up the dry ravine and
ends at the Mahoosuc Trail at Carlo Col. There is a fine outlook ledge a short
distance to the right (southwest) on the Mahoosuc Trail.

Distance from Success Pond Rd.

  to Mahoosuc Trail: 2.7 mi., 2 hr. 5 min.

Mount Success (3565 ft.)

Mt. Success, in Success NH (reached also from Shelburne on the south via the
Austin Brook and Mahoosuc trails), is accessible from Success Pond Rd., 5.5
mi. from Berlin NH and 14.5 mi. from ME 26.

Success Trail (AMC) (map 7: B2)

This trail ascends to the Mahoosuc Trail 0.6 mi. north of Mt. Success from
Success Pond Rd. 5.4 mi. from Hutchins St. Note that the trail sign is easy to

miss and the lower part of the trail must be followed with care through logged areas. The trail follows a logging road, bears right at a fork (sign) at 0.2 mi., and passes straight through a clearing, entering the woods at a sign in 0.5 mi. Here the trail runs along the bank of an old eroded roadbed, then begins to climb at a moderate grade along an old woods road. At 1.4 mi., it reaches the upper edge of an area of small second-growth trees, swings right, and ascends steeply along an eroded streambed, where care must be taken due to slippery rocks. At 1.6 mi., a loop path 0.3 mi. long diverges right to a spectacular ledge outlook with fine views of the Presidentials and the mountains of the North Country. In a little over 100 yd., the upper end of the loop path rejoins, and the main trail ascends to a ridgecrest, from which it descends to a brook (unreliable water source) at an old logging camp site. The trail soon enters a wet, boggy area, climbs over a small ridge, passes through another boggy area, and then makes a short steep ascent to the Mahoosuc Trail at the main ridgecrest.

Distances from Success Pond Rd.

to Mahoosuc Trail: 2.4 mi., 2 hr.

to Success summit (via Mahoosuc Trail): 3 mi., 2 hr. 30 min.

Austin Brook Trail (AMC) (map 7: B1)

This trail ascends to the Mahoosuc Trail at Gentian Pond from North Rd., 0.6 mi. west of Meadow Rd. (which crosses the Androscoggin at Shelburne village). There is limited parking on the south side of the road. The trail passes through a turnstile on private land and follows the western side of Austin Brook, crossing the Yellow Trail at 0.4 mi. The trail follows logging roads along the brook, then crosses it and reaches gravel Mill Brook Rd. at 1.1 mi. (Austin Brook and Mill Brook are different names for the same stream.) This gravel road leaves North Rd. 0.5 mi. east of the Austin Brook Trail trailhead and just west of the jct. with Meadow Rd; this road may be gated at North Rd. or it may be possible to drive in for 1.6 mi. to a turnout on the right just before a brook crossing, a point 0.3 mi above where the trail enters the road. From the point where the trail enters the road, it turn left onto the road and follows it past the parking spot and the brook mentioned above at 1.4 mi., bears right at a fork in another 0.1 mi., and bears left at a fork at 2.1 mi. At 2.5 mi. the Dryad Fall Trail diverges left. Here the Austin Brook Trail turns right; markings must be followed carefully through logged areas as the trail climbs to a plateau and at

3.1 mi., the trail crosses the brook that drains Gentian Pond in an area of beaver activity where the trail may be flooded. It then swings left and climbs steeply to the Mahoosuc Trail at the Gentian Pond Shelter.

Distance from North Rd.

> *to*   Dryad Fall Trail: 2.5 mi., 1 hr. 40 min.
>
> *to*   Gentian Pond Campsite: 3.5 mi., 2 hr. 30 min.

Lary Flume (map 7: B1)

This is a wild chasm in the southern slope of the Mahoosuc Range that resembles the Ice Gulch and Devils Hopyard, with many boulder caves and one fissure cave. There is no trail, but experienced climbers have followed the brook, which can be reached by going east where the Austin Brook Trail begins its last 0.5 mi. of ascent to Gentian Pond.

Dryad Fall Trail (AMC) (map 7: B1)

This trail runs from the Austin Brook Trail to the Peabody Brook Trail near Dream Lake, passing Dryad Fall, one of the highest cascades in the mountains. Dryad is particularly interesting for a few days after a rainstorm, since its several cascades fall at least 300 ft. over steep ledges. The trail is blazed in yellow.

The trail leaves the Austin Brook Trail on the left 2.5 mi. from North Rd., where that trail turns right. The trail immediately crosses a brook and follows an old woods road, climbing gradually across the slope. At 0.4 mi. a spur trail descends left to the bottom of the falls and provides an outlook. *Caution: Rocks in the vicinity of the falls are very slippery and hazardous.* From here, the trail climbs steeply northeast of the falls. At 0.6 mi., it turns right, away from the falls, then turns left onto an old road and comes back to the top of the falls. The trail follows the brook above the falls then it turns left on another road and crosses Dryad Brook at 0.8 mi., then climbs at mostly moderate grades to the Peabody Brook Trail near Dream Lake 0.1 mi. east of the Mahoosuc Trail. (Descending, watch carefully for the junction where the trail turns down steeply to the right off the logging road above the falls.)

Distances from Austin Brook Trail

> *to*   spur trail to Dryad Fall and view: 0.4 mi., 20 min.
>
> *to*   Peabody Brook Trail: 1.5mi., 1 hr. 30 min.

Peabody Brook Trail (AMC) (map 7: B1)

This trail ascends to the Mahoosuc Trail at Dream Lake from North Rd., 1.3 mi. east of US 2. Park on the shoulder of the road, taking care not to block any driveways. Overnight parking is not permitted at the base of this trail.

The trail follows a logging road between two houses, soon bears right at a fork, crosses Peabody Brook, and turns right onto an old logging road at 0.5 mi. It continues north along the brook and bears left at a fork at 0.8 mi., soon becomes a footpath, and begins to ascend moderately. At 1.2 mi., a path leaves left and leads, in 0.3 mi., to Giant Falls. The main trail rises more steeply, and at 1.5 mi., you will see a glimpse of Mt. Washington and Mt. Adams through open trees. The trail climbs a short ladder just beyond. Care must be taken traversing in this area where a slide has occurred. At 2.1 mi., it crosses the eastern branch of the brook, then recrosses it at 2.4 mi. From here, the trail climbs easily to Dream Lake and the jct. on the right with the Dryad Fall Trail at 3 mi., then continues along the southeast shore of the lake, with views across the water to the Presidential Range, to the Mahoosuc Trail.

Distance from North Rd.

   to Mahoosuc Trail: 3.1 mi., 2 hr. 30 min.

Centennial Trail (AMC) (map 7: A1–B1)

This trail, part of the Appalachian Trail, begins on Hogan Rd.; this dirt road turns west from North Rd. north of where it crosses the Androscoggin River, just before it swings abruptly to the east. There is a small parking area 0.2 mi. from North Rd., and parking is also permitted at the jct. of North Rd. and Hogan Rd.; in either case, do not block the road. The Centennial Trail was constructed by the AMC in 1976, its centennial year.

From the parking area on Hogan Rd., the trail runs generally northwest. After 50 yd. on an old road, it bears left up a steep bank into the woods, levels off, and reaches the first of many stone steps in 0.1 mi. The trail ascends rather steeply, then more gradually, with a limited view of the Androscoggin River. It turns left onto a woods road and crosses a brook at 0.7 mi. (last water). The trail then crosses a logging road and climbs past several restricted viewpoints, then descends to a sag in a birch grove at 1.6 mi. Climbing again, it soon turns sharply left and continues upward past ledges that provide increasingly open views. At 2.8 mi., the trail reaches an easterly summit of Mt. Hayes, where there is an excellent view of the Carter–Moriah Range and northern Presidentials from open ledges. The trail descends slightly, then ascends across a series of open ledges to end at the Mahoosuc Trail at 3.1 mi. The summit of Mt. Hayes, with fine views, is 0.2 mi. left; the Appalachian Trail turns right (north) on the Mahoosuc Trail.

Distance from Hogan Rd.

   to   Mahoosuc Trail: 3.1 mi., 2 hr. 30 min.

Mahoosuc Range Area

This section includes the region along the Maine/New Hampshire border from Lake Umbagog southward to the big loop of the Androscoggin River from Gorham to Bethel. The area is drained principally by this river and its branches.

The Mahoosuc Trail extends the entire length of the Mahoosuc Range, from Gorham to Old Speck, and there are many side trails. All of the trails in this section are east of NH 16, north of US 2, and west of ME 26.

Grafton Notch State Park includes the highway corridor of ME 26 and the summit of Old Speck. The remainder of the ridgecrest, followed by the Appalachian Trail from the Maine/New Hampshire boundary to Dunn Notch, passes through Maine Public Reserve Land.

In 1976, the state of Maine negotiated an exchange of land with the Brown Paper Company, which had owned most of the Mahoosuc Range summits. The state gave up rights in public lots and lands in various townships along the Mahoosuc Range extending west and south from the boundary of Grafton Notch State Park.

State laws restrict wood and charcoal fires to designated sites (shelters and Trident Col).

Access Roads

Success Pond Road. This road runs from the eastern side of the Androscoggin River in Berlin NH to Success Pond in about 14 mi., and continues to ME 26 north of Grafton Notch. Over the years, this has been perhaps the most difficult road in the White Mountains for someone unfamiliar with the region to find; important landmarks have disappeared or changed, and the first section of the road itself was moved with astounding but unpredictable regularity. However, it now appears that the situation has become sufficiently stable to give cause for hope, though even at the best of times, following Success Pond Rd. requires a good deal of care and often some trial and error. To find it, leave NH 16 just south of the city of Berlin, 4.5 mi. north of the eastern jct. of US 2 and NH 16 in Gorham, and cross the Androscoggin on the Cleveland Bridge. At the eastern end of the bridge, the road (Unity St.) swings left and passes straight through a set of traffic lights in 0.7 mi. from NH 16. At 0.8 mi., the road bears right across railroad tracks and becomes Hutchins St. It turns sharply left at 1.6 mi. at Frank's Village Store and continues past the mill yard. At 1.9 mi. from NH 16, where there has usually been a large sign reading OHRV Parking 1 Mile, Success Pond Rd. begins on the right (east). It no longer winds among the huge wood piles of the mill yard, but you should still watch out for large trucks, especially those entering from the right. The first part of the road has frequently been difficult to distinguish from branch roads, but once you are past this area, it is well defined—though it is often easy to take a dead-end branch road by mistake. The road is not generally open to public vehicular use in winter, and it can be very rough and muddy, particularly in spring and early summer before yearly maintenance is carried out. Trailheads are marked only with small AMC standard trail signs, often at old diverging logging roads with no well-defined parking area, so you must look for them carefully. The lower parts of the trails originating on this road have been disrupted frequently in the past by construction of new logging roads; great care is necessary to follow the blazes that mark the proper roads, ascending or descending.

Success Pond Rd. leaves ME 26 southwesterly about 2.8 mi. north of the Old Speck trailhead in Grafton Notch.

Distances from ME 26

- *to* Speck Pond Trail, marked by a blue blaze and sign on low post, leaves left at about 7.0 mi.
- *to* Notch Trail spur road (sign), about 8.5 mi.
- *to* Carlo Col/Goose Eye trailhead, about 11.5 mi. (signs)
- *to* Success Trail (unmarked), about 14.0 mi.
- *to* Hutchins St., Berlin NH, about 20.0 mi.

North Road. This road provides access to the trails on the southern side of the Mahoosuc Range. It leaves US 2 about 2.8 mi. east of its easterly jct. with NH 16 in Gorham, and crosses the Androscoggin River on the Lead Mine Bridge; the Appalachian Trail follows this part of the road. North Rd. then swings east and runs along the northern side of the river to rejoin US 2 just north of Bethel ME. Bridges connect North Rd. with US 2 at the villages of Shelburne NH and Gilead ME.

Mahoosuc Trail (AMC/MDP) (map 7: A1–C3)

This trail extends along the entire length of the Mahoosuc Range from Gorham NH to the summit of Old Speck. Beyond its jct. with the Centennial Trail, the Mahoosuc Trail is a link in the Appalachian Trail. Camping is limited to the tentsites at Trident Col and to the four shelters: Gentian Pond, Carlo Col, Full Goose, and Speck Pond (all of which also have tentsites). These sites may have a caretaker, in which case a fee is charged. Some of these shelters are slated for removal, but the tentsites will remain. Water is scarce, particularly in dry weather, and its purity is always in question. Do not be deceived by the relatively low elevations; this trail is among the most rugged of its kind in the White Mtns., a very strenuous trail—particularly for those with heavy packs—with numerous minor humps and cols, and many ledges, some of them quite steep, that are likely to be slippery when wet. Many parts of the trail may require significantly more time than that provided by the formula, particularly for backpackers, and Mahoosuc Notch may require several extra hours, depending in part on how much time one spends enjoying the spectacular scenery. Mahoosuc Notch is regarded by many who have hiked the entire length of the Appalachian Trail as its most difficult mile. *Caution: Mahoosuc Notch can be hazardous in wet or icy conditions and can remain impassable due to unmelted snowdrifts through the end of May and perhaps even longer.*

Part I. Gorham to Centennial Trail. To reach the trail, cross the Androscoggin River by the footbridge under the Boston & Maine Railroad bridge, 1.3 mi. north of the Gorham Post Office on NH 16. On the east bank, follow the road to the right (southeast) along the river for 0.4 mi., then cross the canal through the open upper level of the powerhouse (left of entrance). At the east end of the dam, keep straight ahead about 100 yd. to the woods, where the trail sign will be found. The trail is sparsely blazed in blue. Turn left and follow an old road north along the side of the canal for 0.1 mi., then turn right uphill on an old logging road. At 0.8 mi. from NH 16 the trail crosses a power-line clearing, then bears right and reaches but does not cross a brook, following it closely for 100 yd. Avoid side paths from recent logging operations. The trail ascends at only a slight grade to a side path at 1.1 mi. that leads right 0.2 mi. to

Mascot Pond, just below the cliffs seen prominently from Gorham. The Mahoosuc Trail crosses a woods road, then ascends the valley of a brook, which it crosses several times. At 2.5 mi. it passes a short spur (sign) that leads left to Popsy Spring, then climbs steeply and emerges on the southwest side of the flat, ledgy summit of Mt. Hayes. An unmarked footway leads a few yards right to the best viewpoint south over the valley. A cairn marks the true summit of Mt. Hayes at 3.1 mi. The trail descends on open ledges with good views north to the junction on the right with the Centennial Trail at 3.2 mi.

Part II. Centennial Trail to Gentian Pond. From here north, the Mahoosuc Trail is part of the Appalachian Trail, marked with white blazes. It descends north to the col between Mt. Hayes and Cascade Mtn. at 4.1 mi., where there is sometimes water. The trail then ascends Cascade Mtn. by a southwest ridge over ledges and large fallen rocks, emerging on the bare summit ledge at 5.1 mi. It turns back sharply into the woods, descending gradually with occasional slight ascents to the east end of the mountain, then enters a fine forest and descends rapidly beside cliffs and ledges to Trident Col at 6.3 mi., where a side path leads left 0.2 mi. to Trident Col Tentsite. Water is available about 50 yd. below (west of) the site. The bare ledges of the rocky cone to the east of Trident Col repay the effort required to scramble to its top; a route ascends between two large cairns near the tentsite side path.

The trail descends rather steeply to the southeast and runs along the side of the ridge at the base of the Trident, which is made up of the previously mentioned cone, the ledgy peak just west of Page Pond, and a somewhat less prominent peak between them. The trail crosses several small brooks, at least one of which usually has water. It follows a logging road for 0.1 mi., then turns left off the road at a sign and ascends to Page Pond at 7.3 mi., where beaver activity may cause wet conditions. The trail passes the south end of the pond, crosses a beaver dam, and climbs gradually, then more steeply, to a short spur path at 7.9 mi. that leads left to a fine outlook from ledges near the summit of Wocket Ledge, a shoulder of Bald Cap. The main trail crosses the height-of-land and descends east, crosses the upper (west) branch of Peabody Brook, then climbs around the nose of a small ridge and descends gradually to the head of Dream Lake. The trail bears left here, then bears right to run around the north end of the lake, and crosses the inlet brook at 9.0 mi. Just beyond, the Peabody Brook Trail leaves on the right.

From this jct., the Mahoosuc Trail follows a lumber road left for 100 yd. It soon recrosses the inlet brook, passes over a slight divide into the watershed of

Austin Brook, ascends through some swampy places, and descends to Moss Pond at 10.5 mi. It continues past the north shore of the pond and follows an old logging road down the outlet brook, then crosses the brook, turns abruptly right downhill from the logging road, and descends to Gentian Pond. It skirts the northeast shore of the pond, then crosses the inlet stream. A few yards beyond, at 11.2 mi., is Gentian Pond Campsite (shelter and tentsites), and here the Austin Brook Trail diverges right for North Rd. in Shelburne.

Part III. Gentian Pond to Carlo Col. From Gentian Pond Shelter the trail climbs to the top of the steep-sided hump whose ledges overlook the pond from the east, then descends moderately to a sag. It then starts up the west end of Mt. Success, climbing rather steeply at first to the lumpy ridge, and passes a small stream at 12.6 mi. in the col that lies under the main mass of Mt. Success. The trail now climbs rather steeply and roughly for about 0.5 mi. to the relatively flat upper part of the mountain, then ascends over open ledges with an outlook to the southwest, passes through a belt of high scrub, crosses an alpine meadow, and finally comes out on the summit of Mt. Success at 14.0 mi.

The trail turns sharp left here and descends through scrub, then forest, to the sag between Mt. Success and a northern subpeak, where the Success Trail enters left at 14.6 mi. The main trail climbs slightly, then descends moderately to the main col between Mt. Success and Mt. Carlo at 15.3 mi. The trail then rises over a low hump and descends to a lesser col, where it turns right, then left, passes the Maine–New Hampshire border signs, and ascends moderately again. At 16.4 mi. it drops sharply past a fine outlook ledge into the little box ravine called Carlo Col. The Carlo Col Trail from Success Pond Rd. enters left here; Carlo Col Campsite is located 0.3 mi. down the Carlo Col Trail, at the head of a small brook.

Part IV. Carlo Col to Mahoosuc Notch. From Carlo Col the trail climbs steadily to the bare southwest summit of Mt. Carlo at 16.8 mi., where there is an excellent view. It then passes a lower knob to the northeast, descends through a mountain meadow—where there is a fine view of Goose Eye ahead—and reaches the col at 17.4 mi. The trail turns more north and climbs steeply to a ledgy knoll below Goose Eye, then passes through a sag and climbs steeply again to the narrow ridge of the main peak of Goose Eye Mtn. at 18.2 mi. Use care on the ledges.

Here, at the ridge top, the Goose Eye Trail branches sharp left, reaching the open summit and its spectacular views in 0.1 mi. and continuing to Success

Pond Rd. From the ridge-top jct. the Mahoosuc Trail turns sharp right (east) and follows the ridgecrest through mixed ledge and scrub to a col at 18.5 mi., where it meets the south branch of the Wright Trail to Bull Branch Rd. in Ketchum ME. The Mahoosuc Trail then climbs steeply through woods and open areas to the bare summit of the East Peak of Goose Eye Mtn. Here it turns north and switchbacks downhill through scrub, meeting the north branch of the Wright Trail at 18.8 mi. Beyond the col the trail runs in the open nearly to the foot of the North Peak, except for two box ravines, where there is often water. At the summit of the North Peak, at 19.8 mi., the trail turns sharp right (east) along the ridgecrest, then swings northeast down the steep slope, winding through several patches of scrub. At the foot of the steep slope it enters the woods and angles down the west face of the ridge to the col at 20.8 mi. Full Goose Campsite is located on a ledgy shelf near here; there is a spring 80 yd. to the right (east of the campsite).

The trail then turns sharp left and ascends, coming into the open about 0.3 mi. below the summit of the South Peak of Fulling Mill Mtn., which is reached at 21.3 mi. Here the trail turns sharp left and runs through a meadow. It descends northwest through woods, first gradually, then steeply, to the head of Mahoosuc Notch at 22.3 mi. Here the Notch Trail to Success Pond Rd. diverges sharp left (southwest).

Part V. Mahoosuc Notch to Old Speck. From the head of Mahoosuc Notch the trail turns sharp right (northeast) and descends the length of the narrow notch along a rough footway, passing through a number of boulder caverns, some with narrow openings where progress will be slow and where ice remains into summer. The trail is blazed on the rocks with white paint.

Caution: Great care should be exercised in the notch because of the numerous slippery rocks and dangerous holes. The notch may be impassable through early June because of snow, even with snowshoes. Heavy backpacks will impede progress considerably.

At the lower end of the notch, at 23.4 mi., the trail bears left and ascends moderately but roughly under the east end of Mahoosuc Mtn. along the valley that leads to Notch 2, then crosses to the north side of the brook at 23.9 mi. The trail then winds upward among rocks and ledges on the very steep wooded slope of Mahoosuc Arm with a steep, rough footway. A little more than halfway up, it passes the head of a little flume, in which there is sometimes water. At 25.0 mi., a few yards past the top of the flat ledges near the summit of Mahoosuc Arm, the May Cutoff diverges left and leads 0.3 mi. over the true summit to the Speck Pond Trail. The Mahoosuc Trail swings right and wanders across the semi-open summit plateau for about 0.5 mi., then drops steeply to Speck Pond (3430 ft.), one of the highest ponds in Maine, bordered with thick woods. The trail crosses the outlet brook and continues around the east side of the pond to Speck Pond Campsite at 25.9 mi. (in summer, there is a caretaker and a fee for overnight camping). Here the Speck Pond Trail to Success Pond Rd. leaves on the left.

The trail then climbs to the southeast end of the next hump on the ridge, passes over it, and runs across the east face of a second small hump. In the gully beyond, a few yards east of the trail, there is an unreliable spring. The trail climbs on the west shoulder of Old Speck, reaching an open area where the footway is well defined on the crest. Near the top of the shoulder the trail bears right, re-enters the woods, and follows the wooded crest with blue blazes that mark the boundary of Grafton Notch State Park. The Old Speck Trail, which continues the Appalachian Trail north, diverges left to Grafton Notch at 27.0 mi., and the Mahoosuc Trail runs straight ahead to the summit of Old Speck and its observation tower, where the recently cleared summit offers fine views in all directions. Here the poorly marked East Spur Trail enters.

Distances from NH 16 in Gorham (800 ft.)

   to Mt. Hayes summit (2555 ft.): 3.1 mi., 1750 ft., 2 hr. 25 min.

   to Centennial Trail (2550 ft.): 3.3 mi., 1750 ft., 2 hr. 30 min.

   to Cascade Mtn. summit (2631 ft.): 5.1 mi., 2450 ft., 3 hr. 45 min.

   to Trident Col (2000 ft.): 6.3 mi., 2500 ft., 4 hr. 25 min.

   to Page Pond (2220 ft.): 7.3 mi., 2850 ft., 5 hr. 5 min.

   to Wocket Ledge (2800 ft.): 7.9 mi., 3450 ft., 5 hr. 40 min.

   to Dream Lake, inlet brook crossing (2620 ft.): 9.0 mi., 3650 ft., 6 hr. 20 min.

   to Gentian Pond Campsite (2166 ft.): 11.2 mi., 3850 ft., 7 hr. 30 min.

   to Mt. Success summit (3565 ft.): 14.0 mi., 5750 ft., 9 hr. 55 min.

   to Success Trail (3170 ft.): 14.6 mi., 5750 ft., 10 hr. 10 min.

   to Carlo Col Trail (3170 ft.): 16.4 mi., 6250 ft., 11 hr. 20 min.

   to Mt. Carlo (3565 ft.): 16.8 mi., 6650 ft., 11 hr. 45 min.

   to Goose Eye Trail (3800 ft.): 18.2 mi., 7350 ft., 12 hr. 45 min.

   to Wright Trail, south junction (3620 ft.): 18.5 mi., 7350 ft., 12 hr. 55 min.

to   Goose Eye Mtn., East Peak (3790 ft.): 18.6 mi., 7500 ft., 13 hr. 5 min.

to   Wright Trail, north junction (3450 ft.): 18.8 mi., 7500 ft., 13 hr. 10 min.

to   Goose Eye Mtn., North Peak (3675 ft.): 19.8 mi., 7800 ft., 13 hr. 50 min.

to   Full Goose Campsite (3030 ft.): 20.8 mi., 7800 ft., 14 hr. 20 min.

to   Notch Trail (2460 ft.): 22.3 mi., 8150 ft., 15 hr. 15 min.

to   foot of Mahoosuc Notch (2150 ft.): 23.4 mi., 8150 ft., 15 hr. 45 min.

to   Mahoosuc Arm summit (3770 ft.): 25.0 mi., 9750 ft., 17 hr. 25 min.

to   Speck Pond Campsite (3400 ft.): 25.9 mi., 9750 ft., 17 hr. 50 min.

to   Old Speck Trail junction (4000 ft.): 27.0 mi., 10,550 ft., 18 hr. 45 min.

to   Old Speck Mtn. summit (4170 ft.): 27.3 mi. (43.9 km.), 10,750 ft., 19 hr.

Distances from Old Speck Mtn. summit (4170ft.)

to   Old Speck Trail junction (4000 ft.): 0.3 mi., 0 ft., 10 min.

to   Speck Pond Campsite (3400 ft.): 1.4 mi., 200 ft., 50 min.

to   Mahoosuc Arm summit (3770 ft.): 2.3 mi., 550 ft., 1 hr. 25 min.

to   foot of Mahoosuc Notch (2150 ft.): 3.9 mi., 550 ft., 2 hr. 15 min.

to   Notch Trail (2460 ft.): 5.0 mi., 850 ft., 2 hr. 55 min.

to   Full Goose Campsite (3030 ft.): 6.5 mi., 1800 ft., 4 hr. 10 min.

to   Goose Eye Mtn., North Peak (3675 ft.): 7.5 mi., 2450 ft., 5 hr.

to   Wright Trail, north junction (3450 ft.): 8.5 mi., 2450 ft., 5 hr. 30 min.

to   Goose Eye Mtn., East Peak (3790 ft.): 8.7 mi., 2800 ft., 5 hr. 45 min.

to   Wright Trail, south junction (3620 ft.): 8.8 mi., 2800 ft., 5 hr. 50 min.

to   Goose Eye Trail (3800 ft.): 9.1 mi., 3000 ft., 6 hr. 5 min.

to   Mt. Carlo (3565 ft.): 10.5 mi., 3450 ft., 7 hr.

to   Carlo Col Trail (3170 ft.): 10.9 mi., 3450 ft., 7 hr. 10 min.

to   Success Trail (3170 ft.): 12.7 mi., 3950 ft., 8 hr. 20 min.

to   Mt. Success summit (3565 ft.): 13.3 mi., 4350 ft., 8 hr. 50 min.

to   Gentian Pond Campsite (2166 ft.): 16.1 mi., 4850 ft., 10 hr. 30 min.

to   Dream Lake, inlet brook crossing (2620 ft.): 18.3 mi., 5500 ft., 11 hr. 55 min.

to   Wocket Ledge (2800 ft.): 19.4 mi., 5900 ft., 12 hr. 40 min.

to   Page Pond (2220 ft.): 20.0 mi., 5900 ft., 13 hr.

to Trident Col (2000 ft.): 21.0 mi., 6050 ft., 13 hr. 30 min.

to Cascade Mtn. summit (2631 ft.): 22.2 mi., 6700 ft., 14 hr. 25 min.

to Centennial Trail (2550 ft.): 24.0 mi., 7300 ft., 15 hr. 40 min.

to Mt. Hayes summit (2555 ft.): 24.2 mi., 7300 ft., 15 hr. 45 min.

to NH 16 in Gorham: 27.3 mi., 7300 ft., 17 hr. 20 min.

Baldpate Mountain (East Peak, 3780 ft. and West Peak, 3662 ft.)

Baldpate Mtn., once known as Saddleback and Bear River Whitecap, rises to the east of Grafton Notch. There are two main summits: the fine, open East Peak, and the West Peak. The Appalachian Trail traverses both. Refer to the USGS Old Speck Mountain quadrangle, 15-min. series; the Old Speck quadrangle, 7.5-min. series; AMC Mahoosuc Range; or map 7 in the MATC's *Appalachian Trail Guide to Maine*.

Table Rock Trail (map 7: C3–D3)

The Table Rock Trail, which climbs 900 ft., offers a short, fairly steep, but spectacular climb to the prominent rock ledge on Baldpate Mtn., which is on the eastern side of Grafton Notch. From this ledge, the trail continues onward to rejoin the Appalachian Trail. There is an extensive slab-cave system, possibly the largest in the state, on this trail.

The trail leaves the Appalachian Trail to the right (south) 0.1 mi. from the trailhead on ME 26 (described below). For 0.3 mi. from this jct., the trail rises gently along the side of a hill above a marsh until it reaches a drop-off. From there, it climbs steadily through mature hardwoods and reaches a rocky, caribou moss–covered area called the boulder patch at 0.6 mi. After several switchbacks along rocky ledges, the trail enters a deep ravine between two rock faces. At the top of the ravine, bear right. The trail climbs less steeply to a prominent outlook at 0.8 mi. At 0.9 mi., it reaches the base of the ledges that form Table Rock, where the slab caves begin. *Caution: Be careful if you explore the caves. Some are quite deep, and a fall could mean serious injury.*

On the trail, continue south around the bottom of Table Rock. (On the ledges above, note the weather-formed rock that looks like a shark's fin.) At 1.0 mi., after swinging behind Table Rock, you will meet a blue-blazed trail. Table Rock is 20 yd. to the left.

To the right, the blue-blazed upper Table Rock Trail continues, with only a slight change in elevation, about 0.5 mi. to the Appalachian Trail. Turn right (east) to reach Baldpate; go left (west) to return to the trailhead on ME 26.

Distances from state parking area on ME 26

- *to* start (via Baldpate Mountain Trail): 0.1 mi.
- *to* Table Rock and junction with upper trail: 1.0 mi.
- *to* state parking area, ME 26 (via Baldpate Mountain Trail): 2.4 mi., 1 hr. 45 min.

Baldpate Mountain via Appalachian Trail (map 7: D3)

The Appalachian Trail, which traverses the range, is maintained by the MATC and blazed in white. The following describes approaches from both the west and east.

From Grafton Notch. The trail leaves the northern side of the state-park parking lot on ME 26 (take the trail to the right). It soon crosses ME 26. Then it runs briefly through woods and beside a marsh until, at 0.1 mi., it crosses a brook on a log footbridge. Almost immediately after this crossing, the trail passes the start of the Table Rock Trail, which leaves right. The trail rises gradually on an old woods road. At 0.9 mi., it passes another blue-blazed trail on the right leading to Table Rock. The main trail climbs steadily and then more steeply to the western knob of Baldpate, with good views to the northwest. The trail then slabs the northern side of the knob to a ridge extending toward the West Peak, soon descending to a brook where, at about 2.0 mi., a side trail leads south to the new Baldpate Shelter. Then it climbs steeply over rough terrain to the West Peak which offers vistas in almost all directions. The trail, turning in a more northerly direction, drops only about 240 ft. before climbing to the East Peak nearly a mile beyond. The East Peak is covered with eastern larch krummholz and offers some of the best views of the western Maine mountain and lake country. The east jct. of the Grafton Loop Trail is on the summit. From there, the trail continues to Andover–East B Hill Rd.

From Andover–East B Hill Road. The trail leaves the left (south) side of East B Hill Rd. about 8.0 mi. west of Andover village. It descends from the road, crosses a small brook, then turns south along the edge of a progressively deeper gorge cut by this brook, which it follows for 0.5 mi. before turning west into the mouth of Dunn Notch. At 0.8 mi., the trail crosses the West Branch of the Ellis River (a large stream at this point) at the top of a double waterfall plunging 60 ft. into Dunn Notch. You can reach the bottom of the falls via an old logging road across the stream. (Upstream, you will find a small, rocky gorge and the beautiful upper falls.) The Appalachian Trail crosses the old road and climbs steeply up the eastern rim of the notch. It then climbs moderately to the south.

At 1.3 mi., the trail turns left and climbs gradually through open hardwoods along the edge of the northern arm of Surplus Mtn. At 3.0 mi., it slabs right (southwest) around the nose of Surplus, climbs gently along a broad ridge, and passes near the summit. In another 1.6 mi., it descends steeply over rough ground to the Frye Notch Lean-to, near the head of Frye Brook. From the lean-to, the trail climbs gradually then more steeply, climbing more than 1300 ft. in less than one mile to the open summit of Baldpate's East Peak. The trail then drops down, climbs the West Peak, and descends into Grafton Notch via the trail from the west (described above).

Distances from state parking area on ME 26

>   *to* lower side trail to Table Rock: 0.1 mi., 5 min.

>   *to* upper side trail to Table Rock: 0.9 mi., 45 min.

>   *to* Baldpate, West Peak: 2.9 mi., 2 hr. 30 min.

>   *to* Baldpate, East Peak: 3.8 mi., 3 hr. 10 min.

>   *to* Andover–East B Hill Road: 10.1 mi., 6 hr. 40 min.

Distances from Andover–East B Hill Rd.

>   *to* waterfall: 0.8 mi., 55 min.

>   *to* Frye Notch Lean-to: 4.6 mi., 3 hr.

>   *to* Baldpate, East Peak: 6.3 mi., 4 hr. 30 min.

>   *to* Baldpate, West Peak: 7.2 mi., 5 hr. 15 min.

>   *to* state parking area on ME 26: 10.1 mi., 7 hr.

Grafton Loop Trail (map 7: C3–E3)

The Grafton Loop Trail (GLT) began as a vision of the landowner of Puzzle Mtn. and grew to encompass a large coalition of 20 partners, including the AMC, MATC, private landowners, non-profit organizations, private companies and Federal and state agencies. The goal of the Grafton Loop Trail coalition is to develop multi-day hiking opportunities that offer alternatives to the heavily used sections of the AT. Construction of the eastern section took more than three years (from the AT crossing at East Baldpate, to Puzzle Mtn. and then to ME 26). In addition to the trail itself, five campsites were cleared. These are for tenting camping only and fires are prohibited. The western section is under construction at time of publication, with an anticipated completion date of late 2005, and will link with the AT at Old Speck. Much of the western section trail construction is being done by the AMC. See www.outdoors.org/bookupdates for a trail description upon its opening.

The majority of the GLT crosses private lands owned by families and timber companies who have generously granted public access. Please stay on the trail; don't build campfires, camp only at designated campsites; and practice the Leave No Trace principles.

Directions to the southern trailhead: Travel approximately 4.7 mi. north on ME 26 from US 2 in Newry. At the jct. of Eddy Rd and ME 26, park in the parking area on the right side of ME 26 about 100 yds. from the trailhead. Do not park along ME 26 or Eddy Rd. The trail begins at a post with a blue blaze on it.

Directions to the northern trailhead: The northern trailhead is located on ME 26 in the Grafton Notch parking area about 12 mi. north of US 2 where the AT crosses ME 26.

Eastern Section from the Southern Trailhead. Leaving the parking lot, the trail heads through a young forest, crossing a small brook, then an overgrown logging road. The trail switches back several times along a gradual incline along parts of an old logging road, passing through a healthy area of young spruce and white birch before passing into an area thick with downed balsam fir. The trail continues gradually uphill, utilizing sections of a logging road and switchbacks. The trail is clearly marked with blue blazes and cairns. Avoid turning left onto smaller unmarked paths. At about 2.0 mi. turn lt. and begin a steep climb. The trail at about 2.4 mi. crosses over several exposed granite boulders and ledges offering views of the Sunday River ski area, Grafton Notch, and the distant Presidentials. The trail cuts back into the woods and then passes over a steep boulder staircase and some mild rock scrambling. *Caution: The exposed granite areas are very slippery in wet weather.*

The South Summit of Puzzle Mtn. (3080 ft.) at 3.2 mi. is marked by a large rock cairn. There are excellent views in all directions. At 3.6 mi. the trail summits the rocky ledge top of Puzzle Mtn. (3120 ft.). The mountain is descended on the north by following the cairns. The trail traverses through rolling terrain with a few boulder scrambles and a steel ladder and then goes through an area that includes stands of balsams and paper birches. The trail then descends fairly gradually using some stone staircases. At 4.9 mi. the trail reaches the jct. with the spur trail to the Stewart Campsite. The campsite is 300 ft. down the spur trail and has raised earth tent sites. No open fires are allowed.

After the jct., the trail takes a winding descent via multiple switchbacks and enters an area of young, new growth hardwood. The trail crosses an overgrown road before flattening out as it approaches Chase Hill Brook. Take care to only follow the blue blazes in this area as there are trails blazed in different colors. At 6.3 mi. cross Chase Hill Brook. This crossing may be difficult during times of high water. At the bottom of the mountain (6.7 mi.), the trail intersects an old road. Turn right go 0.25 mi., and re-enter the woods at the cairn on the left side of the road. The trail winds up Long Mountain through new growth hardwood forests, crossing, following, and leaving the logging road several times. The trail eventually leaves the logging road for good and continues through an older forest, comprised largely of spruce and paper birch. The trail contours the ridge in this area, using long, fairly gradual switchbacks with occasional steep climbs. As the trail gains altitude, gaps in the trees afford views of Sunday River ski area and the summit of Mt. Washington. The trail becomes steeper and uses a stone staircase and wooden staircase/ladder to assist with the ascension.

At 9.4 mi, a short spur trail near the summit of Long Mountain goes off to a viewpoint. The trail reaches a high point on Long Mountain at 9.5 mi. The true summit (3021 ft.) is a short distance to the east. Leaving the high point, the trail winds easily downhill, crossing several small streams along the way including the headwaters of Stony Brook. The trail at 10.4 mi. reaches the spur trail (440 ft. long) to the Town Corner Campsite where there are raised earthen tent sites. No open fires are allowed. At 11.1 mi., the trail crosses a snowmobile trail and a log bridge. The trail then descends along a brook to the jct. at 11.9 mi. with the spur to the Knoll Campsite. The 400 ft. spur leads to the raised earth tentsite area. No open fires are allowed. Passing the campsite, the trail follows Wight Brook through a fairly flat area, crossing it several times. In times of high water, it may be difficult to cross Wight Brook.

At 13.2 mi., the spur to the Lane Campsite intersects with the trail. The campsite is on the opposite side of Wight Brook, 435 ft. from the main trail and has raised earthen tent sites. No open fires are allowed. The spur trail continues 400 ft. beyond the campsite to a waterfall that is worthwhile to visit. After the spur trail to the Lane Campsite, the incline on the trail steepens as the trail ascends up to Lightening Ledge. After a short, steep ascent over some boulders, the trail reaches at 14.2, a short spur to Lightening Ledge, which provides clear view of Puzzle Mtn. and the Bear River Valley. In 14.5 mi., the trail reaches the knob of Lightening Ledge (2644 ft.) where there are good views of the Baldpates.

The trail heads back into the woods and descends through a diverse forest with rugged rock faces to the left of the trail. A short, moderately steep downhill descent brings the trail back to Wight Brook and at 14.9 mi. the trail crosses the brook. A short ascent leads to the jct. at 15.0 mi. with the spur trail to the East Baldpate Campsite. The campsite is 300 ft. to the right with raised earthen tent sites. No open fires are allowed. The trail then continues on to the summit passing at 16.4 mi. a huge glacial erratic and reaches the summit at 17.1 mi. The summit of East Baldpate (3812 ft.) is high and clear allowing spectacular views of the mountains and lakes in all directions. The granite surface is laced with alpine shrubs, eastern larch krummholz, delicate mosses and lichen, and fragile flowers. Care needs to be taken to step only on the bare rock surfaces so as to not damage any of the plants. As with all areas above treeline, camping is not permitted and extreme caution should be taken in inclement weather. The GLT joins the AT on the summit for the descent 4.0 mi. down to ME 26 and the Grafton Notch parking area.

Distances from southern trailhead:

> *to* Puzzle Mtn.: 3.2 mi., 3 hr. 30 min.
>
> *to* Stewart Campsite spur trail: 4.9 mi., 4 hr. 30 min.
>
> *to* Long Mtn. spur trail: 9.4 mi., 8 hr. 45 min.
>
> *to* Town Corner Campsite spur trail: 10.4 mi., 9 hr. 30 min.
>
> *to* Knoll Campsite spur trail: 11.9 mi., 10 hr. 15 min.
>
> *to* Lane Campsite sour trail: 13.2 mi., 11 hr.
>
> *to* Knob of Lightening Ledge: 14.5 mi., 12 hr. 15 min.
>
> *to* East Baldpate Campsite spur trail: 15.0 mi., 13 hr.
>
> *to* East Baldpate Summit: 17.1 mi., 16 hr. 30 min.
>
> *to* Grafton Notch parking area ME 26: 21.1 mi., 19 hr. 45 min.

Mount Will (1736 ft.)

The mountain is located in Bethel on the border of Newry. The blue-green-blazed trails are maintained by the Bethel Conservation Commission. The North Ledge trail section goes through the Bethel Town Forest; the rest of the trail is on private land. Refer to the USGS Bethel quadrangle, 7.5 min.-series. The marked trailhead is on the western side of ME 2, 1.9 mi. north of the state rest area, just opposite the Bethel Transfer Station. There is a parking area on the west side (north) of the road.

Not far from the trailhead, the trail divides. The right fork goes up a nature trail to the North Ledges. This section of the trail provides good views of the valley and surrounding mountains from an elevation of 1350 ft. and relatively open ledges. From the North Ledges, the trail proceeds through a series of higher ledges on the way to the South Cliffs. The trail has numerous overlooks of the Androscoggin and Bear valleys north and east. At South Cliffs, there are fully open views south and east. From the cliffs, the trail drops steeply and then more easily back to the jct. and out to ME 2.

Distances from trailhead

> *to* North Ledges (via Nature Trail): 0.75 mi., 45 min.

> *to* South Cliffs: 2.25 mi., 1 hr.

>   Complete loop: 3.25 mi., 2 hr. 30 min.

Rumford Whitecap (2200 ft.)

This mountain is a long, bare-topped ridge in the northwestern part of Rumford. It yields excellent views with relatively little effort. Refer to the USGS East Andover quadrangle, 7.5-min. series.

To reach the trailhead., from US 2, 0.5 mi. west of Rumford Point, go north on ME 5 toward Andover. About three miles from US 2, turn right (east) and cross the Ellis River. Turn left on East Andover Rd. and immediately on the left is a parking area. The trail begins across the road between two large boulders. Follow the trail as it steadily climbs up to the ledges. Avoid taking the right fork about half way up. From the summit, the antenna on Black Mountain and the satellite station at Andover are visible. The trail along the ridge is marked by cairns and with a few paint blazes. Descending, take great care to find and follow the correct trail into the woods; there are many cairns and paths leading in different directions.

Distances from East Andover Rd.

> *to* ledges: 1.5 mi.

> *to* Rumford Whitecap summit: 2.0 mi., 1 hr. 40 min.

Old Blue Mountain (3600 ft.)

The Appalachian Trail (AT) crosses Old Blue Mtn., which is south of Elephant Mtn. and east of the road from Andover to the South Arm of Lower Richardson Lake. The summit of Old Blue is covered with dense evergreen trees 2–3 ft. high, allowing excellent views in all directions. Refer to the USGS Old Speck Mtn. and Rangeley quadrangles, 15-min. series; the East Andover quadrangle, 7.5-min. series, or map 7 in the MATC's *Appalachian Trail Guide to Maine*.

To reach the AT from ME 5 in Andover go 0.6 mi. east on ME 120 to South Arm Rd. Turn left onto South Arm Rd and go north for about 7.7 mi. to the AT crossing at Black Brook Notch. There is limited parking on the right side of the road. From South Arm Rd., the AT climbs very steeply up the eastern wall of Black Brook Notch gaining 900 ft. At 0.6 mi., the trail reaches the top of the notch, then it gradually climbs to the base of Old Blue, which it reaches at 2.3 mi. Here, the trail begins its final 0.5-mi. ascent to the open white granite summit with a 360-degree view.

From the summit, the AT descends north 800 ft. into the high valley between Old Blue Mtn. and Elephant Mtn. In this valley, the AT runs through a virgin red spruce forest for more than a mile.

For detailed information about the AT north of Old Blue, see the latest edition of the MATC's *Appalachian Trail Guide to Maine*.

Distances from South Arm Rd.

to top of Black Brook Notch: 0.6 mi.

to base of Old Blue: 2.3 mi.

to Old Blue summit: 2.8 mi., 2 hr. 40 min.

Bemis Mountain (3592 ft.)

Bemis Mtn. is an open ridge with outstanding views. It rises south of Mooselookmeguntic Lake. The ridge, which runs northeast–southwest, has four peaks descending in elevation to the northeast. The highest peak is wooded. The three lower peaks all have excellent views. The Appalachian Trail crosses Bemis Ridge, and there is a new lean-to near Third Peak. Refer to the USGS Oquossoc and Rangeley quadrangles, 15-min. series; the Houghton and Metallak Mtn. quadrangles, 7.5-min. series; or map 7 in the MATC's *Appalachian Trail Guide to Maine*.

Via Appalachian Trail

Access to the AT is from ME 17 at a turnout (Height of the Land) 11.0 mi. south of Oquossoc and 26 mi. north of Rumford. Parking is at a clearing 0.5 mi. south at the Bemis Stream trailhead.

The trail descends 0.8 mi. to a foot bridge over Bemis Stream. At 1.0 mi., cross the gravel logging road, which was the bed of the old Rumford and Rangeley Lakes Railroad in the 1930s. There is a small spring at 1.2 mi. that is the last sure source of water. After climbing steeply through woods, emerge onto open ledges at 1.6 mi. and cross a series of rocky knobs, the first at 1.7 mi. The ridge trail following cairns and white blazes crosses three peaks: First Peak (2604 ft.) at 2.2 mi.; Second Peak (2923 ft.) at 3.1 mi.; the lean-to at 4.6 mi.; and Third Peak (3138 ft.) at 5.0 mi. At 5.1 mi., the trail begins the ascent to the two wooded knobs of Fourth Peak (3592 ft.), which are reached at 6.2 and 6.3 mi.

For an interesting loop hike, climb Bemis by way of the Appalachian Trail and return via the Bemis Stream Trail, a total of almost 14.0 mi.

Via Bemis Stream Trail

This trail starts from a cleared parking area off ME 17, 0.5 mi. south of the Appalachian Trail crossing mentioned above. Hikers on either trail should park here. The trail is blue blazed and the blazes need to be carefully followed particularly near the summit of Fourth Summit due to logging activity.

The trail fords a brook at 0.2 mi., winds down to the gravel railroad-bed road at 1.1 mi., and climbs to reach Bemis Stream. It follows the western bank up to ford the stream at about two miles, recrossing to the western side at 2.8 mi. Climbing, it crosses again at 4.6 mi. and 5.0 mi. Then the trail swings up and west to join the Appalachian Trail at 6.5 mi. (This point is 7.3 mi. along the Appalachian Trail from ME 17.) The summit of Fourth Peak offers outstanding views in almost all directions.

For a detailed description of the Appalachian Trail beyond Fourth Peak, see the latest edition of the MATC's *Appalachian Trail Guide to Maine*.

Distances from ME 17 via Appalachian Trail

- *to* Fourth Peak: 6.3 mi., 4 hr. 30 min.

- *to* Bemis Mountain Lean-to: 4.6 mi.

  Complete loop (via Appalachian Trail, Bemis Stream Trail, and ME 17): 14 mi., 9 hr.

Section 10

Weld Region

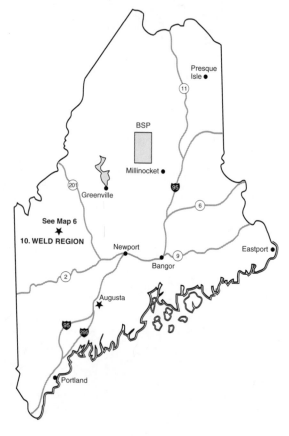

See AMC Maine Trail Map 6: Weld Region.

RECOMMENDED HIKES

Easy

Sugarloaf Mountain (Dixfield) (rt: 4.6 mi., 2 hr. 15 min.) A nice woods hike with a moderately steep section near the summit of Sugarloaf Mtn. The summit offers almost a 360 degree view, which includes the mountains in the Weld area.

Bald Mountain (Weld) (rt: 3.0 mi., 2 hr.) Although the first part of this trail is through a recently lumbered area, the views from the ledges and summit of Bald Mtn. make the hike worthwhile particularly in the fall.

Moderate

Mount Blue (rt: 3.4 mi., 3 hr.) A steady, steep climb to a wooded summit where there are views of the western mountains from the rocky outcrops.

Strenuous

Tumbledown Mountain via the Loop and Tumbledown Ridge Trails (rt: 4.4 mi., 3 hr. 45 min.) A steep ascent through boulder fields to the East and West peaks of Tumbledown Mtn. with spectacular views of the western mountains and beautiful Tumbledown Pond.

LIST OF MOUNTAINS

W eld village lies on the eastern shore of Lake Webb (678 ft.) and is almost encircled by mountains. Tumbledown Mtn. (3090 ft.), with its tremendous cliffs, three peaks, and high pond, is the most interesting mountain in the area and one of the state's outstanding summits. Little Jackson Mtn. (3470 ft.), Jackson Mtn. (3568 ft.), and Blueberry Mtn. (2962 ft.) are also in the Tumbledown Range, which forms the northern and northwestern walls of the valley. Mt. Blue (3190 ft.) lies to the east. The ledgy summits of Bald Mtn. (2370 ft.) and Saddleback Wind Mtn. (2572 ft.) close the valley on the southeast. Brush Mtn. (2430 ft.) and West Mtn. (2782 ft.) are to the west.

In the last decade, efforts by conservation groups including the AMC, TPL, and the Tumbledown Conservation Alliance have focused on conserving additional lands in the Tumbledown Mtn. Range and around Mt. Blue State Park. Mt. Blue State Park (7864 acres) has two sections. The area along the western shore of Lake Webb offers picnicking, boating, swimming, and camping facilities. The section east of the lake and Weld includes the Center Hill parking overlook and picnic area, and Mt. Blue itself. The park has a variety of trails within its boundaries. There is an interesting self-guided trail around Center Hill, the 2.0 mi. Swett Brook Trail at Webb Beach, as well as a 25 mi. multi-use trail system. Information on accommodations and trail conditions can be obtained at the supervisor's headquarters 1.5 mi. from Weld on the road toward Center Hill and Mt. Blue.

Tumbledown Mountain (3090 ft.)

Although not the highest peak of the Tumbledown Range, Tumbledown Mtn. is in many ways the most interesting. The enormous cliff on the southern side of this mountain attracts many rock climbers. Of the three summits, the 3090-ft. West Peak is slightly higher than the others. Another feature of the mountain is Tumbledown Pond (called Beaver or Crater by some), located on the eastern slope of the mountain and surrounded on three sides by higher elevations. The views from the summit ridges are good, except where higher mountains in the range block them to the north and northeast. There are four trails to the pond. In addition to the map in this guide, you can refer to the USGS Dixfield and Rangeley quadrangles, 15-min. series, and the Roxbury quadrangle, 7.5-min. series.

Loop Trail

The Loop Trail leaves Byron Notch Rd. 5.8 mi. west of Weld Corner, heading north on the eastern side of a brook. There is a sign at the start of the trail, as well as a clearing diagonally opposite the trail's entrance into the woods. The trail (blue-blazed) rises gradually, crossing a brook twice, and at 1.0 mi. passes the huge Tumbledown Boulder. From there, it rises steeply, coming out on the open Great Ledges, from which there are splendid views of the 700-ft. cliffs of Tumbledown Mtn. On the ledges, at a large cairn, the Loop Trail to the saddle turns right.

The trail crosses a brook and then climbs steeply in a gully. Near the top of the gully, a side trail leads right to a fissure cave (Fat Man's Misery). Above this is an opening in the boulders with iron rungs. (This section makes the trail unsuitable for dogs.) At 0.6 mi. from the Great Ledges cairn, reach the saddle with a spring (unreliable in dry weather). From here, the Tumbledown Ridge Trail leads east and west.

There are no trails on the North Peak of Tumbledown, but you can reach it by bushwhacking through the valley between the East and North peaks or by going east around Tumbledown Pond and up the upper reaches of Parker Ridge. *Caution: Hikers and rock climbers have been seriously injured on Tumbledown when bushwacking or following closed trails on Tumbledown's cliffs. See section on Bushwhacking in the Maine Mountains in the Introduction.*

Distances from Byron Notch Rd.

- *to* Tumbledown Boulder: 1.0 mi.

- *to* Great Ledges (cairn): 1.3 mi.

- *to* saddle (Tumbledown Ridge Trail): 1.9 mi., 1 hr. 45 min.

Brook Trail (map 6: E2)

This is a direct route to Tumbledown Pond from Byron Notch Rd. It leaves the road 1.8 mi. west of the start of the Parker's Ridge Trail and 4.4 mi. west of Weld Corner. The trail diverges north just before the spot where the road crosses a large double-steel culvert over Tumbledown Brook. The trail is marked Brook Trail on a rock at the start and is blue-blazed throughout its length. For the first mile, it is a logging road. At 1.0 mi., the trail diverges to the right into a low spot; then it climbs steeply, generally following the brook to the pond.

Distances from Byron Notch Rd.

> *to* right turn off logging road: 1.0 mi.
>
> *to* Tumbledown Pond: 1.5 mi., 1 hr. 30 min.

Parker's Ridge Trail (map 6: E2)

This is the oldest of the trails up Tumbledown. From Weld Village, take Rt. 142N, turn left onto West Side Rd. and at 0.5 mi bear right onto Byron Rd. Travel along Byron Road for 2.1 mi. and turn right onto another dirt road just past a cemetery. At 0.6 mi after making turn, bear left and park in the field just before the road re-enters the woods. From here walk up the road to the left (northwest) to a clearing and shelter. The Little Jackson Trail leaves on a logging road behind the shelter (northwest).

The Parker Ridge Trail, blazed blue, enters the woods left (west), crosses a brook, and turns northwest, joining a logging road. For 1.0 mi., the trail rises gently through second growth, then steeply for a short distance over three ledges. After that, the trail rises steadily. Then it crosses the open ledges of Parker Ridge with views of Tumbledown's three peaks ahead, and descends west to Tumbledown Pond.

Distances from parking area

> *to* Parker Ridge: 1.9 mi., 2 hr.
>
> *to* pond (outlet): 2.2 mi., 2 hr. 10 min.

Tumbledown Ridge Trail (map 6: E2)

From the pond outlet junction with the Brook Trail and Parker Ridge Trail, the Tumbledown Ridge Trail ascends west over mostly open ledge to East Peak and to the junction with the Loop Trail. A short spur extends to the summit of the West Peak, offering views into the Swift River Valley and to Old Blue and Elephant mountains to the west.

Distances from pond outlet

> *to* East Peak: 0.4 mi.
>
> *to* Loop Trail junction: 0.6 mi.
>
> *to* West Peak: 0.7 mi., 45 min.

Pond Link Trail (map 6: E2)

From the Parker Ridge Trail 0.1 mi. east of the pond, the Pond Link Trail, blazed blue, heads north, skirting the eastern end of the pond for about 100 yd. It then turns east to ascend to the height-of-land between Parker's Ridge and Little Jackson Mtn. at 0.3 mi. from the pond. The trail continues generally east to a jct. with the Little Jackson Trail. This makes an interesting loop.

Distances from the pond

  to start of Pond Link Trail: 0.1 mi.

  to height-of-land: 0.3 mi.

  to Little Jackson Trail: est. 1 mi., 40 min.

Little Jackson Mountain (3470 ft.)

For the road approach, see the Parker Ridge Trail section. If you want to supplement the map in this guide, refer to the USGS Rangeley quadrangle, 15-min. series, and the Roxbury quadrangle, 7.5-min. series.

The trail leaves behind the shelter area northwest on a logging road. There is a sign at this trailhead and the trail is well blazed and fairly well worn. There are many intersecting logging roads. Stay close to the edge of the valley that leads toward the Jacksons. About half a mile from the shelter, the route heads north toward the col between Little Jackson on the west and Jackson on the east. At about 1.5 mi., the trail turns right (northeast), and the blue-blazed Pond Link Trail (sign) leads straight ahead (northwest). At about 2.3 mi., the trail crosses a brook and continues onto open ledges 0.3 mi. beyond. At the ledges, the trail turns left and, ascending across open ledges with fine outlooks, climbs to the summit of Little Jackson.

The distance from the col to the summit is about one mile. Just below the summit to the west are open ledges with spectacular view of Tumbledown Pond. There are several trails heading toward the pond and they appear well-established and easy to follow, but are not. They all become very difficult if not impossible to follow below treeline and are not recommended. See section on Bushwhacking in the Maine Mountains in the Introduction.

Distances from parking area

  to Pond Link Trail junction: est. 1.5 mi.

  to col: 2.5 mi., 2 hr.

> *to* Jackson summit (via bushwhack from col): est. 3.5 mi.
>
> *to* Little Jackson summit (via trail): 3.3 mi., 2 hr. 30 min.

Jackson Mountain (3568 ft.)

Jackson is a large, rambling mountain partially covered with spruce, with a 100-ft.-square clear-cut, helicopter landing pad, and a radio structure on top. There are limited and obstructed views from the summit but excellent views looking south, east and west from open ledges about halfway up. The trail is narrow and caution should be exercised in following it.

The trail begins at the Little Jackson Trail approximately 120 ft. west of the first open ledges on the Little Jackson Trail. Turn right (north) at the trail jct. and continue over open ledges for about 300 ft., where the trail turns sharply left (west) and descends gradually. In another 180 ft., the trail turns right (north) and continues in a northerly direction to the summit of Jackson Mtn.

Distance from junction with Little Jackson Trail

> *to* Jackson summit: est. 1.0 mi.

Blueberry Mountain (2962 ft.)

See the USGS Phillips quadrangle, 15-min. series, or the Madrid quadrangle, 7.5-min. series, if you want to supplement the map in this guide.

The trail leaves ME 142 1.5 mi. from Weld Corner toward Phillips. Blueberry Mountain Bible Camp maintains a road that runs 1.8 mi. to a clearing above the buildings. A gate near the base may be locked, blocking cars, but to date, personnel at the camp have been cooperative about letting people use their road. They ask that you park across from the main building, not up in the clearing. From the parking lot, follow the roadway left (west) to a field and continue straight across (west), where the road enters the woods, about 0.5 mi from the parking area. The trail is blazed blue and follows a logging road. The trail rises steeply, first through conifers and then over ledges, to the summit. There are interesting geological formations at the top, which is bare and offers excellent views in all directions. There is no water on the trail.

Distances from ME 142

> *to* parking area (via Bible camp road): 1.8 mi.
>
> *to* Blueberry summit: 3.5 mi., 2 hr. 30 min.

Mount Blue (3190 ft.)

From Mt. Washington, this peak is one of the most perfect cones on the skyline. Only the frame of a former fire tower remains on the summit. In addition to the map in this guide, you can refer to the USGS Dixfield quadrangle, 15-min. series, and the Mt. Blue quadrangle, 7.5-min. series.

In Weld village, take the road that leads uphill east from the four corners and bear left at the fork at 0.5 mi. Take the right fork (Mt. Blue Road) at a little over thre miles and continue to the parking place at about six miles (signs). The trailhead is marked by a large sign and bulletin board. The path is broad and well worn and passes the old fire warden's cabin, where there is a spring. Above the cabin site, the gradient is the same for a half-mile; it then begins to lessen as the ridge is approached, although the footway becomes narrower and rougher. The tower has collapsed and woodwork has been removed from the tower frame, but there are paths to four rock outcrops, which offer views in various directions.

Distances from parking place

   to   fire warden's cabin: 0.6 mi.

   to   Mt. Blue summit: 1.7 mi., 1 hr. 40 min.

Bald Mountain (2370 ft.)

The trail up Bald Mtn. leaves the southern side of ME 156 about 8.5 mi. west of Wilton and about 5.0 mi. east of Weld, just southeast of two bridges and a logging road. In addition to the map in this guide, you can refer to the USGS Dixfield quadrangle, 15-min. series, and the Mt. Blue quadrangle, 7.5-min. series. At the time of publication, the trail is undergoing significant rebuilding, and caution should be exercised in following it.

Cross the brook immediately (last sure water) and enter the woods. The trail climbs steadily through the woods, marked by occasional red paint blazes. On the open ledges, it is marked by paint and cairns to the summit, where there are fine views in every direction. A faint trail may be followed 2.0 mi. farther to the summit of Saddleback Wind Mtn., which is slightly higher but attracts fewer visitors.

Distances from ME 156

   to   ledges: 0.9 mi., 45 min.

   to   Bald Mtn. summit: 1.5 mi., 1 hr. 15 min.

Sugarloaf Mountain (1521 ft.)

Sugarloaf Mtn. in Dixfield is conspicuous because of its two prominent summits. It offers fine vistas from its open northern summit. Refer to the USGS Dixfield quadrangle, 7.5- and 15-min. series.

For the route to the summit go north from the corner of Main St. (US 2) and Weld St. (ME 142) in Dixfield. Take ME 142 for 1.2 mi. to Holt Hill Rd. Turn right onto Holt Hill Rd. for 0.5 mi. to Moxie Heights Rd. Turn left, then immediately right onto Red Ledge Rd. Go 0.1 mi. and park along the side of the road where it narrows and an unnamed road goes left. The trail follows the old road/track. At 0.5 mi., take left fork. Do not follow the snowmobile trail that is on the right fork. At 0.7 mi. the Bull Rock trail takes off on the left. Avoid turning onto any trails/tracks that intersect with the Bull Rock trail. Follow the trail for 1.7 mi. Turn right onto a blue-blazed trail. The trail climbs steeply for 0.2 mi. to the col between the northern and southern peaks. At the northern summit there is a plaque commemorating the first cable TV in Maine. From the ledges on the summit there are excellent views to the west and north.

Distances from Red Ledge Rd.

 to Bull Rock Trail: 0.7 mi.

 to blue-blazed trail: 1.7mi.

 to northern summit: 2.3 mi., 1 hr. 45 min.

Bull Rock (920 ft.)

Perched on the side of Sugarloaf Mtn. in Dixfield, Bull Rock offers a delightful preview of the views from Sugarloaf. There are good views to the west and south.

For the trailhead for Bull Rock go north from the corner of Main St. (US 2) and Weld St. (ME 142) in Dixfield for 1.2 mi. to Holt Hill Rd. Turn right onto Holt Hill Rd. for 0.5 mi. to Moxie Heights Rd. Turn left, then immediately right onto Red Ledge Rd. Go 0.1 mi. and park along the side of the road where it narrows and an unnamed road goes left. The trail follows the old road/track. At 0.5 mi., take left fork. Do not follow the snowmobile trail that is on the right fork. At 0.7 mi. turn left on a deeply rutted track/trail. Follow the trail for 0.9 mi. to Bull Rock.

Distance from Red Ledge Rd.

 to Bull Rock ledges: 1.6 mi., 1 hr.

Section 11

Rangeley/Stratton Region

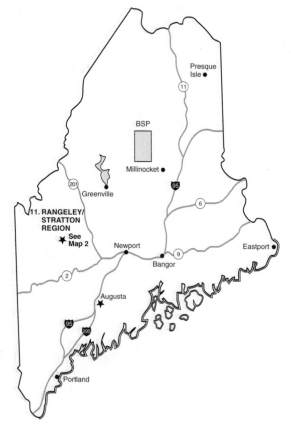

See AMC Maine Trail Map 2: Rangeley/Stratton Region.

RECOMMENDED HIKES

Easy

Bald Mountain (Oquossoc) (rt: 2.0 mi., 1 hr. 30 min.) This trail climbs steadily on easy grades to the summit of Bald Mtn., where there are excellent lake and mountain views from the ledges just south of the summit.

Moderate

Mount Aziscohos via the North Trail (rt: 4.2 mi., 3 hr. 45 min.) A steady, moderate climb through varied terrain to the east peak of Mt. Aziscohos, where there are excellent views of the Rangeley Lakes region.

Kibby Mountain (rt: 4.6 mi., 2 hr. 30 min.) A delightful hike up an old woods road with some steep sections to the summit of Kibby Mtn., where there is an old fire tower that provides extensive views of western Maine and Quebec.

Strenuous

Bigelow Mountain Loop via Horns Pond and Fire Warden's Trails and the AT (lp: 12.4 mi., 7 hr. 30 min.) This loop hike to the Avery Peak summit of Bigelow Mtn. ascends using the less steep and more interesting Horns Pond Trail to the AT passing beautiful Horn Pond. The AT crosses Bigelow's West Peak where there are spectacular views to the north, south, and west, and continues on to Avery Peak. Avery Peak provides excellent views to the east. To complete the loop, descend down the Fire Warden's Trail.

Mount Abraham via Fire Warden's Trail (rt: 9.0 mi., 7 hr. 15 min.) An interesting but strenuous hike to the exposed summit of Mt. Abraham, where the views are some of the best in Maine.

LIST OF MOUNTAINS

This section includes the mountains north of Rangeley Lakes; the area westward to Lake Aziscohos and the New Hampshire border; the isolated mountains north toward the Canadian border, reached by a network of private logging roads and ME 27; and the important and outstanding cluster of 4000-ft. mountains, including Saddleback, Abraham, Sugarloaf, Crocker, Spaulding, Redington, and Bigelow, reached through the towns of Rangeley, Stratton, Kingfield, and Phillips. This last group includes 10 of the state's 4000-ft. peaks. Sugarloaf Mtn., at 4250 ft., is Maine's second-highest mountain (aside from the subsidiary summits of Katahdin), although Mt. Abraham (4050 ft.), Saddleback Mtn. (4120 ft.), and especially Bigelow Mtn. (4145 ft.) are more interesting for hiking. Redington doesn't have an established trail to the summit and experienced hikers may be able to reach it by bushwhacking.

There are two large ski areas in this region, on Sugarloaf Mtn. and Saddleback Mtn.

Accommodations are ample along ME 16/27 between Rangeley, Stratton, and Kingfield. Rangeley Lake State Park on the southern shore opened in 1967, with full camping, boating, and swimming facilities. You can drive to the park via ME 17 or ME 4. There are additional public facilities at Mount Blue State Park in Weld, just south of this section.

The town of Eustis maintains the Cathedral Pines Campground and trailer park, with laundry facilities and a recreation building, on ME 27, 3.0 mi. north of the ME 16 and ME 27 junction at Stratton and 2.3 mi. south of Eustis.

The MFS maintains the following camping areas (fires permitted): on the northern side of ME 16 about 5.0 mi. east of Rangeley and near Dallas; on the western shore of Flagstaff Lake at the end of Old Flagstaff Rd., 2.0 mi. east of a junction with ME 27 (near Flagstaff Memorial Church) and 0.8 mi. north of the Cathedral Pines Campground. On the western side of ME 27, the MFS maintains a camping area about 3.0 mi. south of the Chain of Ponds; at Upper Farm on the eastern shore of the Chain of Ponds just off ME 27; and on the eastern shore of the Chain of Ponds at its northern end, off ME 27.

Several additional camping areas may be found within the Bigelow Preserve; these sites are included in the description of the Bigelow Range trails.

Mount Aziscohos (3215 ft.)

South of Lake Aziscohos (pronounced uh-ZIS-kuh-hahs), this mountain offers excellent views of the Rangeley Lakes region. Fifteen lakes are visible from the summit. The trails lead to the eastern, and slightly lower, of the two peaks, where an abandoned MFS fire tower is down. Refer to the USGS Oquossoc and Errol quadrangles, 15-min. series, and the Richardson Pond and Wilsons Mills quadrangles, 7.5-min. series.

There are two routes up the mountain. Both have discreet blue blazes. Opinions differ as to what they should be named; therefore, the descriptions here are titled simply From the Northwest and From the North.

From the Northwest

Sometimes called the Tower Man's Trail or South Trail, this route begins on the southern side of ME 16, at a small parking area 100 yd. east of the bridge over the Magalloway River at the Aziscohos Dam. The trail, gated by a cable, follows a relatively large logging road; at about 0.7 mi., it turns left (east) onto a narrower, older logging road. At 0.8 mi., it crosses the remains of a bridge and continues gradually uphill. Then, after crossing extensive open space, it bears left into the woods. Cross the small stream at 1.1 mi. and take the left (south) fork. At 1.7 mi., the road reaches the clearing at the site of the former MFS fire warden's cabin, where there is an enclosed spring. Hike on the left side of the clearing and enter the open softwood forest. The trail continues on steeper but relatively easy grades, and at 2.4 mi., the trail from the north comes in on the left. Turn right and continue to the summit at 2.5 mi.

Distances from ME 16

> *to* cabin site: 1.7 mi.
>
> *to* junction with trail from the north: 2.4 mi.
>
> *to* Aziscohos summit: 2.5 mi., 2 hr. 30 min.

From the North

The route from the north begins on ME 16, 1.0 mi. east of the bridge over the Magalloway River at the Aziscohos Dam. Approximately 50 paces east of a graveled logging road, the trailhead is marked with a sign that may be difficult to see. It leads gradually uphill on an old tote road through open hardwood and mixed forest, then turns sharply left at 0.5 mi. At 1.0 mi., the trail enters conifers, and it crosses a brook at 1.1 mi. After that, it continues more steeply, becoming rougher over boulders and exposed roots. It reaches the Tower

Man's Trail coming in from the northwest at 2.0 mi. To the left, it is 0.1 mi. over ledges to the summit.

Distances from ME 16

   to brook crossing: 1.1 mi.

   to junction with trail from the northwest: 2.0 mi.

   to Aziscohos summit: 2.1 mi., 2 hr. 10 min.

Bald Mountain (2443 ft.)

This small mountain is in a prime location between Mooselookmeguntic and Rangeley lakes. A ski area on the northern slope has been out of business for many years, and the ski trails are overgrown. Refer to the USGS Oquossoc quadrangle, 7.5 and 15-min. series.

To reach the hiking trail, go west from Oquossoc on ME 4 about one mile to the terminus of that highway at Haines Landing. Turn left (south) onto Bald Mtn. Rd. before the landing and follow it for about just under one mile to the parking area and trail on the left. A short distance from the start of the trail, take the right fork and climb east and southeast to the summit. The blue-blazed trail is well used and easy to see in the hardwood forest at the base of the mountain. Some minor boulder scrambling is required at the higher elevations, where you must take a little care to stay on the main trail. The bedrock summit has a variety of terrain and excellent views from different outlooks through the spruce.

Distance from road

   to Bald Mtn. summit: 1.0 mi., 1 hr.

West Kennebago Mountain (3705 ft.)

This isolated mountain is north of the Rangeley Lakes and west of Kennebago Lake. There is a fire tower on the southern peak, which also offers fine views of the area and is the highest of the several summits of the north–south ridge that forms the mountain. Refer to the USGS Cupsuptic quadrangle, 15-min. series, and the Kennebago quadrangle, 7.5-min. series.

Access to the fire warden's trail currently is via the Seven Island Land Company system of private roads. Turn right (north) from ME 16 onto a Morton Cutoff Rd. 4.8 mi. west of the ME 4 and ME 16 jct. in Oquossoc and 0.3

mi. west of the MFS buildings at Cupsuptic. Drive 3.2 mi. from ME 16 to a jct. with a well-maintained, wide gravel road, Lincoln Pond Rd. Turn right (east); in 5.5 mi., the road reaches a parking area on the left. The fire tower trail begins at the right end of the parking area.

The trail, blazed with red blazes, starts as a road but soon becomes a path and climbs rather steeply. At 0.9 mi., it levels out among conifers and bears left. Then it begins to climb again, crosses a small stream, and turns sharply right. At 1.4 mi., the trail reaches the warden's camp (3186 ft.), a picturesque log cabin built in 1911. There is a spring behind the camp 100 yd. to the left. The trail leaves the camp from the upper right (northwest) corner of the clearing. At 1.7 mi., it reaches the ridge, where the trail turns left (south) to follow the ridge to the fire tower.

Distances from road

   to warden's camp: 1.4 mi.

   to West Kennebago, southern summit: 2.1 mi., 2 hr.

East Kennebago Mountain (3791 ft., 3728 ft., and 3650 ft.)

East of Kennebago Lake, this is a long, wooded ridge running east–west in T2 R4 and T2 R5. (T and R stand for "township" and "range": Maine uses this system to designate its unincorporated towns.)

This is in part a bushwhack trip. Refer to the USGS Kennebago Lake quadrangle, 15-min. series, and the Kennebago Lake and Quill Hill quadrangles, 7.5-min. series. East Kennebago also appears on the Rangeley-Stratton map in this guide. East Kennebago is listed on the New England Hundred Highest list and more explicit directions may be obtained from that organization.

To reach the trailhead, take ME 16, 8.7 mi. from ME 16/27 in Stratton, or 9.8 mi. from ME 4/16 in Rangeley, turn left on Langtown Main Road, a dirt road, cross a bridge over the river, and turn right at the T in 0.9 mi. At next fork, turn right and bear left at the next fork. Go 1.4 mi. and then bear left on a rocky road for 0.8 mi. Turn left onto another rocky road and go another 0.8 mi. to an open area at a point where the road further deteriorates and turns slightly to left and starts uphill. This is the parking area.

The path is straight ahead on the woods road. Take the woods road for 1.4 mi. (altimeter reading about 2960 ft.) avoiding taking a 90-degree left onto a grassy road that heads steeply uphill. At this point, watch carefully for a yellow post off the road to the right in the woods and on the left a small cairn with a yellow painted rock in it. At this point, the trail heads steeply uphill into the woods marked with yellow blazes. Follow this rough path to about 3300 ft. where the yellow blazes vanish as the path enters an area with some blow-downs. Continue through this area to where you pick up the path and yellow blazes again. Follow the path for 4 to 5 minutes to a point where it starts to descend. From this point it becomes a bushwhack to the summit. Ascend to the summit by going due magnetic north (3600 ft.) through a spruce forest. The summit at 3825 ft. is a broad ridge without any views. A NEHH canister is present. It is suggested to return by reversing the route as the southeastern slopes of this peak are steep with cliffs and ringed with thick spruce.

Distance from parking area

  to East Kennebago summit: est. 3.0 mi., 2 hr. 45 min.

Snow Mountain (3948 ft.)

Snow Mtn. is southwest of the Chain of Ponds. There is an abandoned MFS fire tower on the summit. The mountain offers extensive views in all directions, including an extended sweep into Canada over Lake Megantic. From the summit, you can see many miles of Benedict Arnold's route to Quebec in 1775, which followed the headwaters of the Dead River past the Chain of Ponds and into Quebec Province. Refer to the USGS Chain Lakes quadrangle, 15-min. series, and the Chain of Ponds and Jim Pond quadrangles, 7.5-min. series.

The approach is via a dirt road leading left (west) from ME 27, 13.7 mi. from the 16/27 junction in Stratton. The land in this area is a part of the Penobscot Indian Territory and overnight camping permits are needed, which may be obtained from the Penobscot Indian Nation Department of Trust Responsibilities. This land is used for sustenance hunting by the Penobscot Indian Nation. The road is gated and may be locked near ME 27, which will add approximately five miles one way to the hike. Follow the logging road 3.9 miles and bear right at the fork. Go another 1.1 mi to the parking area where there is a sign for the trail. The trail is over old logging roads marked by snowmobile signs to Snow Mtn. Pond. At about two miles, the road to the left leads to Snow Mtn. Pond. The former fire warden's cabin there is now private property. Turn right to the fire warden's trail (sign) and climb steeply north, passing a spring. At a point where the trail from Big Island Pond comes in on the left, turn right and climb northeast to the summit. There is a viewpoint to the south near the summit. Excellent views of the area may be had by climbing the fire tower.

Descending, don't miss the point where the fire warden's trail turns left and the trail from Big Island Pond goes right.

Distances from parking area

to Snow Mtn. Pond: 2.0 mi., 1 hr. 15 min.

to Snow summit: 1.3 mi., 2 hr.

Kibby Mountain (3638 ft.)

This remote mountain is in the heart of the wilderness area north of Flagstaff Lake, east of the Chain of Ponds, and south of the Canadian Atlantic Railroad, which runs through Lac-Megantic in Quebec and Jackman. The Kibby Mountain Trail was restored in 1989, and is periodically maintained. Refer to the USGS Kibby Mtn. quadrangle, 7.5-min. series, and the DeLorme Maine Atlas and Gazetteer maps 28, 29, 38, and 39.

From the jct. with ME 16 in Stratton, drive north on ME 27 for 16.8 mi. (3.1 mi. northwest from the Snow Mtn. Rd. entrance). Turn right onto the wide dirt logging road, Gold Brook Rd., which runs parallel to Gold Brook. Drive 9.4 mi. to wide logging road on the right. Turn right on this road and go 0.4 mi. to a clearing on the left with a large cairn. Park here.

The trail follows an old jeep trail through a balsam spruce forest and ascends about 1.6 mi at an easy grade via two long switchbacks on grassy terrain. The upper half-mile section to the summit is a steeper foot path. There is an old MFS fire tower stand with outstanding and extensive views of the surrounding wilderness.

Distance from parking area

to Kibby summit: est. 2.3 mi., 1 hr. 30 min.

Saddleback Mountain and The Horn (summit, 4120 ft. and The Horn, 4041 ft.)

Saddleback Mtn., southeast of Rangeley, is one of Maine's outstanding mountains. It is a long range extending east–west. Pronounced saddles separate its several peaks. Two of the peaks are over 4000 ft.—the Saddleback summit and The Horn. The bare summits of both offer far-flung views in all directions. Saddleback, with its widespread areas above treeline, is also unusually exposed. *Caution: High winds and restricted visibility can be dangerous, and the trail is difficult to follow in bad weather.* You can refer to the USGS Phillips and Rangeley quadrangles, 15-min. series, and the Redington and Saddleback Mtn. quadrangles, 7.5-min. series, as well as to the map in this guide or map 6 in the MATC's *Appalachian Trail Guide to Maine.*

There are several points of interest on the southwestern side of the mountain. Piazza Rock is an enormous overhanging flat boulder with a growth of mature trees; nearby, the Caves offer ample opportunities for exploration. Both are on the Appalachian Trail, 1.4 mi. north of ME 4. Eddy Pond, one of several small ponds on Saddleback, is particularly attractive.

The Saddleback Mountain Ski Area is on the northwestern slope of the mountain.

Appalachian Trail (elevation gain: 2750 ft.) (map 2: A6–E1)

To approach Saddleback from the west, follow ME 4 for 32.0 mi. north from the ME 4 and US 2 jct. in Farmington or for 9.9 mi. south from the ME 4 and ME 16 jct. in Rangeley. The AT crosses ME 4 in a steep, winding section of the road. Use the parking lot (approximately 16 car capacity) on the western side of the highway. This hike along the Saddleback ridge should be considered a strenuous hike, and caution should be used in bad weather, as portions of the trail are obscured and difficult to follow.

From ME 4, the AT descends and crosses the Sandy River via a bridge at 0.1 mi. The trail climbs out of the valley, crossing a gravel logging road at 1.1 mi. At 1.8 mi., the trail passes the Piazza Rock Lean-to (built in 1935 by the Civilian Conservation Corps; reconditioned by the MATC in 1993; accommodates eight; tent platforms are also available). A side trail leads left 1.9 mi. to the top of Piazza Rock. Not far beyond along the trail are the Caves, a series of boulder caves with narrow passages.

The AT then climbs steeply, passes along Ethel Pond's western shore, and turns sharply left, away from the end of the pond. The trail then continues to rise, passes Mud Pond, and descends slightly to Eddy Pond (last sure water). Watch for a point near the eastern shore of Eddy Pond about 3.7 mi. from ME 4 where the trail, after turning left onto a road for a few feet, turns sharply right from the road onto a trail. It rises steeply through conifers, emerging in 0.8 mi. on a scrub-covered slope.

This open crest is particularly interesting, but the cairns are small, the path is not well worn, and the trail is fully exposed. It should not be traveled in bad weather. After nearly 0.8 mi. over rocky slopes and heath, the trail descends slightly into a sag, where a blue-blazed side path (may be hard to see) leads right (south) about 0.1 mi. through scrub to a spring (not dependable). The main trail climbs 0.1 mi. farther to the summit.

The AT continues over open slopes, descends steeply into the col between Saddleback and The Horn, and reaches the summit of The Horn 1.6 mi. from the main summit.

For the continuation of the AT beyond The Horn, see the MATC's *Appalachian Trail Guide to Maine*.

Distances from ME 4

> *to* junction with logging road: 1.1 mi.
>
> *to* Piazza Rock Lean-to: 1.8 mi.
>
> *to* Piazza Rock (via side trail): 1.9 mi.
>
> *to* Saddleback summit: 5.7 mi., 3 hr. 45 min.
>
> *to* The Horn summit: 7.3 mi., 4 hr. 15 min.

Mount Abraham (4050 ft.)

Mt. Abraham (or "Ab'ram") lies northwest of Kingfield and south of Sugarloaf Mtn. and Spaulding Mtn. It is an impressive ridge about 4.5 mi. long that runs on a northwest–southeast axis and consists of about eight peaks ranging from 3400 to more than 4000 ft. The highest peak, with an abandoned MFS firetower, lies north of the middle of the ridge. The extensive areas above timberline on Abraham give it an unusually alpine appearance for its height. Although the trailless ridge south of the tower has been traversed, that route is not advisable, since the distances are deceptive and the scrub is very dense between peaks. *Caution: The mountain's openness makes sudden electrical storms unusually dangerous. Watch your weather!*

Two trails ascend to the abandoned fire tower. The Fire Warden's Trail approaches the mountain from Kingfield. The Mt. Abraham Side Trail, cut in 1987, approaches from the Appalachian Trail north of Mt. Abraham and west of Spaulding Mtn. Refer to the USGS Kingfield and Phillips quadrangles, 15-min. series, and Mt. Abraham quadrangle, 7.5-min. series, or map 6 in the MATC's *Appalachian Trail Guide to Maine*, if you want to supplement the map in this guide.

Fire Warden's Trail (map 2: D4–D5)

To reach the trail, follow ME 27 north from Kingfield. Turn left (west) onto the paved road (West Kingfield St.) at the Jordan's Lumber Company store, 0.2 mi. north of the bridge over the Carrabassett River. At 3.0 mi. from ME 27, the road becomes gravel. Go straight through a crossroads at 3.5 mi. to 3.7 mi. (road becomes Rapid Stream Road), where the road forks. From this point, the road is partially private. At 6.0 mi., a road turns left to a new bridge over Rapid Stream. Cross the stream and follow the road for about 0.5 mi. to the trailhead at a crossroads. The trail begins straight into the woods.

The blue-blazed trail follows the southern bank of Norton Brook, crosses the brook, and continues along the northern bank, gradually climbing. In another 0.3 mi., it turns northwest and then crosses another logging road. To reach this point by car, turn right at the trailhead and turn left in about one mile. In approximately 200 yd., the road crosses the trail (marked by a cairn). The road is actively used by logging trucks; use caution. The next 2.0 mi. of the trail, to the abandoned warden's cabin, skirt the northeastern flank of the mountain, crossing four major brooks. Grades are easy. There is a good spring to the right of the cabin.

From the old cabin (2127 ft.), the trail turns left straight up the slope and climbs steeply through the woods for a mile, then comes out on an old slide with good views. At about 0.1 mi. above the cabin, a side trail leads left to a brook (last sure water). The remainder of the trail is completely exposed, except for a few short stretches of scrub. In this section, an abandoned telephone line and the few cairns should be followed carefully in bad weather. The trail rises steadily across a boulder field to the fire tower.

Distances from Rapid Stream

> *to* crossroads near Norton Brook: 0.5 mi.
>
> *to* fire warden's cabin: 3.0 mi.
>
> *to* Abraham summit: 4.5 mi., 3 hr. 45 min.

Mount Abraham Side Trail (map 2: C4–D4)

For the approach to this trail, see the description of the Appalachian Trail route to Spaulding Mtn. in this guide.

From the jct. of the Appalachian Trail and the blue-blazed side trail to the Spaulding Mtn. summit, continue south on the Appalachian Trail, descending the cone of Spaulding Mtn. to the site of the Spaulding Mtn. Lean-to, with two tentsites, a spring, and a privy. A temporary side trail marked by orange tape leads 0.6 mi. north to the old Spaulding Mtn. Lean-to, which is still functional.

Continue south on the Appalachian Trail to the jct. of the Mt. Abraham Side Trail. The Appalachian Trail continues southwest, climbing Lone Mtn. Refer to the MATC's *Appalachian Trail Guide to Maine*. The Mt. Abraham Side Trail leads 1.7 mi. southeast following a very old tote road, climbing gradually then steeply up the southern ridge of Mt. Abraham, which is characterized by very dense forest. The trail emerges from the trees and ascends a rock field to the tower.

Distances from Caribou Valley Rd.

> *to* junction of Appalachian Trail and Spaulding summit trail: 3.9 mi.
>
> *to* site of new Spaulding Mtn. Lean-to: est. 4.5 mi.
>
> *to* junction of Appalachian Trail and Mount Abraham Side Trail: est. 4.9 mi.
>
> *to* Abraham summit: 6.6 mi., 5 hr. 25 min.

Crocker Mountain (northern peak, 4228 ft.; southern peak, 4050 ft.)

The northern extension of the Crocker–Redington Pond Range, these mountains are 3.5 mi. west of Sugarloaf Mtn. and separated from it by Caribou Valley (South Branch of the Carrabassett). The summit of Crocker, despite its height, has few views and is heavily wooded to the top. South Crocker Mtn., 1.0 mi. to the south, has a definite summit with fine views and rises 380 ft. above the col between it and Crocker Mtn. Hikers can approach the mountain via the Appalachian Trail from ME 27 or Caribou Valley Rd. However, the last mile of the Caribou Valley Road is poorly maintained; drive it with caution. Low-clearance vehicles are advised not to use Caribou Valley Road.

Approach via ME 27

For the approach from the north and ME 27, follow the highway 2.6 mi. northwest from the Sugarloaf access road. Park off the highway at this point (sign reading Appalachian Trail Crossing); the newly expanded parking area holds at least 15 vehicles. Leaving the southern side of the highway, the Appalachian Trail climbs steadily through woods for nearly 1.5 mi. before reaching the northernmost knoll of Crocker. A spruce section begins at about one mile and continues to about two miles, where the trail slabs the western side of the ridge through birches. It continues up the western side of the ridge, reenters conifers at about 3.5 mi., and passes a small stream at 4.2 miles (usually reliable—last water). After that, the trail rises more steeply to the crest and reaches the summit of Crocker at 5.2 mi. The descent into the col begins immediately. The trail leads to the low point of the col and soon begins to climb toward the rocky summit of South Crocker. To reach the summit, take the 50 yd., blue-blazed path (sign) to the right (west), where the Appalachian Trail makes a sharp left turn for the descent to Caribou Valley.

Distances from ME 27 via Appalachian Trail

   to Crocker, northern ridge: 1.5 mi.

   to stream in conifers: 4.2 mi.

   to Crocker summit: 5.2 mi., 4 hr.

   to South Crocker summit (via blue-blazed summit trail): 6.2 mi., 4 hr. 30 min.

   to Caribou Valley Rd.: 8.3 mi., 5 hr. 30 min.

Approach via Caribou Valley Road

This road leads south from ME 27, 1.0 mi. northwest of the entrance to Sugarloaf. The Appalachian Trail crosses the road 4.5 mi. south of ME 27; 50 yd. beyond this crossing, an old metal gate is usually open. Note that the last mile of the Caribou Valley Road is in poor shape; low-clearance vehicles should use caution. Parking at the Appalachian Trail crossing is available for up to six vehicles. This trailhead is also used to reach Sugarloaf Mtn. to the east.

The Appalachian Trail leaves the road to the right (west) and climbs steadily but not too steeply through birch woods. Nearly a mile from the road, a blue-blazed trail leads right 0.2 mi. to the Crocker Cirque Campsite (built by the MATC in 1975; it has a two-tent platform, fireplace, and latrine). On the side trail to this campsite is the last sure water. Beyond the turnoff to the campsite, the Appalachian Trail begins the steep climb to the shoulder of South Crocker. The trail leads up the shoulder through woods for the next mile to the crest of South Crocker. Then it turns sharply right, and at the same point, the 50-yd. side trail (sign) to the actual summit of South Crocker leaves to the left. The Appalachian Trail then descends into the col, from which it climbs steadily to the summit of North Crocker.

Distances from Caribou Valley Rd.

> *to* side trail to campsite: 0.9 mi., 35 min.
>
> *to* South Crocker summit: 2.1 mi., 2 hr.
>
> *to* Crocker summit: 3.1 mi., 2 hr. 45 min.
>
> *to* ME 27: 8.3 mi., 5 hr.

Sugarloaf Mountain (4250 ft.)

Sugarloaf Mtn. is the second-highest mountain in Maine. Many other peaks are more popular with hikers, however; Sugarloaf is known and frequented chiefly for skiing. The ski area is on the northern slope, and since it is in one of the heaviest snowbelts in the northeastern United States, spring skiing is frequently good after other areas farther to the south have closed for the season. For the hiker, the view from the symmetrical, bare cone is well worth the climb of almost 2500 ft. The number of peaks visible is perhaps unequaled in the state, except from Katahdin. Spaulding Mtn. is about 2.5 mi. to the south of Sugarloaf and is connected with it by a high ridge.

A rough road (not good enough for cars but easy to follow on foot in bad weather) has been built to the summit. It starts behind the maintenance-vehicle storage building at the base, near the ski-area parking lot, and climbs at first west, then south, and finally east to the summit. This road, or the network of ski trails on the mountain, provides an approach from the north. The road is about four miles long; the ski trails are shorter but steeper.

For ski-trail route, drive in toward the ski area off ME 27. Take a right at the fork. Stay left at sign reading Country Club Condos. Go to the very top of the big loop, and take the dead-end road right at the highest point. The parking area is 75 yd. from this point. A summer mountain-bike trail leads to the woods and ski slope. Stay right and pass Bullwinkles, then follow power lines to a building (weather shelter) and the summit.

You can also approach Sugarloaf from the south. The Appalachian Trail leaves Caribou Valley Rd. 4.5 mi. south of ME 27. Note that the last mile of the Caribou Valley Road is in poor shape; low-clearance vehicles should use caution. Parking at the Appalachian Trail crossing is available for up to six vehicles. This trailhead is also used to reach Crocker Mountain to the west.

After leaving the road to the east (left), the trail soon crosses the South Branch of the Carrabassett (dangerous in high water), follows up the stream for a time, and then begins to climb, at first gently and then more steeply. After that, it crosses ledges and skirts the top of a cirque on the western side of Sugarloaf. The last water is a stream 1.8 mi. from the road. At 2.3 mi., the Appalachian Trail turns right toward Spaulding Mtn., while the blue-blazed Sugarloaf Side Trail leaves to the left and reaches the summit in 0.6 mi.

Distances from Caribou Valley Rd.

>   *to*   Sugarloaf Side Trail junction (via Appalachian Trail): 2.3 mi., 2 hr.

>   *to*   Sugarloaf summit: 2.9 mi., 2 hr. 30 min.

Spaulding Mountain (4010 ft.)

From its jct. with the Sugarloaf Side Trail, the Appalachian Trail (south) traverses the crest of the ridge between Sugarloaf and Spaulding, with views and steep cliffs on the left. At 1.5 mi., the trail begins the ascent of Spaulding, first steeply, then gradually. Near the top, a blue-blazed trail leads left 167 yds. to the summit.

For a description of the Appalachian Trail south of Spaulding, see the Mt. Abraham Side Trail description in this guide or the MATC's *Appalachian Trail Guide to Maine*.

Distances from Caribou Valley Rd.

>   *to*   Sugarloaf summit side trail: 2.3 mi.

>   *to*   Spaulding side trail: 4.4 mi.

>   *to*   Spaulding summit (via Appalachian Trail): 4.5 mi., 3 hr. 25 min.

Bigelow Range (Little Bigelow [3025 ft.], Avery Peak [4088 ft.], West Peak [4145 ft.], South Horn [3805 ft.], North Horn [3792 ft.], Cranberry Peak [3194 ft.]

The Bigelow Range runs east–west for some twelve miles. It is second only to the Katahdin region in interest and opportunities for superb ridge walking. The central features are the twin "cones," Avery Peak and West Peak, which project above the ridge. The equally symmetrical twin "horns," farther west and only slightly lower, are North Horn and South Horn. Still farther west is Cranberry Peak, with its bare ledges. To the east of Avery Peak, but separated from it by a deep notch, lies Little Bigelow Mtn.

The Bigelow Mountain Preserve, established by the people of Maine in a June 1976 referendum, includes the Bigelow Range and the land surrounding it. The 33,000-acre preserve is administered by the Maine Bureau of Parks and Lands.

Backpackers can find campsites at Cranberry Stream and Moose Falls (both stoves only; no fires) and Safford Notch, with Horns Pond Lean-to and Avery Memorial Lean-to (both stoves only; no fires), and Little Bigelow Lean-to. Prior to the New England hurricane of 1938, the western portion of the range was an almost unbroken, uncut softwood forest. That and subsequent storms greatly damaged the forest, and only small uncut sections remain. Water is scarce in some areas of this range.

From Avery Peak, there is a magnificent outlook over the rugged wilderness of peaks, ponds, streams, and extensive Flagstaff Lake—perhaps the best view in the state, except for the one from Katahdin.

Flagstaff Lake, a man-made reservoir (Maine's fourth-largest body of water), lies just north of the Bigelow Range. Like the range, the lake stretches east–west.

West of the Horns lies Horns Pond, a beautiful mountain tarn. Cranberry Pond, Arnolds Well, and other landmarks are farther west.

In addition to the map in this guide, you can refer to the USGS Stratton and Little Bigelow quadrangles, 15-min. series; the Little Bigelow Mtn. and Horns quadrangles, 7.5-min. series; or map 5 in the MATC's *Appalachian Trail Guide to Maine*.

The Fire Warden's Trail is the shortest approach to the main peaks of the Bigelow Range, but the Horns Pond Trail is less steep and more interesting. It leads to the Horns Pond, where it joins the Appalachian Trail (AT) to follow the ridge between the Horns, over South Horn and West Peak, and on to Avery Peak. As a third approach to the west of the first two trails, the AT runs from ME 27 to the ridge west of Horns Pond. These trails approach from the south (ME 16/27). A fourth and longer approach, the Bigelow Range Trail from Stratton east to the AT, east of Cranberry Pond, involves more ridge travel up and down the many peaks of the range. It extends the range's full length, from the western end to Avery Peak. A road runs along the southern shore of Flagstaff Lake from Long Falls Dam Rd. toward Stratton. It offers a fifth approach to the highest peaks via the Safford Brook Trail.

Fire Warden's Trail (map 2: A4–B4)

A rough dirt road, Stratton Brook Rd. (usually passable) runs east from ME 27 about 3.2 mi. northwest of the Sugarloaf ski area access road and 4.5 mi. southeast of Stratton. Drive in, cross the AT at 1.0 mi., and continue straight ahead, turning left at 1.6 mi. into a limited parking area. The road beyond is very rough. The bridge over Stratton Brook is washed out. Cross Stratton Brook on foot (use caution in high water) and continue on the road. At 0.2 mi., reach a fork and go left. (The right fork descends to a partially destroyed bridge.) From this point, the trail leads north for 0.2 mi., then runs east on the level for about half a mile. After that, it climbs steeply over ledges to a shelf. The grade is easy for the next 1.5 mi., during which the trail crosses several brooks. At 1.6 mi. from the parking area, the Horns Pond Trail leaves left (northwest). At 3.1 mi. from Stratton Brook, the trail runs under the West Peak of Bigelow, and its grade becomes increasingly steep. The trail gains nearly 1700 ft. in the next 1.5 mi. as it climbs north–northeast to Bigelow Col. The trail passes the Moose Falls Campsite at 3.6 mi., and meets the AT at 4.6 mi. The caretaker uses the old fire warden's cabin, which is kept locked.

From the col, go right (east) via the AT 0.4 mi. to reach Avery Peak and its abandoned fire tower. To reach West Peak from the col, go left (west) on the AT about 0.4 mi.

Descending, the trail diverges from the AT in Bigelow Col and goes down to the southwest.

Distances from parking area

> *to* Horns Pond Trail junction: 1.6 mi., 1 hr. 10 min.

> *to* Moose Falls Campsite: 3.6 mi.

> *to* Bigelow Col and AT junction: 4.6 mi.

> *to* Avery Peak summit: 5.0 mi., 4 hr.

> *to* West Peak summit: 5.0 mi., 4 hr.

Horns Pond Trail (map 2: A4)

This trail starts at the same point as the Fire Warden's Trail (see above). The Horns Pond Trail diverges left (northwest) from the Fire Warden's Trail 1.6 mi. from Stratton Brook. The Horns Pond Trail heads northwest, climbing gradually. At 3.0 mi., the trail skirts the southern edge of a former bog area with an excellent view of the South Horn. The trail continues to rise gradually, then gets steeper. At 4.1 mi., the Horns Pond Trail intersects the white-blazed AT. Bear right on the AT for 0.1 mi. to the two newly-built Horns Pond lean-tos (caretaker; accommodate eight each; MFS campsite). A 50-yd., blue-blazed trail behind the eastern lean-to leads to Horns Pond.

Distances from Stratton Brook

　　to　start (via Fire Warden's Trail): 1.6 mi., 1 hr. 10 min.

　　to　AT: 4.1 mi.

　　to　Horns Pond lean-tos: 4.2 mi., 3 hr.

Appalachian Trail from the South (map 2: A6–B4)

This trail (partly maintained by the Maine Chapter of the AMC) leaves ME 27 2.6 mi. northwest of the Sugarloaf Mtn. access road. In the first mile, the trail descends slowly and crosses Stratton Brook Rd. at 0.9 mi. (This road and the so-called Jones Pond Rd., soon after it, form alternative starting points for the hike.) After Jones Pond Rd., the trail descends immediately to cross Stratton Brook on a footbridge. In the next mile, the trail passes through spruce woods and then joins an old tote road. Turn left on the tote road, which soon crosses a stream. At 1.9 mi., turn right off the road and cross a tote road 2.5 mi. from ME 27. The trail passes an abandoned beaver pond and then climbs gradually but steadily as it approaches the basin of Cranberry Pond, where it passes a spring (last sure water before Horns Pond).

　　At 3.4 mi., the AT turns sharply right (north). The Bigelow Range Trail (sign) continues straight ahead (west). The AT climbs steeply through a boulder field. At 4.0 mi., it reaches the crest of the ridge. There, it turns right (east) and follows the ridge, crossing a minor summit. At 5.0 mi., where the trail takes a sharp left, there is a lookout 17 yd. to the right over Horns Pond to the Horns. The trail descends steeply. At 5.1 mi., the Horns Pond Trail comes in on the right. The AT continues along the southern shore of Horns Pond, passing the two Horns Pond lean-tos at 5.2 mi.

　　From Horns Pond, the AT continues east, climbing South Horn. At 5.8 mi., the blue-blazed North Horn Trail leads 0.2 mi. left to the North Horn. A little farther on, the AT crosses the South Horn. Then it continues along the crest of the Bigelow Range, reaching West Peak at 8.0 mi. The trail then descends to the Avery Memorial Lean-to at 8.4 mi.; the Fire Warden's Trail comes in on the right directly in front of the lean-to. The AT continues east, climbing to the summit of Avery Peak at 8.8 mi.

　　From Avery Peak, the AT descends east to its jct. with the Safford Brook Trail. For a description of the AT east of the Safford Brook Trail, see the MATC's *Appalachian Trail Guide to Maine*.

Distances from ME 27

- *to* Stratton Brook Rd.: 0.9 mi.
- *to* Stratton Brook: 1.0 mi.
- *to* Bigelow Range Trail junction: 3.4 mi.
- *to* Horns Pond Trail junction: 5.1 mi.
- *to* Horns Pond lean-tos: 5.2 mi., 3 hr. 40 min.
- *to* South Horn summit: 5.9 mi.
- *to* West Peak summit: 8.0 mi.
- *to* Avery Lean-to and Fire Warden's Trail junction: 8.4 mi., 5 hr. 55 min.
- *to* Avery Peak: 8.8 mi., 6 hr. 15 min.

Bigelow Range Trail (map 2: A3–A4)

This blue-blazed trail starts at the western end of the range, on ME 27/16, 0.5 mi. southeast of Stratton and about 100 yd. northwest of the Eustis–Coplin town line. From the highway, follow a dirt road east. At 0.5 mi. from ME 27/16, the road ends at a clearing. The trail passes through woods for 0.3 mi. Then it climbs gradually about 0.2 mi. on a wide logging road. The trail reaches the first barren ledges at 1.9 mi. and bears right. Arnolds Well (a deep cleft in the rocks; no drinking water) is 7 yd. to the right. The trail turns up the ledges. There is a good view from the top of the first ledges. The trail leads through scrub and logged areas along the northern edge of the ridge with fine views. After reaching open ledges, it makes a short, steep ascent to Cranberry Peak at 3.2 mi.

After a short, steep descent, the trail descends more gradually. Then it follows the northern shore of Cranberry Pond, to end at a jct. with the AT at 4.9 mi.

Distances from ME 27

- *to* clearing: 0.5 mi.
- *to* first ledges: 1.9 mi.
- *to* Cranberry Peak: 3.2 mi., 2 hr. 40 min.
- *to* AT junction: 4.9 mi., 3 hr. 50 min.

Bigelow Range from the North (Safford Brook Trail and Appalachian Trail) (map 2: A5)

This trail begins at Round Barn Field on the shore of Flagstaff Lake, crosses East Flagstaff Rd., and climbs to the AT at Safford Notch.

The trail can be approached by water or by road. Round Barn Field is located on the eastern side of a cove on the southern shore of Flagstaff Lake; this cove can be identified from the lake by a large sawdust pile on the lakeshore. To reach the trail by road, turn north off ME 16 onto the blacktop Long Falls Dam Rd. in North New Portland. At 17.3 mi., turn left (northwest) onto Bog Brook Rd. (gravel). At about 0.7 mi., East Flagstaff Rd. leads left (north and west); it crosses the AT in 0.1 mi. East Flagstaff Rd. crosses Safford Brook then reaches the trailhead at 4.3 mi.

From Round Barn Field, the trail passes through the woods and crosses East Flagstaff Rd. at 0.3 mi. The trail follows a graded tote road, then climbs steeply, crosses Safford Brook, and enters Safford Notch. At 2.6 mi., you will reach a jct. with the AT.

Fifty yd. east (left) on the AT is a blue-blazed trail that leads south (right) 0.2 mi. to the Safford Notch Campsite, with two tent platforms and a privy. (Traveling eastward, the AT reaches the highest peak of Little Bigelow at 3.7 mi.) The AT rises steeply west toward Avery Peak for a mile, with several excellent vistas. At 3.4 mi., it reaches the crest of the ridge. There, a side trail leads left 167 yd. to the top of Old Man's Head (a cliff on the side of the mountain). The trail continues to climb steeply, reaching the timberline and, shortly thereafter, the abandoned tower on Avery Peak.

Distances from Round Barn Field

- *to* East Flagstaff Rd.: 0.3 mi.
- *to* AT junction (via Safford Brook Trail): 2.6 mi.
- *to* Little Bigelow summit (via AT east): 6.4 mi., 4 hr.
- *to* Avery Peak (via AT west): 4.7 mi., 3 hr. 45 min.

Little Bigelow Mountain (3025 ft.)

Little Bigelow lies to the east of the main Bigelow Range, separated from it by a deep notch, known as Safford Notch. It is a long, narrow ridge, with steep cliffs along its southern side. The northern slope descends steadily for some two miles to Flagstaff Lake. The natural structure of the mountain makes extremely rough terrain. The trail is part of the Appalachian Trail and therefore marked with white paint blazes. Refer to the USGS Little Bigelow Mtn. quadrangle, 15-min. series and 7.5-min. series, or map 5 in the MATC's *Appalachian Trail Guide to Maine*, if you want to supplement the map in this guide.

The approaches are via the AT. See the Safford Brook description above for Avery Peak for the approach from the west. To approach from the east, follow Long Falls Dam Rd. north from North New Portland. At 17.3 mi., the former route of ME 16, Bog Brook Rd. (flooded out by Flagstaff Lake), diverges left. Follow this well-graded road for 0.7 mi. Turn left onto East Flagstaff Rd., which crosses the Appalachian Trail in 0.1 mi.

The Appalachian Trail leads through hardwoods and follows a brook. At 1.2 mi., a blue-blazed side trail leads right 0.1 mi. across the brook to the Little Bigelow Lean-to. The trail continues through the woods, leaving the brook, and climbs on a series of open ledges that comprise the northeastern buttress of the mountain. At 3.0 mi., it reaches a viewpoint at the southeastern end of the summit ridge. The true summit is about half a mile farther northwest along the trail.

Distances from East Flagstaff Rd. (via Appalachian Trail)

  to Little Bigelow Lean-to: 1.3 mi.

  to Little Bigelow summit: 3.5 mi., 2 hr. 45 min.

  to Safford Brook Trail junction: 6.4 mi.

  to Avery Peak: 8.3 mi., 7 hr.

Section 12

Kennebec Valley

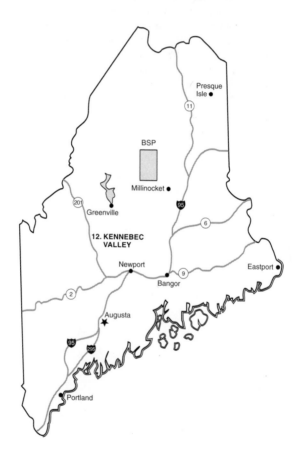

Presque
Isle ●

⑪

BSP

Millinocket ●

⑳⑤

⑥

Greenville

12. KENNEBEC
VALLEY

Newport ●

② ⑨

Bangor ●

Eastport ●

②

Augusta
★

⑨⑤ ②⑨⑤

● Portland

RECOMMENDED HIKES

Easy

Mount Pisgah (rt: 2.0 mi., 1 hr.) An easy hike with limited elevation gain to a fire tower, from which there are extensive views in all directions.

Moderate

Sally Mountain (rt: 6.0 mi., 3 hr.) Although the first part of this hike is along some railroad tracks, the views from the open ledges and the summit of Sally Mtn., plus the blueberries, are worth the hike. From the foundation of a former fire tower, there is a panoramic view that includes Katahdin to the Bigelows.

Strenuous

Moxie Bald Mountain via the AT (rt: 9.6 mi. 5 hr. 30 min.) The AT ascends, sometimes steeply to the open crests and ledges of Moxie Bald Mtn. From the site of a former fire tower, there is an excellent panoramic view that includes Katahdin to the northeast, the peaks of Piscataquis County, and the peaks to the west.

LIST OF MOUNTAINS

This section includes several mountains on the lower and middle sections of the Kennebec River, and other mountains accessible from US 201 and roads running off this highway. There are MFS firetowers on several of these summits. US 201 generally follows the Kennebec River as far as The Forks. It then runs through mountainous country past Parlin Pond to Jackman and on to the Quebec border. ME 15 diverges east from US 201 at Jackman and follows down the Moose River Valley to reach Moosehead Lake at Rockwood.

The highest mountain in this section is Coburn Mtn. (3718 ft.). Boundary Bald Mtn. is 3640 ft., but the majority of the rest are much lower. Most of the mountains described in this section are in Somerset County; two are in Kennebec County.

Mount Pisgah (809 ft.)

On the summit of Mt. Pisgah in Winthrop are a MFS fire tower and a telecommunications tower with a one-story equipment building. Refer to the USGS Wayne quadrangle, 7.5-min. series.

From Lewiston, go east on US 202 toward Monmouth. Just past the intersection of 202 and ME 132, turn left onto North Main Street. Go 0.8 mi. to the crossroads in North Monmouth. Turn right onto Wilson Pond Rd. and go 0.2 mi. Turn left onto Pisgah Rd. and go 1.6 mi. to the trailhead. (Tappen Farm Rd. merges from the left after 1.0 mi.) The trailhead is on the right with a sign for Tower Rd. and a sign reading Trail to Fire Tower. A dirt parking area accommodates six cars.

The trail (a dirt road) leaves from the parking area and immediately (260 ft.) meets a gate with a sign on the right reading, Mt. Pisgah Conservation Area – No Unauthorized Vehicles. A sign on the left directs hikers to Mt. Pisgah Tower via an alternative 0.7 mi. trail through the woods.

To continue on the main trail, go straight up the fairly steep dirt road, following an overhead utility line. After 0.3 mi., the trail levels out, and one should look back to the northwest to see nice views of the lakes and the Presidentials. In another 200 ft., a rutted jeep road joins from the right. Bear left at this junction and follow the trail, which rises gently, for another 0.7 mi. to the summit. The trail's last 100 ft. traverses open ledges to the summit, where views open up to the west. From the fire tower platform, views in all directions take in the nearby lakes and the entire sweep of western Maine's mountains, from Pleasant Mtn. to Sugarloaf, as well as the Presidentials in New Hampshire.

Distance from parking lot

  to Pisgah summit: 1.0 mi., 30 min.

Monument Hill (660 ft.)

Monument Hill in Leeds is just west of Androscoggin Lake and offers good views of the Presidentials to the west and Maine's western mountains to the northwest from its summit, with limited views of Androscoggin Lake through the trees to the east. On the summit is a granite monument to Leeds soldiers and sailors of the Civil War. An obelisk Peace Monument is inscribed with the words, "Peace was sure 1865." Refer to the USGS Turner Center quadrangle, 7.5-min. series.

To reach the trail from US 202 between Lewiston and Augusta, take ME 106 north for 6.2 mi. to Leeds. Take Church Hill Rd. left for 0.9 mi. to North Rd. on the right. The trailhead is at 0.9 mi. (sign) with roadside parking. Occasional wooden signs with black arrows mark the well-worn trail. After 220 ft., the trail forks to offer a 0.9 mi. hiking loop. The left fork is 0.5 mi., and the right fork is 0.4 mi. Both forks rise gently east and southeast through varied forest and berry patches to the rocky summit.

Distance from North Rd.

  to Monument summit via left fork: 0.5 mi., 20 min.

  to Monument summit via right fork: 0.4 mi., 15 min.

Chase Hill (780 ft.)

This summit in Canaan offers a 360-degree view from the fire tower on its summit. Refer to the USGS Skowhegan quadrangle, 15-min. series, or the Canaan quadrangle, 7.5-min. series.

From the jct. of US 2 and ME 23 east of Canaan Village, drive 4.0 mi. northeast on ME 23 to Lancaster Rd. on the left (west). From the junction of ME 151 and ME 23 in Hartland, drive 6.0 mi. southwest on ME 23 to the same road on the right. After turning onto the Lancaster Rd., drive 0.2 mi. to Chase Hill Rd on the right. Follow the Chase Hill Rd. (a small cemetery is just past the jct.) for 0.9 mi. to a house on the right, with a jeep road on the left. Chase Hill Road narrows after this point. Park by the jeep road and walk up the jeep road past the warden's cabin. It is 0.3 mi. to the tower rising above the trees on the wooded summit. The tower is safe to climb and offers excellent views of the surrounding area.

Distance from parking lot

   to Chase summit: 0.3 mi., 10 min.

Moxie Bald Mountain (2630 ft.)

This mountain, located in Bald Mtn. Township northeast of Bingham, is a long ridge running north–south for about four miles. Although the summit is not very high, it has many features of above-timberline summits because of its extended ledges and open crest. In winter, snowshoes could be used to climb Moxie Bald Mtn. The trailless North Peak, easy to reach from the Appalachian Trail, is worth exploring. Refer to the USGS The Forks and Bingham quadrangles, 15-min. series; the Bald Mtn. Pond and Moxie Pond quadrangles, 7.5-min. series; or map 4 in the MATC's *Appalachian Trail Guide to Maine*.

The views from the summit are excellent. Katahdin is to the northeast, beyond many other peaks in Piscataquis County: Bigelow, Sugarloaf, and Abraham are to the west; and Coburn and Boundary Bald are to the north.

The approach is via the Appalachian Trail, which leaves from a point on a paper-company road just south of Joe's Hole, the southernmost point on Moxie Pond. To reach the trailhead from the south, turn off US 201 in Bingham onto ME 16. At 0.8 mi, two roads join the highway from the left; take the rightmost, Deadwater Road. This is a paper-company road that turns immediately to gravel and follows Austin Stream for much of its length. At the four corners (2.5 mi.) proceed straight; at 7.0 mi. a road will join from the right; at 7.1 mi. bear left; at 8.6 mi. cross Austin Stream; at 8.8 mi. stay right; at 9.2 mi. bear right; at 11.0 mi. take the left fork where the road splits; and at 13.9 mi. stay straight. At 15.6 mi., you will see the Appalachian Trail sign on the right. Pull into a parking area (four cars) on the left, being careful not to block camp driveways. (The Appalachian Trail approach to Pleasant Pond Mtn. from the east begins a little more than 100 yd., north, just beyond a power line crossing and across from a small boat landing)

To reach the trailhead from the north, leave US 201 at The Forks on Lake Moxie Road toward Indian Pond. At Lake Moxie Station (5.3 mi.), turn right onto Troutdale Road, following the old railroad bed along Moxie Pond. This road is rough and narrow in places, and there are many camps located on this shore of the lake, so drive carefully. At 12.6 mi., the sign for the Appalachian

Trail and Moxie Bald is located on the left. Parking as described above may be found immediately to the right.

The Appalachian Trail up Moxie Bald leaves the eastern side of the road and immediately crosses Baker Brook near the inlet to Moxie Pond. Even in times of moderate water levels this crossing may be difficult. At 0.5 mi., a power line is crossed. The trail ascends gradually, then more steeply over open ledges before breaking out above the tree line. At 4.2 mi., reach a jct. with a 0.5-mi., blue-blazed side trail used to bypass the summit in bad weather. It rejoins the Appalachian Trail north of the summit along the crest of the mountain. From this jct. Moxie Bold lean-to is 2.4 mi. north; Bald Mountain Brook lean-to is 1.6 mi. south; and Moxie Pond Road is 3.8 mi. south. At 4.8 mi., reach the open summit of Moxie Bald. The former tower has been removed.

Distance from paper-company road via Appalachian Trail

　to　Moxie Bald summit: 4.8 mi., 3 hr. 15 min.

Pleasant Pond Mountain (2480 ft.)

On the Appalachian Trail between Moxie Pond and the Kennebec River at Caratunk, Pleasant Pond Mtn. has open ledges that offer fine views in all directions. Hikers can approach the mountain from either the east or the west, although the eastern approach is recommended for its super views from several open ledges and varied ecology. Refer to the USGS The Forks quadrangle, 15- or 7.5-min. series.

From the east, the approach by road is the same as for Moxie Bald Mtn. Walk 800 ft. north along the approach road from the described parking area to where the trail leads west up the mountain from a spot near Joe's Hole, the southernmost tip of Moxie Pond. After 300 ft., the trail crosses under a power line, passes through low beaver bogs, and ascends to a long ridge, which it follows to the summit 4.7 mi. from the gravel road. A small spring is 0.1 mi. east. At about the halfway point, a great view of Pleasant Pond Mountain may be had as the trail crosses a large rock outcropping.

The road approach from the west starts in the village of Caratunk at the post office where Pleasant Pond Road leaves the village heading uphill. Arrive at this point from the south by turning off US 201 at a sign for Caratunk/Pleasant Pond and proceeding 0.8 mi. From the north, leave US 201 at a similar sign for Caratunk/Pleasant Pond and proceed 0.5 mi. to the post office. From the start of Pleasant Point Road at the post office follow signs northeast to Pleasant

Pond. At 3.1 mi. take the left fork onto North Shore Road; at 3.4 mi. the pavement ends; at 4.5 mi. bear right into the woods as the Boise Cascade Crossover Road bears left. Notice trailhead parking signs as you proceed to a grassy opening and the trail at 4.7 mi.

The Appalachian Trail leaves the parking area north toward Pleasant Pond Mtn. and finds the Pleasant Pond Mtn. Lean-to spur trail at approximately 0.1 mi. and a blue-blazed trail to the pond at 0.2 mi. The rocky trail then leads steeply uphill through dense woods. At 1.3 mi. the trail is re-routed over a rock ledge and shortly thereafter breaks out onto open ledges where all that remains of the old fire tower are concrete footings and broken glass (1.4 mi.).

Distances from paper-company road via Appalachian Trail (from the east)

  to power line: 0.1 mi.

  to Pleasant Pond summit: 4.7 mi., 3 hr. 10 min.

Distances from parking via Appalachian Trail (from the west)

  to Pleasant Pond summit: 1.4 mi., 1 hr. 15 min.

Coburn Mountain (3718 ft.)

This mountain, west of US 201 between The Forks and Jackman, is the highest in the region with spectacular views rivaling the best in Maine. The top of the abandoned MFS fire tower has been replaced with a nice observation deck. Coburn formerly supported the Enchanted Mountain ski area, but this has been shut down for several years. The ski trails have rapidly grown in and all buildings have been removed.

Turn west off US 201 onto a dirt road 10.6 mi. north of the bridge in The Forks and 14.3 mi. south of the US 201 and ME 15 jct. in Jackman. This typical logging road is eroded. The first 0.2 miles are easily passable; high clearance vehicles can make it another two miles to the location of the former ski-area buildings. If in doubt, vehicles may easily be parked on the wide shoulders at any point on the 2.2 mi. drive from US 201 to the mountain.

At the base of the mountain, a four-corner intersection is found at a large clearing. Turn right and pass the old ski lodge foundation to find parking 100 yd. further on the left and across from a second concrete foundation. Exit on foot from the northwestern corner of this clearing on a course of about 280-degree magnetic north. Follow an old jeep trail steeply up hill for a while, changing to alternating footpath and former ski slope. About 0.7 mi. from the trailhead parking, reach the first of two new solar-powered radio repeating stations. A snowmobile trail leaves the station coursing uphill to the summit. About 150 ft. along this trail find the footpath exiting right and proceeding very steeply uphill about 0.4 mi. The trail exits the woods onto the summit at the solar panels of the second new repeating station. The old fire tower is just north on the ridge.

Past the fire tower and the summit building is the old fire warden's trail, which leads off the northeastern ridge and circles down past the few remains of the old warden's cabin onto an old logging track that intersects a jeep/snowmobile trail about halfway down the mountain. For those with compass skills and some bushwhacking experience, it can make a nice loop trip when combined with the previously described route.

Another alternative worth considering is a wide, rocky snowmobile trail that runs from the base of the mountain past the first radio-repeater station and on to the summit. From the aforementioned parking area, walk 0.1 mi. further along the entry road to the clearly marked snowmobile trail.

Distances from US 201

> *to*　base of mountain (via access road): est. 2.2 mi.
>
> *to*　first repeater station and summit footpath: est. 2.9 mi.
>
> *to*　Coburn summit via summit footpath: est. 3.3 mi.

Sally Mountain (2221 ft.)

Sally Mt. is southwest of Jackman, between Wood Pond and Attean Pond. It has a long summit ridge running northeast–southwest, with the highest point at the southwestern end. The northeastern and southeastern slopes rise fairly steeply above two ponds, and the climb to the summit ridge is very steep from these directions. The MFS fire tower has been removed and although the trail is infrequently maintained, it gets sufficient use to keep the route clear. Refer to the USGS Attean quadrangle, 15-min. series, and the Attean Pond quadrangle, 7.5-min. series.

Leave US 201 on Attean Road, which is nearly opposite ME 15 east in Jackman. At 1.4 mi the road turns to dirt; park in an open area to the right from where Sally Mtn. and the Canadian Pacific railroad trestle may be seen. From the parking area, backtrack along Attean Road a short distance to a gated camp road that leads to the railroad tracks. Follow the railroad line to the west for about 1.8 mi. being careful when crossing the trestle over the Moose River. The

Sally Mountain trail crosses the track just beyond power pole #3112 and signal post #770. A white painted board nailed to a tree points toward Sally Mtn.

The blue-blazed trail runs fairly level for a time before climbing steeply through a pleasant forest of mixed hardwoods to the summit ridge. Among the rocks and scrub growth of the summit ridge, the trail becomes fainter, but it generally runs along the east-facing edge of the ridge on a gradual ascent toward the summit. At the summit, four pieces of steel bolted to the rocks mark the site of the former fire tower. The views from the top are excellent, taking in several large ponds and mountains, from Katahdin to Bigelow to the border peaks.

A more pleasant alternative to hiking along the railroad tracks is making the approach to the trail by canoe. From the above mentioned parking area a canoe may be carried across a field to the river's edge. Launching left (upriver) and soon arriving in Attean Pond at a private boat dock, follow the northern shore of the pond west. The trail begins at the second established campsite in a small cove directly opposite Birch Island and Attean Lake Lodge. Trail mileage signs are evident as the trail leads through level forest for about 0.1 mi. to a spot where it crosses the Canadian Pacific tracks.

Distances from road

> *to* start of trail (via railroad line): 1.8 mi.
>
> *to* Sally summit: 3 mi., 2 hr.

Boundary Bald Mountain (3640 ft.)

This rocky summit is north–northeast of Jackman and about eight miles southwest of the Canadian border. Its long, open summit ridge offers 360-degree views of the mountain and lake country of northern Somerset County, the Moosehead Lake Region, and southern Canada. The mountain and the collapsed fire tower at its top can be reached by a 1.2-mi. blue-blazed trail. Refer to the USGS Penobscot Lake and Long Pond quadrangles, 15-min. series, and the Boundary Bald Mtn. quadrangle, 7.5-min. series.

From the bridge on US 201 in Jackman, drive north towards Canada for 7.6 mi. Pass The Falls picnic area on the right (7.2 mi.). Take the second right (7.6 mi.) after the picnic area. Bald Mountain Road is an unmaintained gravel road that leads 5.6 mi. to the trailhead. It is generally suitable for high-clearance and four-wheel-drive vehicles. Drivers may want to carry a shovel to deal with deep washouts and drainage dips.

After leaving US 201, follow Bald Mountain Road and bear right at the fork after the Heald Stream Bridge (2.4 mi.). Do not be drawn left by Heald Stream Rd. Bear left onto Notch Rd. (4.1 mi.). Bear right onto Trail Road (4.3 mi.). For low clearance vehicles, a small clearing on the right (4.5 mi.) provides parking for six cars. High clearance vehicles may find additional parking for three cars on the right (5.0 mi. and 5.4 mi.). Only the most rugged 4-wheel drive vehicles can find parking for two vehicles at the trailhead (5.6 mi.). An old wooden sign reading Bald Mt. Tower marks the beginning of the footpath.

The trail, which heads up a slatey seasonal streambed, is marked with blue blazes. It is easily followed to the bald summit. Proceed across the bald summit to a communications tower facility where excellent views await. While not easily lost above tree line, pay particular attention to the trail on the return trip as it drops into the tree line.

Distance from trailhead on Trail Rd.

to Boundary Bald summit: 1.2 mi.

Appendix A

New England
Four Thousand Footers

The Four Thousand Footer Committee was established in 1957 by AMC to bring together hikers who had climbed in some of the less frequented areas of the White Mountains. The committee developed a list of the four thousand footers in the White Mountains, using the criterion that for a peak to be included, it must be 4000 feet or higher and has to rise 200 feet above the low point on the ridge connecting it to a higher neighbor. This criterion is still in used to determine those peaks that belong on the lists.

The Four Thousand Footer Committee recognizes three official lists and the clubs associated with those lists: the White Mountain Four Thousand Footers, the New England Four Thousand Footers, and the New England Hundred Highest. Each club gives separate awards. Additionally, awards are given for climbing all of the peaks on a given list in the winter. A "winter ascent" is defined as occurring after the hour and minute of the beginning of winter (winter solstice) and ending before the hour and minute of the end of winter (spring equinox). An awards ceremony is held usually each spring.

All of the peaks listed on the New England Four Thousand Footers have well-defined trails, with the exception of Redington Mountain, which may be reached by a bushwhack, and Owl's Head (in the White Mountains of New Hampshire), on which there is an unofficial and unmaintained trail to the summit. Many of the peaks on the New England Hundred Highest don't have trails and to summit them requires skill in the use of map and compass.

Anyone interested in becoming a member of one or more of the clubs may obtain information and an application by sending a self-addressed stamp envelope to the Four Thousand Footer Committee, 42 Eastman Street, Concord, NH 03301. If you wish to receive the list of the New England Four Thousand Footers and/or the New England Hundred Highest, you need to specifically ask for them as well (only the White Mountain Four Thousand Footers are included in the information packet). The Four Thousand Footer Committee also provides the lists at www.amc4000footer.org, along with a FAQ. Applicants for any of the clubs do not need to be members of the AMC, although the committee strongly encourages any hiker using the trails to contribute to the maintenance of the trails in some manner.

On the lists developed by the Four Thousand Footer Committee, the elevations have been obtained from the latest USGS maps, some which are now metric, requiring conversion from meters to feet. Where no exact elevation is on the map, the elevation has been estimated by adding half of the contour interval to the highest contour shown on the map; elevations so obtained are marked on the list with an asterisk. The elevations given here for several of the peaks in Maine may differ from those listed elsewhere in this book, because the Four Thousand Footer Committee uses USGS maps as the authority for all elevations, while AMC (and one of its outside sources, DeLorme) uses GPS in recording elevations.

Maine Four Thousand Footers

Mountain	Elevation	Date Climbed
Katahdin, Baxter Peak	5268*	_____
Katahdin, Hamlin Peak	4756	_____
Sugarloaf Mtn.	4250	_____
Old Speck	4170	_____
Crocker Mtn., North Peak	4228	_____
Bigelow Mtn., West Peak	4145	_____
North Brother	4151	_____
Saddleback Mtn.	4120	_____
Bigelow Mtn., Avery Peak	4090*	_____
Mt. Abraham	4050	_____
Crocker Mtn., South Peak	4050	_____
Saddleback Mtn., The Horn	4041	_____
Redington Mtn.	4010	_____
Spaulding Mtn.	4010	_____

New Hampshire Four Thousand Footers

Mountain	Elevation	Date Climbed
Washington	6288	_____
Adams	5774	_____
Jefferson	5712	_____
Monroe	5384*	_____
Madison	5367	_____
Lafayette	5260*	_____
Lincoln	5089	_____
South Twin	4902	_____
Carter Dome	4832	_____
Moosilauke	4802	_____
Eisenhower	4780*	_____
North Twin	4761	_____
Carrigain	4700*	_____
Bond	4698	_____
Middle Carter	4610*	_____
West Bond	4540*	_____
Garfield	4500*	_____
Liberty	4459	_____
South Carter	4430*	_____
Wildcat	4422	_____
Hancock	4420*	_____
South Kinsman	4358	_____
Field	4340*	_____
Osceola	4340*	_____
Flume	4328	_____
South Hancock	4319	_____
Pierce (Clinton)	4310	_____
North Kinsman	4293	_____
Willey	4285	_____
Bondcliff	4265	_____

Zealand	4260*	_____
North Tripyramid	4180*	_____
Cabot	4170*	_____
East Osceola	4156	_____
Middle Tripyramid	4140*	_____
Cannon	4100*	_____
Hale	4054	_____
Jackson	4052	_____
Tom	4051	_____
Wildcat D	4050*	_____
Moriah	4049	_____
Passaconaway	4043	_____
Owl's Head	4025	_____
Galehead	4024	_____
Whiteface	4020*	_____
Waumbek	4006	_____
Isolation	4004	_____
Tecumseh	4003	_____

Vermont Four Thousand Footers

Mountain	Elevation	Date Climbed
Mt. Mansfield, the Chin	4393	_____
Killington Peak	4235	_____
Camel's Hump	4083	_____
Mt. Ellen	4083	_____
Mt. Abraham	4006	_____

Appendix B

New England Hundred Highest

This list excludes the previously listed New England Four Thousand Footers. Those peaks must also be climbed to achieve the goal of climbing the New England hundred highest peaks. Where no exact elevation is on the map, the elevation has been estimated by adding half of the contour interval to the highest contour shown on the map; elevations so obtained are marked on the list with an asterisk.

Maine

Mountain	Elevation	Date Climbed
Snow (Chain of Ponds quad)	3960*	_____
South Brother	3937*	_____
Goose Eye	3774	_____
Fort Mtn.	3867	_____
White Cap	3856*	_____
Boundary Peak	3855	_____
Bigelow, South Horn	3805	_____
Coe	3795	_____
East Kennebago	3791*	_____
Baldpate	3790*	_____
Snow (Little Kennebago Lake)	3784	_____
N. Peak Kennebago Divide	3775	_____
Elephant	3774	_____

New Hampshire

Mountain	Elevation	Date Climbed
Sandwich	3980	_____
The Bulge	3950	_____

Nancy	3926	_____
The Horn	3905	_____
North Weeks	3901	_____
South Weeks	3885	_____
Vose Spur	3862	_____
East Sleeper	3860	_____
Peak Above the Nubble	3813	_____
Scar Ridge, West Peak	3774	_____
NE Cannonball	3769	_____

Vermont

Mountain	Elevation	Date Climbed
Pico Peak	3957	_____
Stratton Mtn.	3940	_____
Jay Peak	3858	_____
Equinox	3850	_____
Mendon Peak	3840	_____
Breadloaf	3835	_____
Mt. Wilson	3790	_____
Big Jay	3786	_____
Dorset Peak	3770	_____

Appendix C

Accident Report

Incident Location:_____ **Date:**_____ **Time:**_____

Description of Lost or Injured Person:

Name_____ Age/Sex_____

Address_____ Phone_____

Reporting Person:

Name_____

Address_____ Phone_____

1. INCIDENT SUMMARY

_____

_____

2. PATIENT INFORMATION

Allergies_____

Medication_____

Previous Injury/Illness_____

Last 24 Hr. Food/Water Intake_____

MedicalConditions/Other_____

Experience_____

Physical/Mental Conditions_____

Patient Clothing (color/style/size):

Jacket_____ Shirt_____ Shorts/Pants_____

Hat/Gloves_____ Pack_____ Footgear_____

Patient Gear (circle all that apply):

Map	Sleeping Bag	Tent/Bivy	Rain/Windgear
Flashlight/Batts	Extra Clothing	Food/Water	Ski Poles/Ice Axe

3. PATIENT EXAMINATION

Problem Areas/Injuries (circle all that apply):

Head	Face	Eyes	Mouth	Neck
Shoulder	Chest	Stomach	Upper Back	Lower Back
Upper Leg (R)	Knee (R)	Lower Leg (R)	Ankle (R)	Foot (R)
Upper Leg (L)	Knee (L)	Lower Leg (L)	Ankle (L)	Foot (L)
Upper Arm (R)	Elbow (R)	Lower Arm (R)	Wrist (R)	Hand (R)
Upper Arm (L)	Elbow (L)	Lower Arm (L)	Wrist (L)	Hand (L)

4. VITAL SIGNS

	Essential			Helpful		
Time	Level of Consciousness	Breathing Rate	Pulse	Blood Pressure	Skin	Pupils

5. NOTES/PLAN

_____

_____

_____

Appendix D

Leave No Trace

The Appalachian Mountain Club is a national educational partner of Leave No Trace, a nonprofit organization dedicated to promoting and inspiring responsible outdoor recreation through education, research, and partnerships. The Leave No Trace Program seeks to develop wildland ethics—ways in which people think and act in the outdoors to minimize their impacts on the areas they visit and to protect our natural resources for future enjoyment. Leave No Trace unites four federal land management agencies—the U.S. Forest Service, National Park Service, Bureau of Land Management, and U.S. Fish and Wildlife Service—with manufacturers, outdoor retailers, user groups, educators, organizations such as the AMC and the National Outdoor Leadership School (NOLS), and individuals.

The Leave No Trace ethic is guided by these seven principles:
- Plan ahead and prepare
- Travel and camp on durable surfaces
- Dispose of waste properly
- Leave what you find
- Minimize campfire impacts
- Respect wildlife
- Be considerate of other visitors

The AMC has joined NOLS—a recognized leader in wilderness education and a founding partner of Leave No Trace—as a national provider of the Leave No Trace Master Educator course. The AMC offers this five-day course, designed especially for outdoor professionals and land managers, as well as the shorter two-day Leave No Trace Trainer course, at locations throughout the Northeast.

For Leave No Trace information and materials, contact:
Leave No Trace Center for Outdoor Ethics
PO Box 997, Boulder, CO 80306
800-332-4100; 303-442-8222; Fax: 303-442-8217
www.lnt.org

247

Glossary

blaze trail marking on a tree or rock, painted and/or cut

blazed marked with paint (blazes) on trees or rocks

bluff high bank or hill with a cliff face overlooking a valley

boggy muddy, swampy

boulder large, detached, somewhat rounded rock

box canyon rock formation with vertical walls and flat bottom

bushwhack to hike through woods or brush without a trail

buttress rock mass projecting outward from a mountain or hill

cairn pile of rocks to mark trail

cataract waterfall

cirque upper end of valley with half-bowl shape (scoured by glacier)

cliff high, steep rock face

col low point on a ridge between two mountains; saddle

crag rugged, often overhanging rock eminence

flume ravine or gorge with a stream running through it

grade steepness of trail or road; ratio of vertical to horizontal distance

graded trail well-constructed trail with smoothed footway

gulf cirque

gully small, steep-sided valley

headwall steep slope at the head of a valley, especially a cirque

height-of-land highest point reached by a trail or road

knob rounded minor summit

lean-to shelter open on one side

ledge large body of rock; or, but not usually in this book, a horizontal shelf across a cliff

ledgy having exposed ledges, usually giving views

outcrops large rocks projecting out of the soil

plateau high, flat area

potable drinkable

ravine steep-sided valley

ridge highest spine joining two or more mountains, or leading up to a mountain

runoff brook brook usually dry (intermittent), except shortly after rain or snowmelt

saddle lowest, flattish part of ridge connecting two mountains; col

scrub low trees near treeline

shelter building, usually of wood, with roof and three or four sides, for camping

shoulder point where rising ridge levels off or descends slightly before rising higher to a summit

slab (n.) smooth, somewhat steeply sloping ledge

slab (v.) to travel in a direction parallel to the contour of a slope

slide steep slope where a landslide has carried away soil and vegetation

spur minor summit projecting from a larger one

spur trail side path to a point off a main trail

strata layers of rock

summit highest point on a mountain; or, a point higher than any other point in its neighborhood

switchback zigzag traverse of a steep slope

tarn small pond, often at high elevation or with no outlet

timberline elevation that marks the upper limit of commercial timber

treeline elevation above which trees do not grow

Index

Each trail's designated name appears in **bold**.
ALL CAPS denotes a section name.

Get Out & Get Active with the AMC

Become an AMC Member!

With the AMC, you can participate in a wide variety of outdoor activities, connect with new people, and help to protect the natural world you love. Join us and each year you'll receive 10 issues of our member magazine, AMC Outdoors, which will keep you informed of environmental issues and outdoor recreation opportunities—including hiking, paddling, biking, and snowshoeing—across the Appalachian region. You'll also enjoy discounts on AMC skills workshops, lodging, and books. You can also join our Conservation Action Network (CAN) and help increase public influence on critical conservation issues today at www.outdoors.org/conservation/can.

AMC Outdoor Adventures

Develop your outdoor skills and knowledge through AMC Outdoor Adventures and Workshops! Learn to rock climb, snowshoe, or navigate by map and compass. From beginner backpacking and family canoeing to dogsledding and guided winter camping trips, you'll find something for any age or interest at spectacular locations throughout the Appalachian region, including the Maine Woods, White Mountains, Adirondacks, Catskills, and the Delaware Water Gap. For a full listing and to make your reservations, go to www.outdoors.org and click on Education.

AMC Books & Maps: Explore the Possibilities

AMC's hiking, biking, and paddling guides lead you to the most spectacular destinations in the Appalachian region. We're also your definitive source for how-to guides, trail maps, and adventure books. Explore the possibilities at www.outdoors.org /publications.

AMC Destinations: Be Our Guest

From the North Woods of Maine to the White Mountains to the Delaware Water Gap, AMC offers a wide variety of accommodations, from full service lodges to backcountry huts, shelters, and campsites. Experience outdoor adventure at its best as our guest. Get trip suggestions, check lodging availability, and make reservations at www.outdoors.org.

Contact Us Today

Appalachian Mountain Club
5 Joy Street
Boston, MA 02108
617-523-0636

www.outdoors.org

AMC Book Updates

AMC Books strives to keep our guidebooks as up-to-date as possible to help you plan safe and enjoyable adventures. If after publishing a book we learn that trails are relocated or route or contact information has changed, we will post the updated information online. Before you hit the trail, check for updates at www.outdoors.org/publications/books/updates.

While hiking or paddling, if you notice discrepancies with the trail description or map, or if you find any other errors in the book, please let us know by submitting them to amcbookupdates@outdoors.org or in writing to Books Editor, c/o AMC, 5 Joy Street, Boston, MA 02108. We will verify all submissions and post key updates each month.

AMC Books is dedicated to being a recognized leader in outdoor publishing. Thank you for your participation.

AMC Books & Maps
Appalachian Mountain Club
5 Joy Street
Boston, MA 02108

AMC BOOKS
EXPLORE THE POSSIBILITIES

Don't get caught in the rain!

Maine Mountain Guide Map
Baxter Park–Katahdin/
Rangeley–Stratton/Gulf Hagas

This waterproof, tear-resistant Tyvek map is full color and GPS digitized—sure to stand up to the elements.

WATERPROOF TYVEK
1-929173-78-4 • $7.95

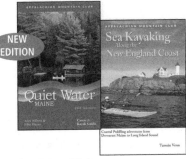

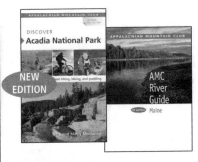

Quiet Water Maine
Canoe and Kayak Guide
2nd edition
BY ALEX WILSON AND JOHN HAYES

1-929173-65-2 • $18.95

Sea Kayaking Along the New England Coast
2nd edition
BY TAMSIN VENN

1-929173-50-4 • $18.95

Discover Acadia National Park
AMC Guide to the Best Hiking, Biking, and Paddling
2nd edition
BY JERRY AND MARCY MONKMAN

1-929173-58-X • $17.95

AMC River Guide: Maine
3rd edition

1-929173-14-8 • $14.95

Sales of AMC Books support our mission of protecting the Northeast outdoors.

Shop Online! www.outdoors.org
Appalachian Mountain Club · 800-262-4455 · 5 Joy Street Boston, MA 02108

little lyford pond camps

LL

A Rustic Retreat in the Maine Wilderness

Spring through fall, enjoy hiking, wildlife watching, paddling, or exceptional fly-fishing. In the winter, explore a snowy paradise on snowshoes or skis. Little Lyford Pond Camps offers the best in summer and winter recreation in a beautiful back-country setting.

Set amidst the famed 100-mile wilderness of the spectacular North Maine Woods, Little Lyford Pond Camps is a serene retreat for outdoor enthusiasts year-round. Travel just 15 miles east of Greenville, Maine, and leave the everyday cares of life behind as you discover this magical setting.

Accommodations

- seven log cabins that sleep one to six people

- delicious breakfast & dinner served in the main lodge

- hot showers in summer; cedar sauna in winter

- woodstoves; gas & kerosene lamps in cabins

Photography: Jerry Monkman, Clare O'Connell, Rob Burbank, Bryan Wentzell, Gerry Whiting

Open December 15–March 31 and May 13–October 31. Call 603-466-2727 for information and reservations.

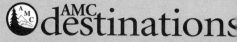

AMC destinations

Five Joy Street, Boston, MA 02108-1490 www.outdoors.org